Social and Emotional Learning in the Classroom

The Guilford Practical Intervention in the Schools Series

Kenneth W. Merrell, Series Editor

This series presents the most reader-friendly resources available in key areas of evidence-based practice in school settings. Practitioners will find trustworthy guides on effective behavioral, mental health, and academic interventions, and assessment and measurement approaches. Covering all aspects of planning, implementing, and evaluating high-quality services for students, books in the series are carefully crafted for everyday utility. Features include ready-to-use reproducibles, lay-flat binding to facilitate photocopying, appealing visual elements, and an oversized format.

Recent Volumes

School-Based Behavioral Assessment: Informing Intervention and Instruction
Sandra Chafouleas, T. Chris Riley-Tillman, and George Sugai

Collaborating with Parents for Early School Success: The Achieving–Behaving–Caring Program
Stephanie H. McConaughy, Pam Kay, Julie A. Welkowitz, Kim Hewitt, and Martha D. Fitzgerald

Helping Students Overcome Depression and Anxiety, Second Edition: A Practical Guide
Kenneth W. Merrell

Inclusive Assessment and Accountability:
A Guide to Accommodations for Students with Diverse Needs
Sara E. Bolt and Andrew T. Roach

Bullying Prevention and Intervention: Realistic Strategies for Schools
Susan M. Swearer, Dorothy L. Espelage, and Scott A. Napolitano

Conducting School-Based Functional Behavioral Assessments, Second Edition:
A Practitioner's Guide
Mark W. Steege and T. Steuart Watson

Evaluating Educational Interventions:
Single-Case Design for Measuring Response to Intervention
T. Chris Riley-Tillman and Matthew K. Burns

Collaborative Home/School Interventions:
Evidence-Based Solutions for Emotional, Behavioral, and Academic Problems
Gretchen Gimpel Peacock and Brent R. Collett

Social and Emotional Learning in the Classroom:
Promoting Mental Health and Academic Success
Kenneth W. Merrell and Barbara A. Gueldner

Executive Skills in Children and Adolescents, Second Edition:
A Practical Guide to Assessment and Intervention
Peg Dawson and Richard Guare

Responding to Problem Behavior in Schools, Second Edition: The Behavior Education Program
Deanne A. Crone, Leanne S. Hawken, and Robert H. Horner

High-Functioning Autism/Asperger Syndrome in Schools: Asessment and Intervention
Frank J. Sansosti, Kelly A. Powell-Smith, and Richard J. Cowan

School Discipline and Self-Discipline: A Practical Guide to Promoting Prosocial Behavior
George G. Bear

Social and Emotional Learning in the Classroom

Promoting Mental Health and Academic Success

KENNETH W. MERRELL
BARBARA A. GUELDNER

THE GUILFORD PRESS
New York   London

© 2010 The Guilford Press
A Division of Guilford Publications, Inc.
72 Spring Street, New York, NY 10012
www.guilford.com

Printed in Canada

This book is printed on acid-free paper.

Last digit is print number: 9   8   7   6   5   4   3   2   1

Library of Congress Cataloging-in-Publication Data

Merrell, Kenneth W.
    Social and emotional learning in the classroom : promoting mental health and academic success /
by Kenneth W. Merrell and Barbara A. Gueldner.
        p. cm. — (The Guilford practical invervention in the schools series)
    Includes bibliographical references and index.
    ISBN 978-1-60623-550-8 (pbk. : alk. paper)
    1. Affective education.   2. Social learning.   I. Gueldner, Barbara A.   II. Title.
    LB1072.M46 2010
    370.15′34—dc22
                                                                                    2009049555

We dedicate this book to the current generation of children who will be entering our nation's schools over the next 5 or 6 years. They live in a world challenged with bewildering problems and astounding possibilities, and we trust that the message of this book will be a positive influence for their benefit. We hope that their generation will benefit from the current and future innovations in social and emotional learning; that they will be resilient, well adjusted, and successful; and that they will leave the world they have inherited in better shape than the one we have left to them. Within this generation we particularly wish to single out some special children in our own lives: Nicholas and Alexa (Barbara Gueldner's nephew and niece) and Madelynn (Kenneth Merrell's granddaughter). May your dreams be realized, and may your world become a better place.

About the Authors

Kenneth W. Merrell, PhD, is Professor of School Psychology at the University of Oregon in Eugene, where he has served as School Psychology Program Director and as head of the Department of Special Education and Clinical Sciences. His research and clinical interests focus on social and emotional learning in schools and social–emotional assessment and intervention with children and adolescents. He has authored numerous journal articles and book chapters on these topics, as well as several books, assessment instruments, and intervention programs. Dr. Merrell has extensive experience in working with children and youth in school settings and in leading academic and research programs.

Barbara A. Gueldner, PhD, is a psychologist with Parker Pediatrics and Adolescents in the greater Denver, Colorado, metro area. She has over a decade of experience working as a school psychologist in the public school systems in Wisconsin and Oregon and with children from infancy through young adulthood in pediatric primary care and intensive medical and psychiatric inpatient care. Dr. Gueldner's research and clinical interests comprise universal prevention of and early intervention into children's mental health concerns, issues in pediatric psychology, consultation, and training mental health professionals. She has coauthored several articles and book chapters on these topics and a social and emotional learning curriculum for students.

Acknowledgments

We wish to acknowledge several people and institutions for their contributions to this book. One of our goals was to make the materials relevant, accessible, and practical. Our experiences as researchers and as practitioners greatly shaped its contents, especially the vignettes and case studies. We specifically acknowledge the educators from Oregon's Springfield, Eugene, and Bethel public school districts, who have lent their expertise and cooperation in many of the social and emotional learning (SEL) activities we have been a part of over the years. While we developed this book, we were fortunate to be working at our respective institutions—the University of Oregon's College of Education in Eugene and The Children's Hospital in Aurora, Colorado—both of which provided a strong foundation and platform from which to develop our ideas. We acknowledge the support of Ayelet Talmi, PhD, and Brian Stafford, MD, MPH, at The Children's Hospital, who are actively engaged in collaborative community advocacy and practice to make SEL concepts universally accessible to all children. We acknowledge the influence and insights of several faculty members at the University of Oregon—too many to mention individually—who served on PhD dissertation committees related to our work in SEL. Our colleague Sara Castro-Olivo, PhD, at the University of California, Riverside, contributed Chapter 5, "One Size Does Not Fit All: Adapting Social and Emotional Learning for Use in Our Multicultural World." Dr. Castro-Olivo is a skilled and passionate advocate for using SEL effectively with culturally and linguistically diverse students, and we look forward to future opportunities for mutual collaboration. Our SEL work has been influenced greatly by many members of the Oregon Resiliency Project research team with whom we have partnered —more than 30 in all between 2001 and 2009—and we are grateful to them for their contributions during this period. The editorial, production, and marketing team at The Guilford Press were a great help during the preparation of this book. We particularly express our thanks to Craig Thomas, Natalie Graham, and Seymour Weingarten for their continued support. As always, special thanks to Chris Jennison, a true gentleman and a scholar and the advocate behind the initial development of The Guilford Practical Intervention in the Schools Series. And finally, we thank the scholars, practitioners, and policy proponents who helped to shape and define SEL as a core entity several years ago, including those who founded the Collaborative for Academic, Social, and Emotional Learning and those involved in spearheading similar efforts. Their vision helped to make our work in this area possible.

About This Book

In 1985, on the 30th anniversary of his discovery of a vaccine for the polio virus—one of the most dramatic innovations of modern times—the legendary scientist Jonas Salk was asked what he would be working on today if he were a young scientist. Without hesitation, Salk replied, "I'd still do immunization, but I'd do it psychologically rather than biologically" (quoted in Buchanan & Seligman, 1995, p. 250). Perhaps the weight of this statement is not fully appreciated at first glance by most readers. Make no mistake about it: What Salk proposed was a radical idea in many ways. Except for the minority of readers who are first-wave baby boomers or older, you probably have no personal experience with polio. But in the early 1950s, polio was the number-one cause of death and disability among all communicable diseases, and it was universally feared by parents. Salk's discovery, after several years of intensely focused work, literally changed the world. Little by little, polio diminished and then disappeared. So, to have the developer of the first safe and effective vaccine for polio indicate that, if given the chance, he would now focus his life's work on inoculation against and prevention of mental health disorders is truly remarkable, in our opinion.

We don't think that you, the reader, need much in the way of convincing that promotion of mental health and prevention of social–emotional disorders among our children is of paramount importance. After all, you are interested enough in a book on mental health promotion in schools to be reading this introduction! But we are also willing to guess that most of you are not quite sure where to start, which may be one of the reasons you have turned to our book. Or perhaps you have already started, but you are frustrated with your efforts and are not seeing the kind of outcomes you anticipated. So how are we doing collectively in our "psychological immunization" efforts? Judging from data compiled by numerous researchers as well as the U.S. National Institute of Mental Health, *not very well*. In fact, about one in five school-age children and youth in the United States have a significant enough mental health problem to warrant intervention, yet only about one in five of these young people actually receive any meaningful services (see Hoagwood & Johnson, 2003). To be blunt about it, we think that despite the incredible efforts of many dedicated educators and mental health professionals, the state of mental health promotion among the young people in our schools is pathetic. We simply must do better.

Please don't take our dismal assessment of the current state of mental health promotion in our schools and communities as just another jeremiad, something to be nodded at and then avoided. The whole point of this book is that we now have the knowledge, tools, and resources at our disposal that, despite our collective challenges and past failures, can make a huge positive difference in promoting mental health and academic success of students. But to make that huge difference, we need to act now, both mindfully and with great care and planning. And we think that you are the ones to act!

Social and emotional learning (SEL) in the classroom is our message in this book for promoting mental health and academic success. Although the specific techniques, strategies, and concepts of SEL are not new, it has only been the past few years—perhaps since the mid-1990s—that SEL has been articulated as a cohesive framework and has gradually evolved into a field with a huge potential reach and influence. Through the efforts of individual prevention scientists and practitioners, such as those who founded the Collaborative for Academic, Social, and Emotional Learning (*www.casel.org*), SEL has matured and expanded to the point where it is beginning to make a significant difference in our schools and communities. As you will see in the research cited, the potential impact of SEL is most impressive, although still in its nascent stages. Hence, we see this book as an "A-to-Z" guide to spur educators and mental health professionals to start using SEL in a cohesive and structured way in schools and related settings.

The eight chapters of this book are not exhaustive by any means, but they will take you through almost every aspect of using SEL, from planning and getting support for it, to selecting curriculum tools, to delivering content in a way that fits your students and communities, to measuring and evaluating the outcomes that you produce. Chapter 1 introduces and defines SEL and realistically assesses what it can offer you and your students. Chapter 2 includes an overview of several of the most widely used and researched SEL programs currently available for adoption. Chapter 3 covers the essentials of using SEL in the classroom, including a wide variety of practical material ranging from preparing your students and selecting materials to developing your own plans for SEL activities if you are not using a packaged program. Chapter 4 explores the link between SEL and academic learning in schools and contains many practical examples and suggestions for how SEL programs and strategies can be woven into the fabric of the curriculum in a manner that supports academic learning. Recognizing that delivery of SEL programming in schools occurs in a complex and increasingly diverse and pluralistic social context, Chapter 5 addresses the need for adapting SEL content to make it culturally appropriate in specific settings and includes a practical, step-by-step guide for doing so. Although we obviously highly value SEL as a mental health promotion tool in schools, we recognize that basic classroom-based SEL programming alone is not enough to fully meet the mental health needs of our students with the most severe and complex problems. Thus, Chapter 6 focuses on enhancing SEL to maximize its benefit to the most distressed students and examines practical ways to help link those students with expanded mental health programming in the broader community. Chapter 7 is a basic primer on using social–emotional assessment, measurement, and evaluation strategies within SEL and briefly overviews some exciting new tools and innovations in this area, some of which are literally "just out the door." And finally, Chapter 8 delves into the intricacies of using SEL within complex organizations such as schools, providing a solid foundation for understanding how systems change, as well as practical strategies for planning and gaining support for using SEL in your own organization.

Is this book the final word on SEL, the *summum bonum* of the field, if you will? Certainly not. There are many important aspects of SEL that we have chosen to skim through, and some are not discussed at all, given our purpose and constraints for the work. Since our aim is directly at practitioners, for whom we have written this book, we have simplified complex ideas to make them accessible and addressed some of the complex research and instructional design issues only summarily. For those readers who desire a more in-depth exploration of SEL, there are several other excellent and more detailed sources, many of which we have cited. We also recognize that there is much still to be learned about SEL and how to best design and implement it in our schools, communities, and families. To us, this is one of the most exciting prospects of SEL, and we eagerly look forward to exploring new frontiers.

If you are unfamiliar with the concept of using structured and articulated curricular materials to promote the mental health of children and adolescents, this book is for you. If you are already somewhat experienced in using SEL or other mental health approaches in schools, this book will help to enhance your SEL planning and delivery. And if you are a veteran of using SEL approaches, the book's overviews of some exciting new SEL tools, practical suggestions for using measurement and evaluation strategies to gauge your impact, and explorations of using strategic planning processes within your organization to maximize your outcomes will appeal to you as well.

The noted anthropologist Margaret Mead famously said, "A small group of thoughtful people could change the world. Indeed, it's the only thing that ever has." Jonas Salk's discovery of the polio vaccine changed the world in ways that could hardly be imagined in the previous generation, yet he said if he could start over as a young scientist, he would focus on "psychological immunization" efforts. We think the time is far gone for only thinking about the state of mental health of our children and adolescents; it's time to do something effective and constructive about it. We are convinced that the carefully planned use of effective SEL strategies in our classrooms is one of the best ways to achieve meaningful results. We wish you well in your journey along this challenging and rewarding path.

Contents

CHAPTER 1

Social and Emotional Learning

What It Is, and What It Can Do for Your Students

INTRODUCTION AND OVERVIEW

As we are beginning to write the first manuscript pages for this book, it's early September. All of the telltale signs of the end of summer are here: the shorter days, the cooler nights, and the first hints of red and yellow in the leaves in the northern climates where we live. The summer camps are shuttered, the swimming pools at the parks have been drained, and the football fields at the high schools are once again lit up on Friday nights. It's back-to-school time. A new school year started for most children and adolescents in this nation within the past 2 weeks. Kids who were running through the sprinkler or playing at the park just days ago are now making their way to school in the morning. For students, parents, and educators, the start of the school year brings both promise and fear: the promise of new possibilities and the fear of new challenges.

Just yesterday, one of us (K. W. M.) was sitting in a meeting with an elementary school principal, as well as other adults who were concerned about children. The school had started a new year only 3 days earlier. The purpose of our meeting was to discuss some of the serious challenges that her students and their families were facing, and what might be done about it.

> Even in bleak circumstances, there are rays of hope: kids who, despite great challenges, somehow manage to beat the odds and succeed. Social and emotional learning (SEL) promotes this hope; *all* students can benefit from the inclusion of SEL at school.

As the group began to recite the familiar litany of problems facing so many students and their families, the pessimism grew thicker. Before long, the problems seemed almost overwhelming and the prospects for a good way out of the quagmire seemed bleak. The conversation reached a pause, and then the principal—a veteran educator in her 50s who presided over an elementary school with a large number of "at-risk" students—made a most profound observation:

"Sometimes the challenges that the kids and families are facing seem overwhelming, and I start to wonder if we are going to be able to make a big enough difference in their lives. It feels discouraging, even depressing at times. But you know what? School started again this week. There's energy and hope in the air. When I see those new kindergarten students arriving at the door on the first day of school, carrying their new backpacks and full of excitement, all seems right with the world."

And so it is. In each of your communities and schools, kids and their families are facing challenges, some that are manageable, and some that are absolutely overwhelming. And yet, hope seems to spring eternal. Most educators and mental health professionals whom we have encountered during our careers started out as optimists. They wanted to make a difference, to change lives, to provide the tools, supports, and inspiration that would lead young people to achieve full and productive lives. And even in bleak circumstances, there are rays of hope, examples of kids who, despite great challenges, somehow managed to beat the odds and succeed.

In a way, this book is about hope. The evolving field of social and emotional learning (SEL) has come together in a relatively brief time and is now poised to offer educators and child mental health professionals hope that the science, instructional methods, and materials now exist and have been carefully articulated to help them make a meaningful difference in promoting mental health, social and emotional adjustment, and academic success of their students. It is our view that *all* students can benefit from the inclusion of SEL at school, that it can be easily infused in many educational contexts, and that it can benefit both the mental health and academic success of children and adolescents. This book is a practical guide for moving forward in this area—a road map for understanding SEL and how it can be applied in schools and classrooms. We are convinced that with only a moderate investment in time and very little, if any, investment in new materials, you can begin to use the tools of SEL in your own classroom or practice setting, with good results, *immediately.*

This introductory chapter begins with a discussion of why SEL efforts are needed in our schools. We argue that children and families in our current society face unprecedented challenges and are in great need of learning social, emotional, cognitive, and behavioral skills that can help buffer and insulate them from the difficulties that are so prevalent and can lead to terribly negative outcomes if left unchecked. An overview of the typical definitions and common elements of SEL is then presented, followed by a description of the essential major components in SEL programs and how they are connected to important outcomes for children and adolescents. Because SEL activities are an ideal adjunct for use in schools that incorporate positive behavior support (PBS) principles for behavior management (but are equally important in schools that do not incorporate PBS), a discussion of using SEL within the three-tiered prevention framework of positive behavior support is provided. We examine some examples of recent legislative actions promoting SEL in schools, because we think (and hope) that these statewide mandates and incentives are a harbinger of things to come on a national level. We also provide a brief discussion of the research base and proven benefits of SEL so that readers can be assured that in this book we are promoting something that has real substance. Finally, we include a vignette that overviews one educator's experience in giving SEL a try in her classroom.

WHY SEL?

Several years ago, on May 20, 1998, we were both happily going about our business in our workplaces in Wisconsin and Iowa, respectively, unaware of a great tragedy that was unfolding on the West Coast, something that would have a significant impact on both of us. As the news began to trickle in throughout the day regarding a tragic shooting incident at Thurston High School in Springfield, Oregon, we, like educators and citizens across the nation, were greatly concerned by the events that had taken place. A troubled 15-year-old student had brought a gun to school and went on a shooting spree that would leave his parents and 2 students dead, 25 students and faculty seriously injured, and a whole school and community traumatized. Although neither of us was involved in the immediate aftermath of these events, they held special interest and would ultimately have an impact on us. One of us (B. A. G.) was working as a school psychologist in Wisconsin that spring, but was hired by Oregon's Springfield School District a year later, with Thurston High School assigned as a site of responsibility. The aftermath of that tragic day was still evident as a traumatized staff, administration, and student body went about the difficult business of trying to move on and get back to normal. One of the most apparent results of these events was that for some time afterward—even 3 or 4 years later—the students at the high school and a nearby middle school who were the most at risk for mental health problems or other adjustment difficulties to begin with were pushed further into the "risk zone" by what had happened, and many of their issues and symptoms were exacerbated. These problems permeated the environment and day-to-day work of providing educational and mental health services to students. The other of us (K. W. M.) was working at a university in Iowa when the Thurston shootings happened, but watched the events unfurl on the news with a particular personal interest. He had attended graduate school in that Oregon community a decade earlier, had been inside the high school briefly to do a practicum observation, and had nephews and a niece who attended school nearby. Later, after returning as a faculty member to the University of Oregon, he worked closely with the Springfield school district's special services coordinator, placing school psychology students for practicum assignments in those schools and became personally aware of the long-term aftermath of that tragic day, as the 10-year anniversary was marked.

> Up to one out of every five students in a typical classroom may experience mental health problems in the course of a school year, but only a few of these students receive appropriate intervention services. SEL provides an alternative approach for delivering preventative classroom-based mental health services that will reach *all* students.

Why do we bring up this awful school shooting in a book on SEL? After all, we are not making any claims that SEL programs would have prevented this tragedy. But let's take a deeper look at the issue and subsequent events. What happened in Oregon in 1998 paralleled similar tragic acts of violence that occurred in the mid- to late 1990s in several U.S. states (Colorado, Kentucky, and Arkansas, among others), and that for a time gripped the attention of education and mental health policymakers and practitioners. In the months immediately afterward, there was increased professional emphasis on crisis prevention and intervention, behavioral and mental health issues in schools, and especially risk assessment and prediction of violence in students. This increased attention was appropriate and necessary. Then, little by little, the interest began to wane and shift, as fewer of these large-scale traumatic events made their way into the news. Many school boards and state legislatures adopted "get-tough" and "zero-tolerance" policies that were punitive rather than preventative, and were more aimed at getting high-risk students out of schools than at providing mental health promotion services. Soon after, in 2001, the U.S. Congress passed the No Child Left Behind Act (NCLB), which emphasized standards, accountability, basic academic skills, and frequent assessment, and which struck terror into the hearts of school administrators nationwide that the assessment data from their schools would place them on the dreaded "failing school" list, or at least not compare favorably with other schools nearby. Although NCLB, in our view, was prompted by some serious issues and has had some important positive effects, it has also resulted in an unfortunate shift away from primary prevention and mental health efforts in many schools, because it placed educators under intense pressure to increase students' scores in certain fundamental academic areas. As the field of SEL has come into its own in the past decade, it has done so in many instances against the grain of the current zeitgeist, where mental health and social–emotional wellness issues have once again taken a back seat to other priorities. In our view it's time for the pendulum to quit swinging so dramatically, and for schools to move mental health promotion from the fringes to the mainstream of educational practice.

Dramatic and highly publicized events such as school shootings tend to create a push–pull dynamic that masks the need for ongoing, rather than reactive, SEL and mental health promotion efforts in schools. In their aftermath, major attention is shifted from other priorities to preventing and responding to high-profile events. And when the concern has lessened and we no longer see reports of dramatic and disturbing incidents in schools, policymakers and administrators often tend to assume that all is well, and that the problem is at least temporarily solved. As many see it, it's now time to move on.

This view is shortsighted and unfortunate. All is *not* well with respect to the mental health status of children and youth in the United States. Although we don't want to take the position of alarmists or to turn this section into a jeremiad of doom and gloom, a few alarming facts are worth considering if we are to fully comprehend the current state of affairs. Although most children are able to successfully cope with the social, emotional, and academic challenges they face, many do not do so well. And of those who seem to have satisfactory personal adjustment, many children are in a surprisingly fragile state, and a single stressful event or situation could push them over the edge and into a crisis mode.

According to researchers who have conducted prevalence estimates and specific epidemiologic studies, an estimated 20% of school-age youth experience mental health problems during the course of any given year (Coie, Miller-Johnson, & Bagwell, 2000; Greenberg et al., 2003). To put this figure into a practical context, that's one out of every five students in a typical classroom. And of the youth experiencing these problems, up to 8.3% experience significant depression (Greenberg, Domitrovich, & Bumbarger, 2001). Often in crisis, approximately 80% of youth with mental health problems do not receive effective intervention services (Greenberg et al., 2003). Without intervention, they may experience a "domino effect" of cumulative problems, in which one thing leads to another, and they are constantly struggling just to get by. These problems, seldom just transitory, have the potential to continue throughout life, especially if they do not receive appropriate supports. For example, a teen fraught with depression may experience sadness, poor concentration, irritability, interpersonal conflict, social isolation, and decreased academic performance. Left undetected and untreated, and without the supporting power of skills and knowledge that could be transmitted through social and emotional learning efforts, academic failure, school dropout, joblessness, poverty, conflicted interpersonal relationships, and sometimes suicide may needlessly result (Michael & Crowley, 2002). To put these challenges into an economic and larger social content, billions of dollars are annually spent in the United States on treatment for existing mental disorders, lost productivity, mortality, and criminal justice costs (Coie et al., 2000). It's fair to say that our society pays a tremendous social, emotional, and monetary price for our collective mental health problems.

Coie et al. (2000) emphasized the urgency with which prevention programs are needed if we are to change the negative trajectory of mental health problems among children and adolescents. The cost of providing treatment for existing and chronic mental health problems far exceeds the cost of providing prevention programs that may deter such problems from occurring in the first place. We also face a future shortage of mental health professionals available to provide treatment to those in need. Many individuals who need help simply may not get it. If you work in a typical school setting, you know exactly what we are talking about here: There are typically not enough psychologists, counselors, and social workers available to meet all of the needs that your students have. We believe that as professionals and as members of a society that should strive for social justice, we have a moral and ethical obligation to provide effective evidence-based prevention services to all who face life's challenges.

One advantage we have in meeting these challenges is that schools are excellent venues for providing prevention and intervention services. In fact, of the minority of affected students who are fortunate enough to receive mental health services, 75% receive these services in a school setting (Hoagwood & Erwin, 1997). Researchers Doll and Lyon (1998) proposed that schools have opportunities to promote competence across academic, personal, and social domains. Schools may prioritize these opportunities because they value skills that are necessary for success in life such as good problem solving, academic proficiency, and social and emotional competence. Because they value these skills, educators may be motivated to mobilize their resources to provide children with the structure and curriculum necessary for success.

Perhaps most evident, schools are increasingly motivated to make sure students are successful since the enactment of the NCLB, a federal law that calls for increased accountability for student performance. Although we have noted that, in many schools, this legislation has removed the focus from mental health prevention because of the pressure to demonstrate higher academic achievement, there is another element to consider here that favors SEL, or that at least could favor SEL. Increasing demands on students' academic performance as well as increasing recognition that social and emotional competence in youth is vital to adjustment into adulthood calls for action. Furthermore, as we show in Chapter 4, SEL can have a very positive effect on academic performance and thus should not be viewed as something that detracts from academics. As Greenberg et al. (2003, p. 470) noted, "There is a national consensus on the need for 21st-century schools to offer more than academic instruction if one is to foster success in school and life for all children." We could not agree more.

DEFINING AND UNDERSTANDING SEL

Although the concerns presented in the previous section are not necessarily new, the field that has come to be known as *social and emotional learning* (SEL) is a relatively recent development. Beginning in the 1990s, when Daniel Goleman's (1995) influential book *Emotional Intelligence* was published, researchers from several related disciplines were beginning to seek common ground in developing a framework for supporting the positive social, emotional, and academic development of children and adolescents in school settings. According to Greenberg et al. (2003) the term *social and emotional learning* was coined by a group of prevention researchers, educators, and child advocates who attended a 1994 meeting hosted by the Fetzer Institute for the purpose of moving the field forward in promoting prevention and mental health efforts. Several of the individuals who were part of this "Fetzer Group" effort later became key players in establishing the Collaborative for Academic, Social and Emotional Learning (CASEL; see *www.casel.org*), which to date has been the most influential organization in promoting the aims of SEL.

> "Through developmentally appropriate classroom instruction and application of learning to everyday situations, SEL programming builds children's skills to recognize and manage their emotions, appreciate the perspectives of others, establish positive goals, make responsible decisions, and handle interpersonal situations" (Greenberg et al., 2003, p. 468).

SEL both incorporates and broadens several areas of focus that have been used to describe and promote educational intervention programs in this area, including *social competency training, positive youth development, violence prevention, character education, primary prevention, mental health promotion*, and others. SEL does not replace these other important efforts; it simply provides a framework by which their best aspects can be incorporated to help meet the educational and mental health needs of children and youth.

The *social* aspect of SEL indicates a concern for fostering positive relationships with others, such as peers, teachers, and family members. This part of SEL reflects *interpersonal* development. The *emotional* aspect of SEL indicates a concern for fostering self-awareness or self-knowledge, especially involving emotions or feelings, but also by implication, the cognitions or thoughts that are connected to our emotions. This part of SEL essentially reflects *intrapersonal* development. The *learning* aspect of SEL implies that both social and emotional growth and adjustment can be taught and learned through instruction, practice, and feedback. By including *learning* in the phrase there is also a natural link to schools or other educational settings, and by implication, the notion that specific instructional activities, lesson activities, and curricula may be used to promote these aims.

There is no "official" definition of SEL. In fact, several definitions have been proposed, and there are some differences among them. These slight points of variance or disagreement are or of no real consequence, nor should they be of concern to you in your efforts to use SEL with students in your own school or agency. That said, definitions are important in establishing working parameters for an idea or a concept in a way that makes them easy to approach and understand. One definition that we like very much is; "Through developmentally and culturally appropriate classroom instruction and application of learning to everyday situations, SEL programming builds children's skills to recognize and manage their emotions, appreciate the perspectives of others, establish positive goals, make responsible decisions, and handle interpersonal situations" (Greenberg et al., 2003, p. 468). Another definition of SEL that we value is "SEL is a process through which we learn to recognize and manage emotions, care about others, make good decisions, behave ethically and responsibly, develop positive relationships, and avoid negative behaviors" (Zins, Bloodworth, Weissberg, & Walberg, 2004, p. 4).

Major Aspects of SEL

Although a definition of SEL provides a brief general idea of what we are concerned with when we speak of social and emotional learning, it lacks the precision to help educators and mental health professionals concentrate on the specific skills, attributes, and areas of focus that they wish to promote with their students. For this reason, we think that some additional exploration is a good idea.

Wellness

An interesting place to start our discussion of aspects of SEL is the concept of *wellness*. All too often, efforts aimed at prevention and treatment of troubled children and youth have focused on erasing or reducing pathology or disorders (the educational equivalent of "disease" in the medical world), without really asking questions such as "What does wellness look like?", "What are the characteristics of a student who exhibits wellness?", or "How do we achieve wellness?" In addressing these questions with respect to mental health promotion, Lorion (2000) noted that "wellness refers to the psychological capacity to cope with the demands arising across time, circumstance, and setting" (p. 15), and stated further, "wellness as a characteristic of individuals across the life span represents the norm rather than the exception across varying situational demands. . . . [It is] a positive state in and of itself rather than merely serving as an index that dysfunction has been avoided" (p. 17). What Lorion's views on wellness seem to imply is that all too often, we have thought of wellness only as the absence of disease or pathology, without giving much consideration to what a state of positive health or wellness really looks like. Human services professionals—particularly psychologists and psychiatrists—have traditionally plied their services armed with the tools for diagnosing and treating disease, with only a minimal amount of consideration for the properties of wellness. And as the old saying, "When the only tool you have is a hammer, everything starts to look like a nail," goes, many of us in these fields have all too often focused our efforts on labeling disorders and prescribing treatments without really venturing into the properties of wellness that we seek to foster in the individuals and groups that we serve.

Pathways to Wellness

Once we understand the importance of wellness as a unique construct, and an idea of what it entails, just how do we arrive there? How does someone who is not well become well? When we and our colleagues began the development of the Strong Kids social and emotional learning programs (which are detailed along with several other SEL programs in Chapter 2), we were interested in a systematic approach for promoting social, emotional, and academic wellness in children. In our predevelopment literature review efforts, we found an intriguing breakdown of five "pathways to wellness," which were articulated by pioneering prevention science researcher Emory Cowen (1994). Cowen and his colleagues at the University of Rochester, through their research and clinical outreach efforts in the groundbreaking Primary Prevention Project, identified the following as the essential pathways by which wellness is fostered:

> **SEL should ideally take place in the home, beginning in infancy, with competent and loving parents providing positive role models and raising successful and happy children. Unfortunately, we are not all on equal footing in our exposure to home settings that favor wellness outcomes.**

- *Forming wholesome early attachments.* Young children need to form positive relationships of trust, warmth, and affection with their parents, other primary caregivers, and siblings. These early positive attachments provide a foundation on which subsequent wholesome attachments and positive relationships are built, such as with peers and teachers. The absence of wholesome early attachments may be a key ingredient in developing subsequent social and emotional problems.
- *Acquiring age-appropriate competencies.* Each stage of infancy, childhood, and adolescence includes particular developmental competencies that must be acquired for optimum wellness and successfully achieving the milestones of development. Although children learn new skills and concepts at differing rates, almost all children who receive the appropriate support, modeling, and mentoring can acquire the competencies for each developmental stage.
- *Exposure to settings that favor wellness outcomes.* The power of the setting or environment in promoting wellness is enormous. Although some children who are exposed to unfavorable settings are still able to achieve wellness, the odds are steeply not in their favor in this regard.
- *Having the empowering sense of being in control of one's fate.* Although one's parents, peers, and environmental surroundings are critically important to achieving wellness, there are also internal variables at play. The belief that one can be instrumental in manag-

ing and seeking one's own destiny—regardless of how small the scenario—seems to be an essential pathway that leads to emotional and social health. Psychologists typically refer to this pattern of believing and thinking as having an "internal locus of control."

• *Coping effectively with stress.* Although they are not equally disbursed among us, life's stresses are an inevitable part of the human condition. Developing the ability to respond in an effective and proactive manner to stressors—both great and small—is another key skill that is likely to promote wellness.

It stands to reason that for optimal effectiveness and impact, any comprehensive SEL curriculum or intervention program should address most—and preferably all—of these five critical pathways. Failure to make sufficient progress along any of these pathways may lead to undesirable outcomes, and may damage one's overall wellness. Fortunately there are specific steps, techniques, and intervention tools available that address each of these pathways.

PERSON-CENTERED SEL COMPETENCIES

Another tool for understanding the major aspects of SEL is the framework of person-centered SEL competencies that was detailed by Zins, Weissberg, Wang, and Walberg (2004). This SEL framework does not have an explicit focus on one's surroundings, but zooms in on the competencies that seem to require extensive use of cognitive, affective, and self-regulatory states. These states, which are for the most part internally regulated, have been thought of as "self-related" forms of social–emotional adjustment (see Merrell & Gimpel, 1998).

Zins et al.'s person-centered SEL framework includes the following key elements:

• *Self-awareness.* This realm is characterized by the ability to identify and recognize emotions; gather accurate self-perceptions; recognize strengths, needs, and values; have a sense of self-efficacy; and develop a sense of spirituality, which is usually defined as a recognition of one's place in the world and relation to other things, including the possibility of a higher power or greater creative force.

• *Social awareness.* Social awareness, or the realm of relating effectively to other people, includes the ability to take the perspective of another person and to have empathy for him or her (the ability to take a different emotional perspective), an appreciation of human diversity in its various forms, and a healthy and appropriate respect for other people.

• *Responsible decision making.* Developing the capacity to make decisions in a responsible way includes the ability to identify problems and evaluate the situations in which problems arise, use effective problem-solving skills, evaluate and reflect on various alternatives in life, and the development of a sense of personal, moral, and ethical responsibility.

• *Self-management.* Characterized by internal self-regulation skills and the ability to translate them into overt action, self-management includes impulse control, stress management, self-motivation and personal discipline, and the ability to set appropriate goals and organize one's actions to attain those goals.

• *Relationship management.* Having successful interpersonal relationships requires more than just social awareness; it also requires effective overt skill enactment. Within this realm of SEL competencies, Zins, Weissberg, et al. stressed communication, social engagement, cooperation, negotiation, conflict management, as well as help-seeking and help-providing skills.

So what's not to like about these specific aspects of SEL (which are illustrated in more detail and examples in Table 1.1) that can and should be addressed in prevention and intervention curricula? In our view, *nothing:* We have yet to find a downside to the notion of promoting these characteristics through systematic instruction in schools. Whether we are considering the pathways to wellness—the avenues by which healthy social and emotional development are promoted—or the specific person-centered aspects that are considered to be essential for effective adjustment and relationship success, we are talking about important and practical characteristics that *everyone* needs. But as is discussed earlier in this chapter,

TABLE 1.1. Descriptions and Examples of Five Key Components of the Framework of Person-Centered SEL Competencies

Skill	Description	Example
Self-awareness	The ability to identify one's own emotions, cognitions, values, strengths, and needs	A student recognizes that he is feeling frustrated while working on math, a subject he knows he struggles with, and that the frustration is leading to negative and unrealistic thoughts.
Social awareness	The ability to recognize other people's perspectives, differences, and emotions	A student playing basketball with friends realizes that a teammate plays harder and seems happier when positive comments are made to her.
Responsible decision making	The ability to recognize challenges and to engage in effective problem-solving routines; ability to evaluate and reflect on one's own actions; development of a sense of personal responsibility	A student plans out a time line for completing a demanding project that is due in several weeks at the end of a grading period.
Self-management	The ability to monitor and control one's emotions, impulses, and behavior in order to achieve personal goals	A student who is feeling very frustrated and anxious taking a challenging test takes deep breaths in an attempt to relax and be able to finish it.
Relationship management	The ability to communicate, cooperate, negotiate, and provide and receive support in order to achieve satisfactory interpersonal relationships	A student who is having a difficult time at home because of conflicts with parents over rules initiates a discussion with her parents in order to discuss the rules and to try and negotiate some changes in them.

Note. Based on Zins, Weissberg, et al. (2004).

we can't just take it for granted that all or even most people will succeed in this regard, or even that most people will develop the minimum competencies needed to be happy, well-adjusted, and successful in life. In fact, many individuals have significant deficits in the various key social–emotional attributes, and we should no longer take it for granted that our students will develop them without an explicit plan for instruction and mastery of the essential elements. Just as we cannot take it for granted that our students will learn to read without being explicitly taught how to do it, we should make social–emotional *resilience* the "fourth R," and move toward universal social and emotional instruction and learning as part of the school curriculum.

Ideally, positive SEL should take place in the home, beginning in infancy, with competent and loving parents providing positive role models and raising children who become successful and happy persons through these efforts. There is no question that such a home environment is the best advantage one can ever receive in growing up to be competent, happy, and independent. But most unfortunately, we are not all on equal footing when it comes to exposure to home settings that favor wellness outcomes. And even for those children who have had every advantage at home in this regard, SEL efforts within classrooms have the potential to help further insulate them against adverse outcomes by providing a scaffold for coping with the ever-increasing social stresses and demands of our modern world. In this vein, Brandt's (1999) comments about the necessity for universal SEL in schools strikes an agreeable chord:

> Social and emotional learning is both a new and very old idea. In all cultures and in every generation, educators and parents have been concerned with children's sense of well-being and ability to get along with others. Certainly in today's social environment, teachers have no choice but to attend to their students' personal and social development, even when their first priorities are academic knowledge and skills. (p. 173)

USING SEL WITHIN POSITIVE BEHAVIOR INTERVENTION AND SUPPORT AND THE THREE-TIERED PREVENTION MODEL

We make no claims that SEL should be a "stand-alone" effort in promoting children's resiliency, mental health, and academic success, disconnected from other programs and initiatives. In fact, such an approach to SEL (or anything else, for that matter) in schools would be profoundly short sighted. Many veteran educators find the perennial recurring school reform efforts or "next great thing" promises and programs to be a source for irritation and dismay. We understand the frustration that comes from seeing trendy new programs and legislative or administrative mandates rolled out every few years, only to see them eat up a significant amount of energy and resources, only to be abandoned in favor of the next trend or mandate after they fail to deliver what was promised. We've been around schools long enough now to be able to look back and see the remains of initiatives and programs that were once trumpeted with great enthusiasm, only to later be found lacking in some important way, and ultimately to be assigned to the scrap heap of things no longer needed after they fall out of favor. So let's be very clear about this issue: SEL is not a fad, a trendy new idea, or a "next great thing" mandate. Neither is SEL a stand-alone solution to our educational and social problems. Rather, we see SEL as a basic premise that should be woven into the fabric of schools to complement, supplement, and enhance existing educational efforts. In our view, SEL is one of four primary components of safe, effective, and caring schools, along with effective academic instruction, a caring and nurturing school environment, and a foundation of positive behavior interventions and supports (PBIS). In essence, when considering the importance and place of these four components, it is important to realize that *we need them all.* Figure 1.1 details the importance of these four primary components, showing how they are interrelated and form necessary and interdependent parts of the entire school milieu.

Positive Behavior Interventions and Supports

Among these other three areas that work with SEL in providing our four primary components, it is easy enough to understand what is meant by effective academic instruction and a caring and nurturing school environment. Positive behavioral interventions and supports—generally referred to as PBIS for short—is a newer concept that may be less familiar to readers. Thus it's worthwhile to briefly mine the workings of PBIS to see how it fits as one of these primary components of safe, caring, and effective schools, and to see how it forms a natural link to SEL.

PBIS is a data-oriented approach to school discipline and behavior management that is based on behavioral principles. It differs from many traditional systems of behavior management because it focuses on teaching, shaping, and reinforcing appropriate behaviors in schools, eschewing the reactionary approach that focuses primarily on punishment for violation of school rules. Proponents of PBIS have convincingly argued that reactionary

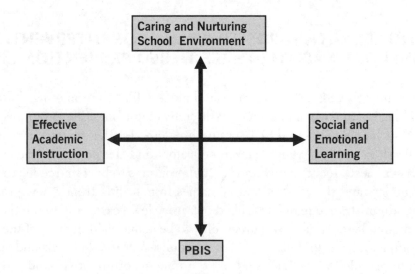

FIGURE 1.1. We need it *all:* Four essential elements of safe, positive, effective, and caring schools.

punishment-based systems that focus on responding to rule violations are simply not very effective, because these efforts do not focus on teaching students the skills that are needed to behave appropriately in school, and because punishment-based efforts tend to only suppress problem behavior in the short term (Crone, Horner, & Hawken, 2004). Another area where PBIS efforts often differ from traditional behavior management systems is that, ideally, they are designed to be implemented on a schoolwide basis rather than in selected individual classrooms within a school. The advantage of a school-wide PBIS effort is that there is consistency in the expectations, rules, and procedures across classrooms and grades. Rather than having to adjust to different behavioral expectations and consequences across a complex school environment, students in PBIS schools should have a predictable routine that is consistent across the school day. Teachers and other school staff who work in PBIS schools also have clear expectations of how they should deal with student behavior, as well as a consistent level of support from their administrators.

The website for the U.S. Department of Education's National Technical Assistance Center on PBIS (see *www.pbis.org*) contains extensive information and resources on PBIS, including basic descriptions of using it schoolwide or districtwide, research references, links, and slides from training sessions conducted by experts. In addition, the best general single source we have found for a practical, comprehensive overview of how to implement PBIS in schools is Crone et al.'s (2004) book, *Responding to Problem Behavior in Schools: The Behavior Education Program*. We recommend readers who desire to learn more about the basics of PBIS to review these sources.

Our purpose in this section is to show how SEL may be integrated with PBIS, and how they are complementary. Without going through an extensive technical orientation on PBIS, we think that the following points provide a good summary of the basic elements of how it is used in schools:

- Staff and administrative "buy-in" and support are necessary to make the system work on a schoolwide basis.
- Staff receive sufficient training in the basic elements of PBIS implementation and have available consultation from a team leader or other inside specialist if there are questions or problems.
- The school adopts a set of very brief, simple, and positively stated rules for behavior (e.g., "be safe," "be respectful," and "be responsible"), and students are provided direct instruction in what the rules mean and how to behave in a manner that is consistent with these expectations.
- Teachers briefly refer to and reteach these expectations and rules in their individual classrooms on a regular basis.
- Students are acknowledged, praised, or otherwise reinforced for engaging in appropriate behavior.
- Behavioral and social skills are taught to all students on a regular basis.
- Students who engage in behaviors that are not in compliance with the PBIS rules and expectations are corrected, retaught the rules, and given warnings and simple consequences (e.g., loss of privileges) for misconduct.

- Students who have repeated problems with behavioral expectations and rule violations are provided with a more intensive support program, such as a daily "check-in/ check-out" procedure or point card that they carry from class to class, which serves as a way of monitoring their progress and praising them for appropriate behavior; they may also receive individualized function-based assessments of their behavior to help link them to more effective individualized services.
- Dangerous or more severe behaviors may be addressed through additional consequences (discipline referrals, removal from a classroom) and provision of more intensive individual supports.
- Ideally, simple data are gathered and evaluated on a frequent basis, at both the classroom and school levels (e.g., number of office discipline referrals), to gauge the success of the PBIS program.
- Staff retraining and consultation are provided as needed.

We see SEL and PBIS as being highly compatible and complementary. In fact, one of the premises of effective instruction with SEL programs is that an effective behavior management system should be in place prior to SEL instruction, and that the onset of new SEL instruction (classwide or in small groups) should include a basic review of behavioral expectations and rules. Our experiences in being part of many structured SEL interventions in school settings has taught us that these programs seem to go much better when an effective and consistent behavioral management system is in place. Some of the schools where we did the initial development and validation work for the Strong Kids program were PBIS schools. In general, implementation of SEL lessons in these schools went more smoothly than in schools where discipline systems were not uniform or were even haphazard. Just as

> **SEL and PBIS are highly compatible and complementary. Our experiences have taught us that SEL programming gets much better results when effective PBIS systems are in place.**

PBIS systems seem to enhance SEL in schools, it's also clear to us that there is a positive reciprocal effect. Use of SEL programs can help to enhance the ongoing skill teaching and acquisition aspect of PBIS. The PBIS focus on positive discipline management seems to be enhanced by adding activities and instruction that teach students how to understand their emotional responses, modify their thought processes, and solve day-to-day problems. And perhaps more important, SEL has the potential to expand the reach of PBIS efforts by moving beyond a basic behavioral focus and into the realm of students' cognitions, emotions, goals, problem-solving abilities, resilience, and relationship concerns. In summary, we see SEL and PBIS as complementary, each area providing a structure for supporting students that expands the reach of the other.

The Three-Tiered Prevention Model

One of the interesting aspects of PBIS is that at its core it is greatly influenced by the field of prevention science and, more specifically, by the public health approach to prevention and treatment of disease. In recent years these fields have begun to influence other aspects of education, including SEL. The prevention science or public health approach to school-based intervention is detailed at length in other sources, to which we refer readers who desire more background in this area (e.g., Merrell & Buchanan, 2006; OSEP Technical Assistance Center, 2008; Walker et al., 1996). We see this prevention science/public health model of providing intervention services as an ideal fit with SEL, one that deserves some space in this chapter.

The basic public health model for prevention and treatment is often visualized as a triangle with three distinct levels. Hence, the term "three-tiered prevention model" is commonly used in describing the ideas on which it is based. For our purposes, the entire triangle represents all students within a school setting, the majority of whom are not experiencing significant difficulties (i.e., the bottom portion of the triangle), some of whom are at risk of developing significant problems (i.e., the middle portion), and an even smaller portion of whom are experiencing significant difficulties (i.e., the top portion). In practice, the bottom portion of the triangle model includes about 80% of students—those who are basically doing okay in school—and is referred to as the *primary level*, which indicates *universal prevention* efforts (in other words, efforts that are aimed at all students). The middle section of the triangle is usually considered to include about 15% of students in a school—those who are showing some concerns or indications of risk—and is referred to as the *secondary level*, which indicates *targeted prevention* efforts (in other words, efforts that are targeted on a smaller portion of the population). The top section of the triangle is a very small portion indeed, and reflects the notion that it includes only about 5% of students in a given school population—those who have the most intense needs—and is referred to as the *tertiary level*, which reflects *indicated prevention* efforts (in other words, efforts that are directed toward only a small number of students who have been indicated to have significant needs). Got it? Perhaps the illustration we have included in Figure 1.2 will help. Remember to think of the triangle and its components as a reflection of the public health model for the school population.

In many school systems, typical practice is to focus most of the available mental health services on those students who are at the *top* of the triangle—those who are currently experiencing significant learning and or social–emotional difficulties. Historically, school-based practitioners such as school psychologists have tended to spend the majority of their time and effort providing tertiary prevention services to these students on a case-by-case basis. Although these Tier 3 students make up the smallest percentage of the school population, they often require the majority of time and resources from school personnel. It's easy to understand why we often work this way. These students at the top of the triangle have intense needs and require a significant amount of support. But with all due respect to past practice and current pressures, this way of doing business is really a prescription for being in a perpetual "crisis intervention" mode, and the way of thinking that accompanies such practices clearly has some drawbacks. There is no question that the number of students with intense needs are not declining. If anything, this population is growing. At the same time, our staffing patterns for professionals who can provide mental health services (not to mention our class sizes) generally don't keep up with the increase in student needs. In other words, we work harder and harder to serve an increasing percentage of students

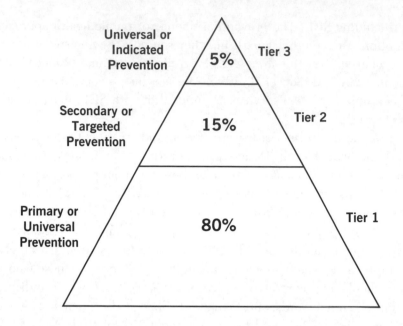

FIGURE 1.2. The three-tiered "triangle of support."

with intense needs, but we ultimately get further behind and end up serving a smaller and smaller percentage of the total population of students, and we ultimately spend little or no effort on prevention. Clearly, there is a better way to go about our business of promoting mental health and academic achievement in schools, and we think that SEL can play an important part in making this shift.

One of the great things about SEL is that it is potentially useful at all levels of the triangle of support, just like PBIS. SEL can be used in general school classrooms as a way to promote mental health and resilience of *all* students. SEL can also be used in a slightly more intensive manner with those students who are struggling and need "a little more." And there is no question that SEL efforts can be used effectively in a more intense manner with the small percentage of students who have significant needs and require "a lot more." Shifting to a systemwide prevention model requires that we look at the "big picture" by considering the needs of *all* students, not just those who are currently experiencing significant difficulties. This idea requires that we begin to move some resources and energy toward those students who are not currently experiencing significant difficulties so that we might help them acquire skills to reduce the probability that they will eventually rise to the "top" of the triangle. More specifically, *primary prevention* for students who are not currently experiencing learning and/or social–behavior difficulties is accomplished through schoolwide and classwide efforts that involve the consistent use of effective practices, ongoing monitoring of these practices and student outcomes, and staff training and professional development. The goal of primary prevention is to create school and classroom environments that promote student learning and health and decrease the number of students at risk for learning and/ or mental health problems. Thus we see SEL as not only having a place to support students who are at risk or who have intense mental health needs, but also as a potentially powerful way of promoting primary prevention among *all* students.

BENEFITS OF SEL: WHAT THE RESEARCH SAYS

So now that you have a solid basic understanding of SEL and what it can do for your students, and now that we have (hopefully) convinced you that SEL can be an important part of your classroom efforts, you might ask the obvious question: "Does it work?" In short, the answer is a resounding "yes," but we don't expect you to just take our word on that. The brief overview of some of the research on effectiveness of SEL programs in schools that we include in this section should provide you with a more convincing answer, and will give you some direction on where to look on your own if you want to learn more.

In *Building Academic Success on Social and Emotional Learning: What Does the Research Say?* Zins, Weissberg, et al. (2004) make a convincing case for the benefits of SEL in schools, with 12 chapters devoted to reviews of the scientific evidence in support of SEL. In their introductory chapter the editors consolidated the findings from across the volume and noted that there is scientific evidence in support of a wide variety of SEL outcomes related to school success. The three primary areas into which these numerous outcomes fit included *school attitudes* (e.g., stronger sense of community, higher motivation, increased sense of coping, better attitude about school, better understanding of behavioral consequences), *school behavior* (e.g., more prosocial behavior, fewer suspensions, higher engagement, reductions in aggressive behavior, fewer absences, more classroom participation), and *school performance* (e.g., higher achievement in math, language arts, and social studies; improvements in achievement test scores, use of higher-level thinking strategies).

> The research is clear: Scientific evidence supports the use of SEL in schools. Three primary areas of research-based positive outcomes of SEL include school attitudes, school behavior, and school performance.

Also offering strong support of the potential effectiveness of SEL practices in schools was an influential meta-analytic (evaluation of research) study by Wilson, Gottfredson, and Najaka (2001), who in their review of 165 separate studies of school-based prevention programs (including positive youth development and SEL) noted many positive effects, particularly focusing on reductions in delinquency and substance abuse among students, reductions in school dropout and nonattendance, and increases in both cognitive and behavioral forms of self-control and social competence.

Another influential review of the research in this area was conducted by Durlak and Wells (1997), who identified 177 school-based prevention programs across three categories: *environment-centered* (e.g., parent training), *transition programs* (e.g., divorce support groups, first-time mothers), and *person-centered programs* (e.g., affective education, problem-solving). The person-centered category is probably the one that is most closely aligned with current SEL practices in schools. The authors concluded that prevention programs, in general, result in small but meaningful gains in improving academic achievement and decreasing internalizing and externalizing behaviors. In examining in more detail the 46 programs identified as affective education (i.e., awareness of emotions and their expressions), the authors concluded that such programs resulted in *robust gains in improving competencies* (e.g., self-assertion, communication skills) and *decreasing problematic behavior* (e.g., anxiety/depression, externalizing behavior problems). An interesting aspect of the findings was that although all ages of students experienced meaningful gains related to affective education, the largest gains were found with children ages 7 and under. Although the study conducted by Durlak and Wells provided general information on the effect of prevention programs and was not focused exclusively on SEL, they were clearly able to document that school-based prevention programs that contain elements that are synonymous with current SEL practices can result in meaningful positive outcomes for students.

The two meta-analysis studies reviewed in this section—those by Wilson and colleagues (2001) and Durlak and Wells (1997)—included more than 300 separate intervention studies when they are combined. These efforts represent an incredible amount of research and are impressive in the consistency of their findings. Many additional individual studies published since these two reviews of research were completed have reached the same conclusion: that SEL programs in schools not only promise a great deal in terms of improved academic, social, and emotional outcomes for students, but they also have a solid track record in delivering on these promises.

CURRENT TRENDS IN LEGISLATION AFFECTING SEL

The importance and potential benefits of social and emotional learning to children and youth in school settings has not escaped the attention of policymakers and other government officials, both at the state and federal levels. In 2003 Illinois became the first U.S. state to formally address child and adolescent mental health needs in an organized and systematic fashion compatible with SEL, by enacting the 2003 Children's Mental Health Act (*www.ivpa.org*) and stimulating the formation of the Illinois Children's Mental Health Partnership. In response to the legislation, the partnership group developed a blueprint that strategically outlined several areas of need with respect to children's mental health and education within the state, and then matched them with recommendations for appropriate action. The blueprint document represented an effort that would be coordinated communitywide in an attempt to avoid the typical pattern of fragmentation of school- and community-based mental health efforts. Identification of prevention, early intervention, and treatment resources for the purpose of providing children and youth from birth to age 21 comprehensive mental health care was the primary aim of these efforts. One of the most innovative and intriguing aspects of these efforts was specifically identified the state's public school systems as primary community resources from which children and youth may receive social and emotional education and support. The Illinois legislation has resulted in significant efforts within the state and is a model for other states. In our view it rates as the single most influential piece of legislation and public policy that has been developed thus far in promoting the aims of SEL on a wide scale.

In 2006 the state of New York enacted major new children's mental health legislation, the Children's Mental Health Act of 2006 (Bill A06931), which, among other things, promotes the use of SEL programs and social–emotional development into elementary and secondary school educational programs. Although the New York legislation is very broad and has multiple goals, it has thus far been a positive force in promoting SEL efforts in that state. In May 2008, a statewide collaborative of individuals appointed to help move the legislation into specific actions within the state's Children's Mental Health plan began to convene to create recommendations around major themes of this law (see *www.omh.state.ny.us/omh-web/engage/* for complete details). Two of the five major themes and recommendations identified by the collaborative have a direct connection to promoting SEL in schools:

- Every action should strengthen our capacity to engage and support families in raising children with emotional health and resilience; and
- Social and emotional development forms a foundation for success in school and in life.

We understand that policy experts and lawmakers in other states have been considering adopting new children's mental health legislation that would help foster the aims of SEL, but these efforts appear to be works in progress at the present time, and it is unclear which state will take the next step. The Illinois and New York legislative accomplishments represent seminal efforts. Supporters of SEL hope that the prominence and influence of these two heavily populated states may help to sway other states to adopt similar measures, particularly if the current legislation results in meaningful positive outcomes.

These state-level initiatives do not yet have parallel legislation at the federal level, but the concerns they have aimed to address have not gone unnoticed by both elected officials and policy administrators in the federal government. The U.S. Department of Education and the National Institute of Mental Health of the U.S. Department of Health and Human Services have both funded research, training grants, and model demonstration projects directly connected to SEL, and have also provided some limited dissemination and training efforts for educators and mental health professionals that focus on SEL. The highest-profile piece of federal legislation in recent years that is connected to or compatible with SEL was enacted in 2004, when the U.S. Congress passed the Garret Lee Smith Memorial Act. This bill specifically addressed the seriousness and urgency in which young adults with mental health problems need prevention and intervention services. Following the tragic death of his son (who had suffered from bipolar disorder and learning problems) by suicide, former Oregon Senator Gordon Smith led this effort to prevent youth suicide by advocating for prevention, early intervention, and treatment services to school- and college-age youth. The Garrett Lee Smith Memorial Act resulted in the creation of a program within the Substance Abuse and Mental Health Services Administration that could facilitate the development of statewide prevention and intervention strategies delivered to community agencies. College campuses were a particular focus of this bill. Although by focusing on suicide these efforts highlight one of the worst negative outcomes of children's mental health difficulties, they have also been responsible for raising awareness regarding the mental health concerns of youth in general, the need to promote wellness, and the necessity of transforming community-based responses into informed, organized, and resourceful prevention and intervention efforts.

Although mandating or encouraging SEL and other children's mental health promotion efforts is not necessarily the only way for these programs to become utilized on a widespread basis, and although we recognize that legal mandates do not always deliver the intended results, such efforts can play a key role in doing so. Let's face it: There is nothing even remotely close to the power of carefully designed legislation or public mandates (especially when they provide appropriate resources and systemic support) in making a dramatic impact on educational practice. Laws such as the Individuals with Disabilities Education Act, the Americans with Disabilities Act, and more recently, NCLB, although not without flaws, have resulted in major reforms in educational practice nationwide. We hope that the time will come when SEL efforts are encouraged and promoted through new policy and legislation on a widespread basis so that all children can receive the benefits of social and emotional learning in schools.

WRAPPING THINGS UP

SEL is a promising and effective way of improving outcomes for children and adolescents in school settings. One of the most intriguing aspects of SEL in general is that its potential benefits are very broad, positively influencing academic achievement, affective or emotional development, cognitive skills such as problem solving and higher-order thinking, social interactions, and behavior. Some of the key elements regarding SEL that are addressed in this introductory chapter, and that are worth a quick recap include:

• Although children and adolescents and their families have faced substantial challenges across societies and throughout history, the current complexities of modern or postmodern life are such that these challenges are often immense, and recent research indicates that as many as 20% of all school-age children and youth in this nation experience significant mental health challenges.

• Unfortunately, a small percentage of children and youth who exhibit notable emotional, social, and behavioral concerns actually receive appropriate prevention and intervention services.

• Most children who do receive prevention and intervention services for mental health concerns obtain these services in school settings.

• SEL—or focused, skill-based efforts in promoting positive social, affective, and cognitive development among students in school settings—is a relatively new term and emphasis, but the needs for these efforts are not new, nor are the approaches that SEL promotes.

• Although SEL may encompass many aspects, the primary elements include self-awareness, social awareness, responsible decision making, self-management, and relationship management.

• Recent emphasis areas within American education and children's mental health—including PBIS and the three-tiered model of prevention and intervention that has been adapted from the field of public health—are ideally suited to incorporate and support SEL efforts.

• Although the SEL field is relatively new, the research basis is extensive and very impressive, indicating that SEL programs not only offer the promise of improving student outcomes in academics, social development, behavioral adjustment, and intrapersonal awareness, but tend to produce meaningful gains across the child and adolescent age span.

• There is a growing trend among public policymakers, state-level legislators, and mental health administrators to promote SEL in schools as a way to enhance mental health efforts, and two states (Illinois and New York) have led the way with far-reaching initiatives designed to use SEL to achieve positive results in schools.

VIGNETTE: A Veteran Teacher Gives SEL a Try

Kathryn's fourth-grade classroom was by no means the kind of school environment that is held up as an example of the troubles teachers face in their work, or of the shortcomings of the educational system. On the contrary, Kathryn was a committed and hard-working teacher with 10 years of experience who was sincerely focused on making a difference in her students' lives. By and large, her classroom, although overcrowded with nearly 30 students, was not as chaotic as would be the case with a less skilled teacher.

Despite the fact that many of her students faced problems endemic to modern life—some had some very serious personal and family challenges—it was hard to tell from an initial visit to the classroom that so many of them were needy and lacked some essential personal and social skills. Still, Kathryn felt increasingly concerned about her ability to meet the complex academic and mental health needs of her students, and she noted that in her 10 years as a teacher, she had noticed an increase in the number of her students who fell into the "at-risk" category. She was aware of the high needs of many of her students, and despite her skill and commitment as a teacher, felt ill equipped to deal with them.

Kathryn was ready for some new tools to help support her efforts as a teacher and was particularly open to the idea of receiving training and materials to infuse SEL into her classroom routine. Even without the benefit of a schoolwide SEL effort and the type of systemic support it could provide, she was willing to give SEL a try and was impressed by how seamlessly it seemed as though it could fit within her weekly classroom routine. Kathryn was a quick study and began to implement a set of brief SEL activities, goals, and lessons into her classroom on a once-per-week basis, with review and support activities interspersed throughout the week on days when the SEL curriculum was not being taught. There were some challenges in getting started. She had a full slate of demands in her classroom, and the infusion of SEL into her routine required some creative revision of the weekly schedule. And although the principal and part-time school counselor both supported her efforts to try SEL, there was no infrastructure in place for external support of her efforts within her school environment. But Kathryn was committed to give SEL a try. The curriculum was brief and structured, and it covered the key SEL components: emotional education, social and interpersonal skills, thinking strategies, coping with stress and uncomfortable feelings, solving problems, setting goals, dealing with conflict, and being a good friend. She was pleased with how naturally the SEL program fit within her teaching routine and how it required relatively little extra preparation and materials, particularly after she had gone through the first 2 weeks of the program and became familiar with its workings. Moreover, she was impressed and surprised by how many of the activities provided practice and support for the academic activities she was focusing on, including reading, writing, social studies, and even mathematics.

Most of all she was surprised by two things: how quickly her students picked up on the concepts and skills that were being taught, and how naturally they seemed to link them to their everyday routines. For example, the social skills and conflict resolution lessons and the unique language and fun activities they included found their way into the playground and lunchtime routines, and it was not unusual for the students to refer to them later in the classroom when they discussed how they approached particular social challenges. Kathryn even found herself benefiting from many of the concepts that she was teaching her students, as she used techniques such as stress-reduction activities and cognitive change strategies in dealing with everyday concerns in her own life. She discussed her successes with SEL with some of her fellow teachers and the school counselor, and some of them expressed interest in looking at the materials and strategies she had acquired and how she was using them in her classroom. The school counselor and one of the other two fourth-grade teachers ultimately decided to make SEL part of their routine as well.

With some assistance from practicum students from a nearby university, some basic data were gathered on her implementation of the new SEL program and how her students were benefiting from it. It was clear that both the teacher and the students liked SEL, and that the students' knowledge of SEL strategies and concepts increased significantly across the weeks in which the program was implemented. Kathryn also noticed how these knowledge and skill gains seemed to help her students moderate and enhance their approaches to dealing with the many challenges some of them faced. And it was very interesting to find that, even 2 and 3 months after the conclusion of the formal SEL program she had experimented with, she and her students were still using many of the skills, techniques, and ideas it had brought to them. In short, Kathryn's experience convinced that SEL was something she could and would use as a regular part of her classroom routine from then on, and she even actively recommended it to her fellow teachers. "There really is no downside to these SEL activities and lessons," she later commented. "The kids like it, they are learning a lot from it, and I can actually see them benefiting over time in their ability to get along with each other, solve problems, understand their feelings, and cope with adversity. I'm all for it."

CHAPTER 2

Social and Emotional Learning Curricula
A Review of Selected Programs

INTRODUCTION AND OVERVIEW

So you think you'd like to give social and emotional learning a try in your classroom or school? We enthusiastically support your decision! We also realize that getting started is often one of the most difficult steps in this process, and we've developed a plan to help you get on board with SEL. In this chapter we focus on so-called "packaged" curricula, that is, structured programs that are specifically designed to improve students' social and emotional functioning. For the most part, these curricula were chosen because they have an "evidence basis," which means they have been researched and found to effectively and positively influence students' social and emotional skills. A brief description of several of the more widely used programs is included, as well as tips on how to choose the most appropriate program for your students' specific needs. A case study is used to illustrate the selection process. Packaged curricula are one way—but not the only way—of teaching social and emotional concepts; in Chapter 4, we review and discuss brief but targeted SEL strategies that are not necessarily part of a curriculum, but can be easily infused into academic programming and instruction.

SEL CAN BE IMPLEMENTED IN VARIOUS WAYS

In Chapter 1 we highlighted the notion that social and emotional learning efforts should complement, supplement, and enhance existing school programming. For some schools or classrooms, this process may mean adding a dash of emotion education programming into a system that already implements positive behavioral supports effectively, but could use some

> **Before implementing specific SEL practices, it is vital to consider the overall vision that this programming aims to enrich.**

strengthening to improve students' ability to recognize a range of feelings in themselves and others. For other schools, existing programming may be faltering, either due to poor implementation, few resources, or a waning belief that a difference can really be made in students' social and emotional health. In this case, the vision of school programming may need an overhaul: heavy lifting, sorting, and restructuring may be necessary. Wherever your school or classroom exists on this continuum, it is vital to step back and consider your primary goals for implementing SEL practices.

CHOOSING AN SEL PROGRAM THAT MATCHES THE NEEDS OF STUDENTS

Ideally, schools will be adopting SEL curricula and practices for the entire student body. We say that such a practice is ideal because we know that organized SEL efforts coordinated across multiple grade levels and receiving ongoing district support are more likely to lead to better outcomes for students (see Greenberg et al., 2003). The Collaborative for Academic, Social, and Emotional Learning (CASEL) recently published a comprehensive rubric for helping schools strategically consider and plan SEL implementation (for additional information, visit *www.casel.org/downloads/Rubric.pdf*). The development of the rubric was based on best practices and has, to date, relied on face validity as a basis for implementation and is currently under a revision and likely modifications (CASEL, personal communication, May 27, 2009). Notwithstanding this inevitable stage of growth and development, what we find innovative about this detailed resource is that the rubric provides the structure whereby schools can methodically think through the phases of implementation that new programs inevitably pass through and consider how the programs apply to the phase of implementation that individual schools are currently in. Figure 2.1 contains a flowchart adapted from the CASEL rubric that illustrates the overall recommended processes of selecting and implementing SEL programs in schools. This approach is a clear departure from the often haphazard and fruitless efforts that result when random "I think it will work" strategies are thrown at unsuspecting students! The rubric reviews three primary and essential stages in the implementation cycle (readiness, planning, and implementation), breaks them down into subphases, and provides a guideline for review when considering sustainability issues.

Let's be realistic for a moment. It can be so very difficult to hold back from jumping into starting a new program when those shiny, colorful, and friendly-looking manuals arrive in the mail. We want to *strongly* encourage you to step away from the manuals or the cata-

> **Strategic planning is *essential* to choosing an SEL program that will make the early stages of implementation logical and sustainable over time.**

log for a moment and advocate that your school team use a strategic plan to implementing SEL, employing a coherent evaluation process such as the CASEL rubric. We hope you have already used such a process to choose the program you just ordered. We know how exciting and, for some, daunting, it can be to get started

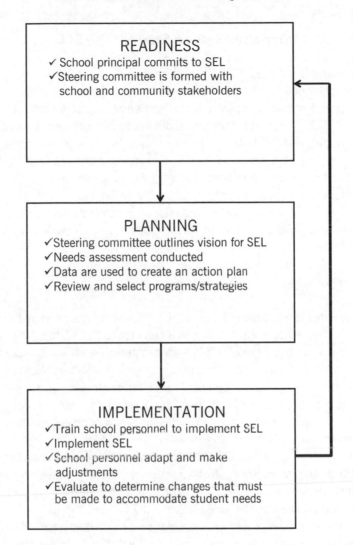

FIGURE 2.1. A flowchart for selecting and implementing SEL programs. Modified 2006 from a rubric by the Collaborative for Academic, Social, and Emotional Learning (*www.casel.org*; link to rubric: *www.casel.org/downloads/Rubric.pdf*). Used by permission. (*Note:* The concepts and graphic illustration are under revision by CASEL during 2009–2010 and are expected to be modified. CASEL has not collected any data on the effectiveness of the SEL implementation and sustainability process and has relied on face validity and best practices to inform its development.)

with an evidence-based SEL program. Being mindful of these feelings and adhering to a strategic plan will help to ensure that your students benefit from this program to the fullest extent. Worksheet 2.1, "Worksheet for Evaluating SEL Programs," might be useful as you go through the strategic planning process prior to selecting a specific SEL program. This worksheet is designed to help you identify the key characteristics of various SEL programs you might be considering, and then analyze how good a fit these programs might be for the particular needs of your students and school system.

Vignette: Getting Started with SEL

The following scenario is provided to help you further consider how this process might play out as you think about the needs of your students and schools, as well as the hope you have for them in acquiring and regularly applying social and emotional strategies. This scenario uses CASEL's rubric for SEL implementation and applies it to a hypothetical case where a school psychologist is committed to SEL development in his or her school, has some ideas regarding the areas that need to be addressed, but requires additional support to get started. We encourage you to use the time you take to read through this section as an opportunity for reflecting on the goals you have for your students and the current status of SEL in your building. We suggest that you jot down some notes to organize your thoughts on how you might begin to realize these goals and build a case that you can present to your colleagues that exudes your commitment and passion.

Scenario

A school's staff is considering a new SEL curriculum that was presented by the school psychologist after she attended a workshop at a national conference that featured a new SEL program. This topic happens to be the psychologist's area of interest, and she is incredibly invested in the social and emotional well-being of elementary school–age children. Not only does she know that SEL is in children's best interest in general, but after many years of reliable implementation that is infused into typical classroom activities, she believes that this approach could cut down on the number of special education or other evaluations on her caseload, thus freeing up more of her time for intervention planning and delivery. This impact is possible because students should acquire some skills they can use to cope with the daily frustrations they deal with, and the infrastructure of school backs up this approach 100% after experiencing success with PBIS. Her dilemma: How does she begin to get this process started in her school?

Using the SEL implementation rubric published by CASEL, she realizes she needs to back up and consider three phases of an "implementation cycle": readiness, planning, and implementation. After reviewing the information on the rubric, she organizes these planning areas with her notes as follows:

CASEL Rubric Phase 1: Readiness

The steps within this phase are:

1. The school principal understands that SEL is more than a one-time program; rather, it is a framework. The principal has committed to using classroom-based instruction to facilitate SEL and wants to support and sustain it.

School psychologist reflection: "I have talked with the principal at length about these issues and she is very supportive. She is looking to me to guide the implementation process."

2. The school principal has started a steering committee with key school and community stakeholders to take leadership of SEL implementation.

School psychologist reflection: "I know that there are many school personnel and community members who have expressed interest in improving students' social and emotional development. I'm not sure they are aware of the strategic planning that it takes to meet this goal. I'll need to talk with the principal and see who might be interested in joining this committee. I may have to ask for some extra release time or support to focus on this area."

> **Initial stages of planning for SEL must involve key members of the school and neighborhood communities. This practice builds an important bridge that will provide bidirectional perspective and support.**

CASEL Rubric Phase 2: Planning

The steps in this phase are:

1. Work with the steering committee to develop and outline a vision for SEL in the school building.

School psychologist reflection: "This might be challenging for our building staff because we sometimes disagree on things like prioritizing academic instruction versus dealing with behavioral problems or how release time is used, because it is so limited. I'll want to talk to the principal about how we might handle disagreements and facilitate consensus so we are not stalled."

2. Conduct a needs assessment to review current SEL practices and compare them to school and state policies, student and staff needs for social and emotional development and program implementation, current school climate and how SEL is perceived and valued, and any barriers to implementation.

School psychologist reflection: "Wow. This could be a lot of work, but I can really see how these components are so important. If there are state policies that we are not implementing, we may have to accelerate this process, which could put some strain on our existing responsibilities. If our teachers are relatively uninformed about SEL and are so overwhelmed with meeting academic benchmarks, there may be a lot of resistance to work through. On the other hand, I know our teachers are really concerned about the lack of coping skills that students have and all the stressors they face in their neighborhoods and families, and I think we can brainstorm some solutions. Regardless of the outcome of the needs assessment, I will need to consult with the district office on how needs assessments have been conducted in the past and whether I can obtain some support with this."

3. Make an action plan based on data collected from the needs assessment.

School psychologist reflection: "It may take 6 months to a year to get to this point, but this process seems organized and well thought out. I think the action plan will really focus our efforts and address some of the issues that would otherwise distract or delay our plan. We can't predict every problem or barrier, but I feel comfortable that we've considered a variety of issues."

4. Review SEL programs and strategies that are evidence based and seem to have the best chance of meeting our goals. Select the program/strategies.

School psychologist reflection: "This step is where I felt really enthused at the conference workshop on the SEL program, and selecting the program is right in the middle of this planning rubric. After going through the readiness and planning phases, I feel much more confident that the program the committee recently selected will be the best match for our needs. I can't wait to get started!"

CASEL Rubric Phase 3: Implementation

The steps in this phase are:

1. Provide training to school personnel about the program and implementation.

School psychologist reflection: "We'll probably use an in-service day at the beginning of the school year to do this training. I'll talk to the principal and the steering committee about the feasibility of this option. I'd like to start the school year with the staff getting ready to implement this program and knowing how this is going to be successful."

2. Implement SEL program in the classroom.

School psychologist reflection: "I'd like to be available to support teachers as they work through the program. I think it might also be helpful for them to write down some notes on how things are going, especially areas that might need more support."

3. Teachers have adapted to the program, made changes, and are becoming more comfortable. School personnel are integrating the program content into other school activities so students are getting used to using SEL language on a regular basis.

School psychologist reflection: "The steering committee should consider focusing on supporting school personnel at this juncture. This is where implementation could disintegrate because of unexpected barriers like frustration or unexpected school events or expectations. I'll mention this at our next meeting to heighten their awareness."

4. Review the planning and implementation activities to determine whether changes should be made.

School psychologist reflection: "We should set up regular meetings to make sure we are reviewing issues that may interfere with or complicate our SEL efforts, as well as review data that we are taking to monitor student progress. We don't want to get too comfortable with thinking that once SEL programming is up and running it can sustain itself. Our school and district undergoes changes every year (e.g., funding cuts, turnover in personnel, state and federal legislation) that may significantly alter our ability to implement SEL and affect student social and emotional development."

Of course, this scenario is just one example of how SEL implementation might work in actual practice. We hope this example provides more breadth and depth to your awareness of the issues that need to be considered before choosing SEL programs and strategies. Certainly it would be extremely helpful to talk with colleagues from other schools about their efforts to implement SEL and the strategies they found to be helpful to get around implementation barriers that are sure to arise. You may even wish to consider working with a consultant or someone else with expertise in implementing SEL. An interesting article recently published in *The Community Psychologist* (Smith, McQuillin, & Shapiro, 2008) narrated such a process when a university, community, and school partnered to implement an after-school program. The authors chronicled everyone's initial enthusiasm, which diminished as the realities of imperfect program implementation set in, despite their strategic planning efforts. We think the primary aim of this narration is one of program and process dissemination, being mindful of the importance of contextual factors (e.g., school priorities, community pressures, and individual values), being flexible and creative as challenges arise, and adhering to implementing an SEL program in the way it was intended and found to be effective.

ADVANTAGES OF USING PACKAGED, EVIDENCE-BASED PROGRAMS

When considering the kind of SEL programming to choose for your setting, there are many options. This section provides a discussion and overview of some programs that are already put together, marketed, and sold as a packaged product or idea. Of course, schools may want to implement very brief strategies that can be quickly and easily infused into the course of a typical academic subject. We review these strategies in Chapter 4. But first let's consider some advantages to already-assembled programs.

Open any publishing catalog that sells educational and psychological materials and you will find quite a selection of programs that tout the promotion of social and emotional development across many ages. I (B. A. G.) sometimes have to review the catalog several times before choosing a book (or several) that seems to fit the topic area I am looking for—the selections can be numerous, intriguing, and full of promise for enhancing my clinical skills. (By the way, we are happy you selected *this* book and appreciate your careful consideration!) What is especially appealing about many packaged SEL programs is that they have often (but not always) been field tested for effectiveness and feasibility—a trial run with data to support the fact that the program produces results and that professionals implementing it are pleased with it as well. We must emphasize *often* because, of course, we live in a free-market society and not all programs have a strong evidence basis; the programs that are reviewed in this chapter do have an evidence basis, which is one reason we chose to include them from among many possible examples we could have selected. But what does the notion of effectiveness really mean? Take, for instance, an SEL program with an emphasis on cognitive and behavioral therapeutic techniques. Cognitive-behavioral therapy (CBT) has been demonstrated consistently over time to be an effective treatment for adults and youth who experience symptoms of depression and anxiety (Merrell, 2008a). The likelihood that these same strategies, infused into a school-based SEL program aimed at improving depression and anxiety symptoms, would have an effect in a school setting seems reasonable. The program is then rigorously studied under school-based conditions and found to indeed be effective and thus have evidence to support it. Schools want programs that have already demonstrated their effectiveness. It is usually a waste of time and resources—and is potentially risky—to implement a program that has no or shaky evidence that it will produce the desired results. Identifying and using programs that have convincing supporting data is an efficient means to a desirable end such as students' social and emotional development.

One aspect of the process of considering the evidence or research base for an SEL program that may not get enough attention is the difference between results of a study that was done using highly controlled scientific conditions ("efficacy research") and a study that was done in real-world conditions, in classrooms and similar settings using typical practice

> **Packaged SEL programs offer several advantages to simply piecing together a variety of ideas and practices. Often they are strategically developed to target a specific area, are field-tested, and are based on theoretical constructs and instructional techniques known to be effective with children in the school setting.**

and with typical research ("effectiveness research"). One form of evidence is not necessarily better than the other, and both forms should ideally be included as evidence. We do wish to caution you that what works in the laboratory or in a tightly controlled scientific field trial may not necessarily translate into what works in the sometimes messy real world of schools. For this reason, don't assume that any program, no matter how much scientific evidence supports it, is necessarily going to be effective in your particular school environment or classroom setting (see Merrell & Buchanan, 2006, for a more detailed discussion of efficacy versus effectiveness). Rather, evidence of effectiveness in various settings should be considered as a good starting point for making a selection, but you also need to consider the unique conditions under which you will be delivering the program and use that information to help inform your choice.

One of the challenges that we've seen many teachers face in using SEL strategies in the classroom is pulling together a variety of materials from multiple sources and experimenting with how and whether they work with their students. Often they do work, and the ideas and materials are sometimes brilliant. We want to emphasize that such an approach may be the best in many situations, and that the use of a commercially packaged program is not always necessary. That said, an advantage to packaged programs is that the materials are already put together with the intention of creating a logical flow of content, minimizing prep time, and providing already-tested ideas regarding implementation. There is always a learning curve when something new is tried in the classroom; fortunately, the work that was put into studying the program has led to working out many of the wrinkles that may have otherwise been incredibly frustrating. Again, we remind you of Worksheet 2.1, "Worksheet for Evaluating SEL Programs," which you might find useful as a tool to help you match the needs of your students and structure of your school with the aims and strengths of specific published SEL programs.

School personnel choose a specific SEL program because it targets a perceived SEL need or requirement. Ideally, this need was identified through a strategic needs assessment. Packaged programs are generally designed with very specific skill sets and goals in mind like teaching empathy, problem-solving skills, emotional education and regulation, and stress management. The programs are developed by researchers who have studied and understand the theoretical concepts regarding particular areas of development, maladjustment, and resilience, and directly link these concepts to instructional strategies that can positively influence change. And speaking of instruction, many of the packaged programs increasingly utilize instructional strategies that are known to affect student learning in the classroom. Successful SEL programs that use effective instructional strategies in conjunction with SEL concepts have a greater opportunity to be successful within a school environment.

It is widely accepted that in order to maximize SEL's impact on students' social and emotional functioning for the long term, the program should ideally be infused across the duration of students' educational tenure. Many SEL program developers are taking this notion into consideration and designing their programs to extend across an entire compulsory educational career. We and our colleagues at the University of Oregon took this very notion into consideration when the Strong Kids series was developed. It was clear that consistently providing instruction of SEL concepts across time (i.e., prekindergarten through high school age) is undeniably paramount to the best chances for healthy development. We would be overwhelmingly delighted to see strategic and community–home–classroom–coordinated SEL programming extend to the birth-to-3 age group, strategically linking the instruction that occurs in the home and in daycare facilities to school-based prevention and intervention efforts. Why not give our children the best start with social and emotional development?

SELECTED SEL PROGRAMS

This section showcases some of the most widely used and studied SEL programs that are implemented in schools. The programs selected are certainly not fully representative of all the commercially available SEL programs. We chose these programs because they focus on SEL promotion in a school setting, are used in classrooms where all students could expect to be exposed to the program content, and have evidence to support their effectiveness. The programs are listed in alphabetical order in Table 2.1. You may notice that all of the programs can be implemented in the general education classroom and primarily focus on student social and emotional development from kindergarten through grade 6. This section does not include programs that are targeted specifically at students who are already experiencing identified social and emotional problems that may be interfering with their daily functioning (e.g., specific phobias, severe depression), although certainly we know there are students in our general education classrooms who are experiencing these problems. Rather, these types of programs are designed to benefit all students to some extent, including those students with higher levels of risk.

Caring School Community

Caring School Community, formerly known as the Child Development Project, (see *www.devstu.org/csc/videos/index.shtml*) was developed by researchers at the Developmental Studies Center, a nonprofit organization that works to develop children's academic, ethical, and social skills, and was designed for students in kindergarten through grade 6. Caring School Community focuses on promoting a positive and healthy school climate through the core principles of fostering relationships, taking responsibility, and teaching respect. Four primary components make up the program, including (1) using class meetings to discuss classroom behavior, (2) pairing students across ages to build relationships and trust, (3) family involvement to inform parents of school activities and allow parents an opportunity to participate, and (4) schoolwide noncompetitive activities that involve school, home, and community. The materials that are used to promote these skills include (1) a Teacher's Guide with lessons taught according to topic (30 lessons for Kindergarten through Grade 1; 35 lessons for Grades 2–6); (2) a Principal's Leadership Guide that also includes the Teacher's Guide; (3) a Cross-Age Buddies book, providing 40 activities for children to interact with others across ages; (4) a Homeside Activity book to further develop the skills taught at school

TABLE 2.1. Selected SEL Programs

Title	Area targeted	Age group	Components	Reference
Caring School Community	School climate	Kindergarten–Grade 6	• In-class meetings to discuss classroom behavior and norms • Cross-age pairings to build relationships and trust • Family involvement to inform and share ideas on school activities • 15 school activities involving staff, students, parents • Optional SEL lessons integrated into literature and math	*www.devstu.org/csc/videos/index.shtml* Solomon, Battistich, Watson, Schaps, and Lewis (2000)
I Can Problem Solve	Violence prevention	Preschool–Grade 6	• Teaches students how to think by contrasting concepts with word pairs • Identifying feelings, listening skills, paying attention • Problem solving with alternative solution skills	Shure (1992a)
Promoting Alternative Thinking Strategies (PATHS)	Emotional awareness self-control, interpersonal problem solving, peer relationships	Kindergarten–Grade 6	• 30–45 lessons, main areas: • ID feelings • Relaxation through deep breathing • Perspective taking • Study skills	*www.prevention.psu.edu/projects/PATHS.html* Conduct Problems Prevention Research Group (1999); Greenberg and Kusche (1998a, 1998b)
Raising Healthy Children	Teacher training to promote healthy social and emotional development in classrooms	Grades 1–2	• Classroom management • Social–emotional skills • Active engagement • Reading strategies • Motivational strategies	*depts.washington.edu/sdrg/* Catalano, Mazza, Harachi, Abbott, and Haggerty (2003)

Program	Focus	Grade Level	Components	Reference
Safe and Caring Schools	Prosocial skills, improve academic functioning	Preschool–Grade 8	Self awareness, social skills, and responsible decision making	*www.researchpress.com/product/item/8331/* *www.safeandcaringschools.com/*
Second Step: A Violence Prevention Curriculum	Prosocial skills to decrease risk of engaging in destructive behavior	Preschool–Grade 9	• Empathy instruction • Problem solving for impulse control • Emotion regulation	*www.cfchildren.org/programs/ssp/overview/* Grossman et al. (1997)
Social Decision Making/Social Problem Solving	Prosocial decision making skills	Grades 2–5	Uses direct instruction and practice FIG TESPN: • Identify feelings • Identify the problem • Goal setting • Think of solutions • Envision consequences • Select the best solution • Plan it/try it • Notice what happens	*www.ubhcisweb.org/sdm/* Elias and Bruene Butler (2005)
Strong Kids: A Social and Emotional Learning Curriculum	Social–emotional wellness via explicit instruction	Preschool–Grade 12	• Emotion awareness • Anger management strategies • Identifying and changing thinking errors • Stress management • Goal setting	*strongkids.uoregon.edu/* Merrell, Carrizales, Feuerborn, Gueldner, and Tran (2007a, 2007b, 2007c)
Thinking, Feeling, Behaving	Emotion education	Grades 1–12	• Uses a rational emotive therapy approach to identifying feelings, changing irrational thoughts, and negative consequences • Activity-based instruction	*www.researchpress.com/product/item/5271/*

in addition to involving parents in school-based activities; (5) a School Community-Building Guide whose activities promote a helpfulness, inclusion, and responsibility within the school community; and (6) an Optional Read-Aloud Library featuring literature that illustrates ethical and social issues that children will encounter. The information associated with these materials is intended to be taught by classroom teachers over the course of a year.

Research over the past 20 years indicates that students who have participated in this program demonstrate a higher motivation to achieve, enjoy school more, and have better conflict resolution skills and empathy and altruism toward others (for additional information see *www.devstu.org/pdfs/cdp/cdp_eval_summary.pdf*). In a study by Solomon, Battistich, Watson, Schaps, and Lewis (2000), students who participated in the program, as compared with those in a control group, reported less alcohol and marijuana use and teachers observed more prosocial and problem-solving behavior.

In summary, Caring School Community is a school-based program that uses as community-oriented approach to developing social and emotional skills in students. It values and thereby includes families in the program materials and has a year-long and organized approach to instruction across multiple grade levels. Research to date is encouraging in showing the effectiveness and durability of outcomes past the sixth grade and across demographically diverse communities.

I Can Problem Solve

I Can Problem Solve (ICPS) (Shure, 1992a) is a prevention program targeting interpersonal problem-solving skills with the goal of preventing antisocial behavior (for more information, visit *www.researchpress.com/product/item/4628/*). There are three versions of ICPS with corresponding lessons, one for preschool-age students (59 lessons), one for kindergarten and early primary grades (83 lessons), and the third for intermediate elementary grades (77 lessons). Note the large number of lessons, which indicates that ICPS is intended for frequent use across a school year, and that it covers many different topics. The lessons can be integrated into academic activities (such as reading), and scripts are provided to teach each lesson along with ideas for stories, games, role plays, and puppets, as well as illustrations to highlight the content of the lesson. Students learn problem-solving skills via a game with hypothetical characters and are then prompted to use these skills throughout the day in typical situations. Students learn to generate solutions to problems by thinking through the outcomes of each potential solution as well as possible roadblocks to achieving their goals.

Research has shown that after participating in this program, students demonstrated a reduction in behaviors associated with impulsivity and inhibition, as well as an increase in prosocial behaviors such as caring and sharing (see Shure & Glaser, 2001, for a review). For those interested in collecting data to track outcomes (as we would highly recommend), there are several evaluation measures that were used specifically with ICPS and could be reasonably used by a school clinician to track progress. For example, the Preschool Interpersonal Problem-Solving Test (Shure, 1992b) measures problem solving in preschool-age children, and the What Happens Next Game (Shure, 1990) measures the extent to which a child can generate solutions to problems.

ICPS is an SEL program that has demonstrated effectiveness in improving interpersonal skills and decreasing externalizing behaviors such as impulsivity. Multiple lessons span preschool through intermediate elementary school grades and progress monitoring has been used with this program to evaluate student progress. A unique aspect of this program is its use of multimedia approaches to delivering the curriculum from visual aids such as puppets and handouts to role-playing realistic life situations.

Promoting Alternative Thinking Strategies

Promoting Alternative Thinking Strategies (PATHS) is a prevention program that was developed by researchers at the Prevention Research Center at the Pennsylvania State University (Kusche & Greenberg, 1994). This program targets the development of self-control, interpersonal relationships, and emotional awareness, all to foster social competency for elementary-age students (for more information visit *www.prevention.psu.edu/projects/PATHS.html*). There are 30 to 45 PATHS lessons that can be taught during the school year in which students learn about and practice identifying feelings, breathing techniques for relaxation, and perspective taking. Academic skills are also targeted such as organizational and study skills, sustaining attention, and goal setting. Families are included in this curriculum through letters that are sent home with information about the lessons so parents can practice the skills at home, with the goal of generalizing the concepts across a variety of settings and situations. A newly developed PATHS for preschool is also available and shows promise in teaching students' emotional awareness and recognition, as well as their competence.

Research to date has demonstrated positive effects for children in general and special education settings, and for children with hearing impairments. It has been found to be useful for general education students as a universal program used throughout the school year and across grade levels. Multiple ethnic groups have been included in the evaluation studies, which demonstrates its value in settings that serve a vastly diverse school population (examples of the research conducted include Greenberg & Kusche, 1998b, and Greenberg, Kusche, Cook, & Quamma, 1995). Specific, positive outcomes have included better understanding of emotional and social situations; improved alternative problem-solving strategies to resolve conflict; ability to tolerate frustration; and decreased sadness and disruptive behaviors. PATHS has been rated as a "model program" by the National Registry of Evidence-Based Programs and has received other top awards (e.g., from the Office of Safe and Drug-Free Schools and Centers for Disease Control and Prevention). Trainings and on-site consultation services are available with this program to assist with implementation procedures.

The PATHS program has a robust evidence basis for its effectiveness in increasing the emotional and social awareness and competency in students in pre-K and throughout elementary school. Of particular interest is its specific focus on emotional literacy, or teaching students about their emotions and how to regulate them. In addition, it appears to have utility across a wide spectrum of children's cultural, ability, and socioeconomic considerations.

Raising Healthy Children

Raising Healthy Children is a multicomponent program for first- and second-grade students that was developed by the Social Development Research Group at the University of Washington (for more information visit *depts.washington.edu/sdrg*). The research for this program was started in 1993 and followed a group of first- and second-grade students through high school, not only tracking progress, but also providing continuous instruction and support to teachers, students, and parents. Its focus was on staff development activities that would train teachers to infuse SEL concepts into everyday classroom activities to promote social and emotional competency skills that can moderate behavioral problems in adolescence and build resilience (Catalano, Mazza, Harachi, Abbott, & Haggerty, 2003). Eight SEL instructional units were developed and delivered in the classroom, each taught over the course of 1 month (approximately 45 minutes to teach the lesson and then brief activities that were practiced daily for the remainder of the month). Teachers also provided additional support around reading skills to ensure basic and functional competency, as well as direct instruction on classroom behaviors such as listening skills. Parent support was provided through parenting groups and home-based services, which also served to orient parents to school-based processes and procedures.

Multiple outcomes studies have provided data regarding the impact this program has had on attachment to school, academic performance, antisocial behaviors, and social competence (see *depts.washington.edu/sdrg/* for a comprehensive list of references to these studies). For example, students who were exposed to SEL-oriented teaching strategies had a more positive attachment to school and their family, fewer suspensions and expulsions, and more social interactions and age-appropriate behavior. This body of evidence has increased the field's understanding of the enormous impact that alterable, ecological classroom characteristics as well as school-to-home outreach and support can have on students' social, emotional, and academic development.

If you are interested in obtaining additional information about or materials regarding the Raising Healthy Children program, we encourage you to contact the Social Development Research Group directly (*depts.washington.edu/sdrg/*). This program successfully utilizes teacher training and classroom instruction as a means to facilitating prosocial behaviors in school and at home, while improving academic achievement.

Safe and Caring Schools: Skills for School, Skills for Life

Safe and Caring Schools: Skills for School, Skills for Life was developed by Petersen (2005) and is a commercially packaged program, published by Research Press (for more information visit *www.researchpress.com/product/item/8331/*). This program is available for students in grades pre-K through 8, with four separate instruction manuals and corresponding activities for different age groupings (e.g., pre-K to kindergarten, grades 1–2, grades 3–5, and grades 6–8). SEL concepts are woven into daily classroom activities and aim to positively influence classroom dynamics, promote prosocial skills that can decrease behavior problems, and build character. Lesson plans and monthly themes for activities and literature-based SEL are provided. Reproducible forms are available on CD-ROM. The Safe and Caring Schools manuals include many activities and modules and are designed to be used across the span of a school year. For example, the suggested theme to be used in the month of November is "My Support System." Within this framework, the middle school version of the curriculum includes five curricular components (Theme at a Glance, What Do You Think?, Extended Activities, Activity Directions, and Activity Reproducibles), with eight separate activity reproducibles.

Although the publisher of Safe and Caring Schools promotes this program as a proven, research-based program, we were not able to find any examples of published research studies in which it was used, either through the usual research search engines or the publisher's catalogue or website. That said, it is probably more accurate to describe this program as promising on the basis of proven principles, rather than tested through research. Advantages of the Safe and Caring Schools programs include the careful sequencing of the curriculum activities across the school year, and the developmentally appropriate versions of the program that span four distinct age ranges from pre-K through high school. Future research efforts appear to be needed to validate this program for effectiveness, but it does appear to have some interesting and engaging aspects, and its many activities could be easily integrated into a classroom routine.

Second Step: A Violence Prevention Curriculum

Second Step: A Violence Prevention Curriculum was developed to teach students in preschool through grade 9 to increase key areas of social competency to reduce problem-externalizing behaviors such as physical and verbal aggression. This program, published by the Committee for Children (1988), has won numerous awards from agencies such as the U.S. Department of Education's Panel on Safe, Disciplined, and Drug-Free Schools (2001) and the U.S. Department of Justice, Office of Juvenile Justice and Delinquency Prevention (2003). The program is one of the most widely used SEL-type interventions that we have seen. Both of us have often worked in and with schools that are actively using this program as part of their typical classroom curriculum, naturally embedded into academic instruction and generally expected to be a part of an elementary school student's classroom experience. Indeed, the program has been widely accepted as such across schools in the United States and internationally. The curricular content in Second Step is broken into three primary domains of instruction: empathy, problem solving, and managing emotions. For preschool through elementary school, each unit uses large photographic cards with the content of the lesson on the reverse side. Program materials also include videos for students and parents, as well as posters that prompt students to use their skills. For middle and high school students, the content is very similar to the elementary school version, but is presented with overhead transparencies and videos and utilizes discussion and activities to rehearse the concepts. Committee for Children provides implementation support such as e-newsletters, consultation support, and trainings.

Second Step has been rigorously evaluated over the last 20 years, producing strong evidence for its effectiveness in rendering prosocial skills and reducing aggression (see Grossman et al., 1997 for a report on a randomized controlled trial, as well as *www.cfchildren.org/programs/ssp/research/* for a list of selected publications). For example, improvements have been measured in students' skills in taking another's perspective and solving problems. Socially aggressive acts in middle school students, such as spreading rumors and insulting or excluding one another, were found to have decreased after students participated in the Second Step curriculum. Students who had not received the program did not show similar gains; in some cases, their behavior worsened.

Second Step has a 20-year track record of producing and improving important social and emotional skills in elementary and middle school students. It has also been widely accepted by school personnel as a viable program to implement during the school day and has won numerous awards. The Committee for Children's website provides useful information for review should you consider implementing this program, and we encourage you to talk with other districts who have done so.

Social Decision Making/Social Problem Solving

Social Decision Making/Social Problem Solving (SDM/SPS) was created by a school principal and psychologist in order to address the need for students to receive systematic instruction in the area of social problem solving (Elias & Bruene Butler, 2005). Classroom teachers teach students problem-solving skills in the classroom, then use examples and opportunities for practice throughout the school day. SDM/SPS is recognized as an "exemplar program" by the U.S. Department of Education and is offered by the University of Medicine and Dentistry of New Jersey (for more information visit *www.ubhcisweb.org/sdm/*). The content is intended for general and special education students in grades K–8, and is designed to be infused across multiple academic content areas so it can be easily applied to daily living situations. Lessons are structured across three domains: teaching self-control and social awareness, social decision making using an eight-step "clear thinking strategy," and applying lesson content to academic and everyday issues. You may recognize the mnemonic used in the eight-step model, FIG TESPN, which stands for (1) identify feelings, (2) identify the problem, (3) goal setting, (4) think of solutions, (5) envision consequences, (6) select the best solution, (7) plan it/try it, and (8) notice what happens. At the core of this program is "overlearning" the concepts to build fluency and generalization across a variety of settings and situations.

There is convincing support for the effectiveness of SDM/SPS (see Elias, Gara, Schuyler, Branden-Muller, & Sayette, 1991). Teachers' ability to lead students through the problem-solving process improved following training in this area. Students' skills improved in the areas of understanding consequences of their actions and understanding other students' feelings and being more sensitive to them, and in problem solving during interpersonal situations and with other problems in general. These skills were also found to generalize to situations outside of school. High school students who had received the program in early grades demonstrated more prosoical behavior and less antisocial behavior, including difficulties in the area of general social interaction skills, suggesting that positive outcomes can be maintained over time.

The widely used SDM/SPS program has demonstrated effectiveness in the short term, as well as generalized effects across settings and over time. Its focus on social problem solving, overlearning the concepts, and eight problem-solving strategies make this a program that can be easily integrated into a typical school day and across grade levels. Those interested in obtaining additional information on this program may wish to visit *www.ubhcisweb.org/sdm/*, where helpful tips for implementation, training support, and research publications and references are posted.

Thinking, Feeling, Behaving: An Emotional Education Curriculum for Children

Thinking, Feeling, Behaving: An Emotional Education Curriculum for Children (Vernon, 2006) is based on the tenets of rational emotive therapy, in which feelings are identified, thoughts and beliefs are challenged, and consequences to behavior are observed (and hopefully change in a positive direction). This commercially packaged program was revised in 2006 from the original version (1989), and is appropriate for students in grades 1 through 12 (for more information visit *www.researchpress.com/product/item/5271/*). There are 105 activities in the K–6 program and 105 activities in the grade 7–12 program; 35 activities are designated according to grade level. For example, the grades 3–4 activity set has 35 activities appropriate for this age group. The activity content is grouped into five areas: self-acceptance, feelings, beliefs and behavior, problem solving and decision making, and interpersonal relationships. The activities illustrate the content for the lesson; worksheets and discussion questions facilitate further understanding and processing of the concepts. Participation and discussions regarding real-life situations are strongly encouraged to generalize the content to everyday issues.

There are several journal articles and book chapters on the use of rational–emotive behavior therapy with elementary-age students in which the Thinking, Feeling, Behaving program is reviewed and positively described, based on its clear connection with the structure of this treatment framework, which has been proven to produce beneficial results. In addition, there is some research evidence supporting the benefits of the Thinking, Feeling, and Behaving program. For example, Donegan and Rust (1998) demonstrated that the use of the program with second-grade students was linked to improvements in students' self-concept. Thus this program appears to be built on a solid foundation and has some supporting research evidence.

Advantages of the Thinking, Feeling, Behaving program include its novel approach (we are not aware of any other SEL program that is based exclusively on the premises of rational emotive behavior therapy), its long history of use in schools, and the large number of engaging activities for students. Teachers and mental health professionals who are influenced by the rational emotive therapy approach to intervention or who are interested in including such an approach in their SEL activities may find this program particularly appealing.

SEL UP CLOSE: THE STRONG KIDS CURRICULUM SERIES

Having provided brief overviews of some of the exemplary and promising SEL programs that are in wide use, we would now like to introduce in more depth a specific SEL program in order to see up close the details of how such programs work in actual practice. For this example we will focus on the SEL program *Strong Kids: A Social and Emotional Learning Curriculum*. Strong Kids is a 10- to 12-lesson curriculum (depending on developmental level), that is considered to be a skill-based SEL program. This program was developed by us and our colleagues at the University of Oregon, based on the notion that social–emotional and resiliency skills can be learned and taught in school, and that they require explicit instruction just like academic skills (see the Strong Kids website at *strong-kids.uoregon.edu/* for more information). Based on instructional design principles such as activating prior knowledge and providing opportunities for practice, Strong Kids was built on Cowen's (1994) five proposed pathways to psychological wellness as a basis for designing specific curricular concepts. These pathways include (1) promoting early attachments, (2) building competence with developmentally appropriate skills, (3) being in a setting that promotes wellness, (4) feeling empowered about the future, and (5) coping with stress using relevant skills. Unlike some of the other programs we reviewed, Strong Kids is not a lengthy program focusing on all social and emotional problems that occur in a school setting, such as school violence or antisocial behavior. Rather, it is designed to be a brief and easy-to-use program that specifically targets social and emotional competence and resiliency and gives students skills to address problems associated with internalizing symptoms (e.g., depression, anxiety, social withdrawal, somatic problems).

The Strong Kids series was originally designed with students in grades 3–8 in mind; however, as the need emerged for programs that could provide SEL instruction across students' academic tenure, it became clear that extension of Strong Kids from preschool to second grade and up through high school was feasible and prudent. Thus there are now five grade-specific versions of the Strong Kids series. These include *Strong Start for Pre-K* (Merrell, Whitcomb, & Parisi, 2009), *Strong Start for Grades K–2* (Merrell, Parisi, & Whitcomb, 2007), *Strong Kids for Grades 3–5* (Merrell, Carrizales, Feuerborn, Gueldner, & Tran, 2007a), *Strong Kids for Grades 6–8* (Merrell, Carrizales, Feuerborn, Gueldner, & Tran, 2007b), and *Strong Teens for Grades 9–12* (Merrell, Carrizales, Feuerborn, Gueldner, & Tran, 2007c). There is a range of 10 to 12 lessons included in the various volumes (fewer lessons for younger children) with a focus on teaching social and emotional learning concepts, building resiliency, finding assets and building on them, setting goals, and learning general coping skills. Skills that can be used to address internalizing problems are specifically reviewed, including emotion identification, behavioral activation, managing stress and anxiety, social problem solving and anger management, and cognitive restructuring. The curriculum was designed to be used in the classroom during a typical school day and integrated naturally into academic areas such as language arts, a health and wellness curriculum, and social studies.

Strong Start comprises 10 lessons, whereas the Strong Kids/Strong Teens programs contain 12 lessons. Each lesson follows the same general instructional format and is organized as follows: the purpose and objectives of the lesson are described, a list of materials that will be needed is provided, concepts from the previous lesson are reviewed, and new content is presented, followed by a brief review of the content covered that day and a homework assignment that teachers hand out to students. Throughout the lesson, students participate in activities specifically designed to promote application to real-life examples and retention of these concepts. Small- and large-group discussions and role-play activities are a major focus, as well as precorrecting, reminding, and reinforcing the concepts and skills during the course of a typical school day and in between lesson administration.

An example of this process is highlighted in *Strong Kids for Grades 6–8*, Lesson Six: Clear Thinking 1. At the beginning of the class, the instructor reviews the content from the previous lesson and introduces the new content—that emotions vary in terms of intensity (a little or a lot) and that students will learn to identify maladaptive thoughts and thinking errors. The students then participate in an activity in which they identify an emotion, rate the emotion on an "intensity thermometer," and begin to discuss the idea that emotions and thoughts can coexist. The following sample script introducing this idea can be adapted as necessary:

"When we feel strong emotions, we have thoughts that go with those emotions that happen at about the same time. It's important to pay attention to both our feelings and our thoughts."

Students are led through an activity, using an overhead transparency, to learn about six thinking errors that can occur when experiencing uncomfortable emotions and thoughts. Figure 2.2 includes the student handout and instructor overhead from the manual that is used to teach these common thinking errors. Students review these thinking errors and discuss six scenarios that could elicit these thoughts. For example:

"Michael's parents are getting a divorce. He thinks that this is all his fault because he has been getting into trouble lately."

A thinking error that is occurring in this scenario is "Making It Personal." The class would review this concept and brainstorm other situations in which they may find themselves that would elicit any of the six thinking errors. The class concludes with a review of the concepts that were covered and a homework assignment is distributed.

Strong Kids was designed with universal or primary prevention purposes in mind and has been used successfully in general education classrooms and in other settings, including secondary and tertiary prevention settings. The lessons can be naturally infused within a language arts, social studies, or health curriculum. Table 2.2 lists the names of the lessons in the Strong Kids series. The programs can be taught by classroom teachers, school counselors and psychologists, and sometimes using a team teaching approach. Typical classroom management strategies should continue with the addition of extra reinforcement for participation via individual or group rewards. We recommend using assessment to not only monitor student outcomes and adjust instructional variables as appropriate, but also whether the

FIGURE 2.2. Common thinking errors. From Merrell, Carrizales, Feuerborn, Gueldner, and Tran (2007b). Copyright 2007 by the University of Oregon. Reprinted by permission.

TABLE 2.2. Program Structure and Lesson Contents of the Strong Kids and Strong Teens SEL Programs

Lesson	Title	Description
1	About Strong Kids: Emotional Strength Training	Overview of the curriculum
2	Understanding Your Feelings: Part 1	Introduction to emotions Identify emotions as comfortable or uncomfortable
3	Understanding Your Feelings: Part 2	Discussion of appropriate and inappropriate ways of expressing emotions
4	Dealing With Anger	Recognizing triggers to anger Practicing ways to change inappropriate responses
5	Understanding Other People's Feelings	Identifying others' emotions by using clues
6	Clear Thinking: Part 1	Recognizing negative thought patterns
7	Clear Thinking: Part 2	Challenging these thought patterns to think more positively
8	The Power of Positive Thinking	Promoting optimistic thinking
9	Solving People Problems	Conflict resolution strategies
10	Letting Go of Stress	Stress reduction and relaxation exercises
11	Behavior Change: Setting Goals and Staying Active	Increasing time spent in enjoyable activities and meeting goals
12	Finishing Up!	Review of the lessons

components of each lesson are taught as they were designed and to determine the extent to which practitioners may need extra support. Of course, cultural adaptations must be considered as well as community climate issues, where persons may be unfamiliar with SEL and have concerns with its content.

Research to date has demonstrated positive, promising results with the Strong Kids programs, most notably in the areas of students retaining the content knowledge, decreasing existing internalizing symptoms, high levels of intervention integrity, and strong social validity (e.g., Gueldner, 2006; Harlacher, 2008; Nakayama, 2008; Merrell, Juskelis, Tran, & Buchanan, 2008; Tran, 2007). Areas of future research include evaluating generalization and maintenance effects across common situations and over time, making appropriate cultural adaptations in the program (see Castro-Olivo, 2006), the use of "booster sessions" to facilitate these effects, and supporting school-to-home partnerships to bolster this relationship and promote wellness throughout.

In summary, Strong Kids provides an example of the level of detail and depth that goes into an SEL program, such as the other programs that we previously reviewed. Although we admit that we have a vested interest in the success and influence of the Strong Kids programs, we do not promote this program or any other program as the "best." Rather, we suggest that what is best will depend on your specific needs, the specific concerns you are attempting to address, the amount of resources and support available to help implement the program, the match between time required and time available, and so forth. It is our view that there are several exemplary programs available, each offering particular advantages and limitations, and each varying widely in terms of time needed, level of structure, cost, training requirements, target focus, and so forth. Again, it is not necessary to use a packaged program in order to achieve benefits from SEL in classrooms, but such programs often provide great advantages because of the careful way they were planned and developed, and the user-friendly approach that they encompass in their design.

HOW TO SELECT A PACKAGED SEL PROGRAM THAT MEETS YOUR NEEDS

> Implementing SEL programming often involves eliminating programs and practices that no longer work or do not apply to the issues that today's students are facing. Letting go and embracing change can lead to renewal and measurable positive outcomes.

Early in this chapter, we discussed the rubric developed by CASEL as a choice for initiating and planning SEL in your school. We hope we have made the case that there is more to implementing SEL than choosing the program. However, it is typically very challenging to know how to choose a program; there are a lot of choices that seem to cover many of the same topics and claim to have an evidence basis. Following are some ideas to get this process started.

Identify the Needs of Your School

Look in the database that tracks behavioral referrals and you are sure to get some idea of the school's "high flyers" and the behaviors that are most frequently occurring or bothersome. SEL is, of course, broader than remediating disciplinary referrals, although its application could lead to improvements in this area. CASEL's rubric addresses the need for forming a steering committee that can evaluate the needs of the school via a needs assessment. Although most school personnel inherently understand the primary concerns of their school population, the most disturbing or disruptive behaviors (e.g., bullying, physical aggression) are often the most logical targets for intervention. But this view could be deceiving. Although these issues must be addressed swiftly, the school climate as a whole must also be considered. Choosing a program that addresses issues affecting the school climate may be a direction that would make sense for your school. On the other hand, if the school climate is generally positive and orderly, a program targeting specific skill areas may be beneficial. Check with your school administrators to find a qualified professional either in your district or in your community who could assist you with designing and implementing a needs assessment that is targeted, efficient, and can yield useful information.

Identify the Short- and Long-Term Goals for Your Students

Perhaps you are convinced that students need a solid social–emotional foundation of skills to be productive and responsible citizens of their communities—a long-term goal with which we would agree. What other long-term goals might you and your colleagues have for your students? How do these goals align with parents' goals for their children? Or the goals of the community or future employers? Perhaps your school would like to increase students' capacity to *apply* social problem-solving strategies, an example of a short-term goal. Many goals will seem equally urgent and valuable. It is important to focus on the big picture (i.e., your mission and long-term goals) as well as understanding the skill sets (short-term goals) that can contribute to growth toward a larger goal. We must emphasize that acquisition of social and emotional learning skills will be most successful when consistent instruction and support over the course of students' academic tenure are provided. This statement means considering and evaluating programs that have the potential to be sustained and delivered over time and naturally embedded into a school day.

Assess the Programs That Are Being and Have Been Used in the School

Other programs may have been tried by school professionals that are either continuing and are successful, are continuing but are viewed with lukewarm or dwindling support, or have "crashed and burned," meaning they did not work as hoped and there may be some collateral damage (e.g., personnel morale may be depressed, and hopelessness regarding future SEL efforts is present). It is vital for your school's planning committee to understand the programs that were tried and the reasons for their success or failure, and consider the programs that are working well and how they might complement a new program. It is also important to be mindful that the need for overall restructuring could include elimination of programs that are not working well and building the case for continuing with a new program in light of pessimism.

Review Programs That Seem to Be the Best Match for Your Needs and Goals

We have provided several very good programs for your review to jump-start your search for evidence-based programs. This list is not exhaustive, and we encourage you to use trusted sources to review and critically evaluate other programs if necessary. Some of these sources include the CASEL website at *www.casel.org* or the Center for Social and Emotional Education (*www.csee.net*). If you have access to a database where you can search the literature for research conducted on a particular program, we encourage you to obtain this information and review it with your steering committee. The point is for you to be an informed consumer and make every effort to assess the extent to which you believe the program can work symbiotically with your school ecology.

Identify the Resources That Are Needed to Sustain Implementation Efforts

Keeping a program going, especially if it is successful, can be an enormous undertaking. All too often we forget that programs need to be monitored for implementation integrity, and that implementers must have support to plan for instruction, pay for materials, and train staff. It is reasonable to expect that regular meetings should be held to provide updates on implementation efforts, review progress and any challenges, and brainstorm problems as they arise. Having your administration on board will help tremendously as the team collaborates.

WRAPPING THINGS UP

This chapter focused on choosing from among packaged SEL programs and considering factors that must be taken into account when making this choice. We provided information regarding several specific programs to give you a starting point from which to think about some of the programs available and their specific areas of focus. We also included issues that warrant consideration when actually choosing the program:

- SEL programs must be implemented over time, have resources to support implementation efforts, and prioritize sustainability.
- Thoughtful planning must precede choosing an SEL program to determine the best fit for your school's environment, priorities, goals, and current climate.
- Ongoing assessment while implementing an SEL program will help you determine when changes are necessary and monitor student and staff progress.
- Advantages to prepackaged SEL programs include a conceptual framework, the inclusion of research, field testing, and organized materials.
- Several evidence-based programs were reviewed in the chapter to jump-start your search for a program that best fits your students' needs.

Worksheet for Evaluating SEL Programs

Name of school: _____

Target grade/age level: _____

Program being considered: _____

Publisher/price: _____

List any costs in addition to curriculum manual: _____

_____

Number of lessons/activities: _____

Time required per lesson/activity: _____

Frequency of lessons/number of weeks: _____

Core SEL competency areas covered in program:

    ☐ Self-awareness   ☐ Social awareness   ☐ Decision making

    ☐ Self-management   ☐ Relationship management

Other competencies covered in program: _____

Training required/available to use program: _____

Are evaluation and progress monitoring tools available?   ☐ YES   ☐ NO

Match of program to needs of our students: ☐ Strong   ☐ Adequate ☐ Weak

Overall recommendation:

    ☐ Strongly recommended ☐ Consider further ☐ Not recommended

ADDITIONAL COMMENTS:

CHAPTER 3

The Essentials of Using Social and Emotional Learning in the Classroom

INTRODUCTION AND OVERVIEW

The preparation required to implement an SEL program is one of the most important steps in producing successful outcomes in students' social, emotional, and academic lives. It's also critical to school personnel satisfaction with using the program or activity. How often have you been asked to add a promising yet unfamiliar concept or lesson into established academic content and you felt excited, but also apprehensive or maybe even annoyed? Through a process of trial and error you taught the new information, found ways of efficiently organizing the materials, and eventually the new content was part of your mastered repertoire. The early stages of implementing SEL programming may be quite similar to what we just described. Because the infusion of SEL into the classroom is still a fairly new idea for many educators, and training in this area was not necessarily part of their undergraduate and graduate training, school professionals may feel a little unprepared. Understandably, it can be challenging to consider infusing a new set of instructional materials into an already full school day.

> **Implementing SEL can be a daunting experience for many educators. Carefully selected planning strategies can make this experience more realistic and manageable.**

This chapter reviews the core elements of planning for SEL implementation. We hope that by highlighting some important guidelines, you will be able to consider any issues that might arise in your unique settings and situations. Our experience with the Strong Kids curriculum, as well as in working with school professionals on other SEL programs, has helped us understand and field test many of the following preparation activities. Core elements of planning include such basics as:

- Making sure you have all the materials that are needed.
- Seeking training opportunities from professionals who have implemented the same program.
- Finding and using strategies to keep materials and activities organized.
- Using existing and potentially new classroom management strategies to ensure attentive and motivated students.
- Creating innovative activities that can help students generalize the material across a variety of life situations and maintain these skills over time.

At nearly every speaking engagement on SEL, we are asked about specific accommodations and modifications that can be made for populations with special needs. For example, how could an SEL program be offered to children with autism spectrum disorders in a meaningful way? What about students who have ADHD or otherwise have difficulty maintaining attention for a 45-minute lesson? We offer some suggestions for your consideration and discuss the importance of including the family and community in school-based SEL efforts. Admittedly, work still needs to be done to refine best practices of delivering SEL programs in the schools. We believe the following suggestions will provide you with an excellent starting point and reference for troubleshooting inevitable and often challenging situations.

PREPARATION AND PLANNING: THE BASICS

You may have had the experience of being in the middle of teaching an academic lesson or giving a professional presentation and realizing that a worksheet for students' homework was forgotten, a key point in the presentation slide was omitted, the directions for the in-class activity were misread or unclear, or your understanding of a key concept that needed to be taught was limited. How frustrating this can be! The same mishaps can occur when delivering SEL content. For example, a worksheet that describes and illustrates common expressions of emotions was not photocopied for distribution or you took longer to grade papers and had no time to prep for the next day's SEL lesson. In addition, through the course of our experiences observing and delivering SEL content, we are continually reminded that in order to teach SEL concepts, we must understand what we are teaching, have a strategic plan to obtain and organize materials, find support when it is needed, and measure students' progress. *Whew!* This section provides you with a guide to getting started with all these tasks that can make your experience with SEL rewarding and enjoyable. We have constructed a reproducible checklist in Worksheet 3.1 that may be used for easy reference to help guide you through this process.

> **Having a basic understanding of general SEL ideas will help the beginning phases of implementation make sense. Information can easily be gleaned from reviewing the program materials, seeking reliable and published resources, and discussing concepts with colleagues.**

Here are several areas that will help you begin organizing the process of implementing an SEL program. They are listed according to priority, or the order in which one would most likely become familiar with the materials and then proceed to some details that can be addressed after understanding some basics about the program.

Obtain the Necessary Materials

This step may seem quite obvious, but in fact, several types of materials may be needed to teach SEL strategies. It helps to know ahead of time to make sure these are available. Some of these materials may include:

- An instructor's manual
- Students' workbooks
- Overhead projector
- Transparencies for classroom instruction
- Reproducible worksheets for class activities or homework
- Posters or other visual aids to use during instruction or to display in the classroom
- Writing instruments, art supplies
- Video or audio playing devices

Of course, other materials may be needed. Typically, the instructor's manual will advise the instructor regarding the materials that are necessary for the curriculum in general, as well as for each lesson. It goes without saying that preparation includes knowing exactly what is needed to implement the lesson *before it is implemented!* Some programs might allow you to obtain materials, such as using worksheets that can be reproduced, directly from the instructor's manual. As you become more familiar with the program, preparation will become much easier and you will find ways to organize the materials for efficient access. Do you have an assistant in your classroom or school who can help you gather these materials and make sure they are ready? Using existing resources in your school to assist you in your preparation is an excellent way to minimize your preparation tasks *and* promote a sense of teamwork in SEL initiatives.

Know and Understand the Content

Similar to your preparation to teach academics and classroom behavioral management, some background and content knowledge is needed to teach social and emotional learning concepts. This does not necessarily mean you must return to a university to obtain a specialization certification or other advanced training in this area. There, however, many resources that can help as you learn about SEL concepts and strategies that are quite possibly very novel to you. We look forward to the day when adults are fluent in social and emotional knowledge because they were exposed to and were able to practice these skills on a regular basis at school, home, and in their community when they were children. When we were attending our respective K–12 educational settings, there was no strategic approach to teaching social and emotional skills. I (B. A. G.) have, on numerous occasions during the course of workshops and trainings, informally surveyed the number of educational and mental health professionals who received exposure to specific instruction in this area during their childhood. An affirmative response is generally quite low. For those of us who did not have this opportunity, we probably found we had some learning to do not only for ourselves and our families, but now also for the benefit of our students. For this reason, we cannot stress enough the importance of engaging in activities that will help you understand the theory and evidence that supports SEL concepts and strategies.

Generally, packaged SEL programs have manuals that provide not only the evidence supporting the effectiveness of the program, but also the "conceptual model" on which these strategies were based. For example, children go through a series of social and emotional stages during the course of their development. Programs are strategically developed with these stages in mind, so that the information they are exposed to is appropriate for their developmental age and facilitates growth to the next stage.

An understanding of how and why the materials were developed and are presented is critical to building your own confidence in delivering the information to your students. For this reason, a review of the program materials and manual is a minimum requirement to getting started with instruction. We encourage you to read them, despite the perception that the material might be a little "dry." Why is this important? Adults generally obtain their knowledge of social and emotional functioning from their own experiences and often use these points of reference to convey or clarify concepts that may be difficult for students to understand. Many of you have taken a course or two in child development, or an introductory course or more in psychology. The field of education has grown exponentially in understanding how theory and evidence-based strategies may be imparted directly to students via educational instruction. Given the field's increased understanding of social and emotional development and how to promote growth, it is incredibly important to access resources that provide *up-to-date* and *accurate* information. In addition to the program materials, there are several online resources available, as well as written materials found in bookstores and catalogs that can help. The following organizations and their associated websites are examples of groups dedicated to helping educators find information to assist in this process:

- Collaborative for Academic, Social, and Emotional Learning (*www.casel.org/*)
- UCLA Center for Mental Health in Schools (*smhp.psych.ucla.edu/*)
- University of Maryland Center for School Mental Health (*csmh.umaryland.edu/*)
- Center for Social and Emotional Education (*www.csee.net/*)

You will find that the program materials, together with additional written resources you locate either through trusted Internet sources, books, or a university course should give you the knowledge you need to confidently begin disseminating SEL to your students. As you peruse these materials in conjunction with teaching the SEL strategies, you will certainly improve your understanding of the content and increase your awareness of the research that supported the conceptual framework used to design SEL programs. You may also develop a sense of mastery and confidence with concepts that may previously have seemed daunting or confusing, as well as learn new skills that can be applied to your own life! We cannot emphasize enough how your understanding and appreciation for SEL theory and research into practice will translate into how you are able to communicate these ideas and skills to your students.

Estimate the Time That Is Needed for Preparation and Implementation

An excellent time-management resource called *Time Management from the Inside Out* (Morgenstern, 2004) recommends that in order to improve day-to-day efficiency, one should estimate the amount of time that it will take to complete each task. Morgenstern suggests that you first list the tasks that need to be accomplished, then estimate how long it will take to complete the task, and, finally, record how long it actually took to complete the task. When applied to newly implementing an SEL program, this strategy can be a lifesaver during an incredibly hectic school or clinic day. In the program materials, estimates may be provided regarding how long it may take to implement one lesson or classroom activity. These estimates are generated from prior observations and measurement of multiple individuals implementing that particular task. What can be difficult to estimate is the amount of time needed to prepare to implement the lesson or activity. So while you are familiarizing yourself with the program materials, you may find it beneficial to list the necessary preparation tasks, as well as how long it may take to teach a particular activity. This will be the estimated time commitment for preparation and teaching per lesson or activity. When you begin preparation and teaching activities, make a note of how long these tasks actually took. Where you able to delegate some responsibilities? Did some tasks require less or more time? It will almost certainly take a little longer to prep and teach when learning a new program, and these same activities will almost certainly require less time as you become more familiar and fluent. This template should provide you with a solid estimate of the amount of time you should reserve for planning and teaching the SEL program or strategies that have been selected.

Technical Support: Training, Consultation, and Feedback

Most schools make time for professional development throughout the course of an academic year. Although the topics may change and vary in degree of participant interest, this tradition of providing information and training can be an excellent starting point to promote staff development regarding SEL initiatives. In fact, training and ongoing support is highly recommended to increase the likelihood that programs will be implemented as they were studied and intended, and with this support students' skills should be enhanced (CASEL, 2003; Fixsen, Naoom, Blasé, Friedman, & Wallace, 2005). Although the specific type of support that works best with SEL programming is not well understood at this time (Gueldner & Merrell, in press), there are several options that we believe can be very helpful given their field testing in educational settings with academic and behavioral needs. But first, how does one go about obtaining support in the first place? The steering committee or similar group that was used to investigate SEL programs and commit to implementation is an appropriate advocacy group to promote support services to administrative staff.

Trainings and Inservicing

We have both had opportunities to gladly serve as trainers during staff development sessions to expose school personnel to SEL and to provide more in-depth training. This type of training can meet several goals, either to get your school started with SEL or to brainstorm and problem solve around the minutiae of implementing SEL in the context of unique and systemic programming issues. Professionals who provide this training can often be found among university faculty who specialize in SEL or school mental health issues, as well as practitioners familiar with SEL program construction and implementation. SEL program publishers and professional organizations also may offer trainings to provide support around a specific program. For example, the Committee for Children offers trainings for their Second Step Program to support school professionals with getting started with the program and sustaining effective programming (for more information, visit *www.cfchildren.org/programs/ssp/training/*). It is important to note that while these often one-time trainings can be motivating and informative to jump-start SEL initiatives, they can be limited in scope and consequently may have limited long-term effects with student outcomes (Fixsen et al., 2005) and teachers' abilities to sustain effective implementation practices (Witt, Noell, LaFleur, & Mortenson, 1997). The reality is that most "train and hope" methods of inservicing—those methods that do not include a comprehensive plan for follow-up—are just a starting point.

Consultation

Consultation services may be an option to consider if support during the course of program implementation would appear beneficial and is feasible. Once again, ongoing support is highly recommended to produce and sustain meaningful outcomes for both educators and students. Consultation can be quite broadly defined; it is important that your steering committee is able to articulate the goals it hopes to accomplish by utilizing these services. Some common uses include either assessing current school and classroom strengths and needs to define how a program will work in the setting and what is needed to maximize results, and/or providing one-on-one assistance during program implementation to observe how the program is running, especially areas that may be addressed to maximize results. There are many school professionals (e.g., school psychologists and counselors) in your school who are excellent resources because they are interested and have training in using universal prevention and early intervention strategies in their schools. Systematic SEL programming may not be a part of their current job responsibilities, but we are willing to guess that many of them would be incredibly interested and willing to serve in this capacity, especially if their current responsibilities can be adjusted to accommodate this role. Some districts also retain specialists, much like reading instruction specialists, who collaborate with teachers and educational support staff to provide support when a new or particularly challenging curriculum is adopted. This section does not allow for a detailed discussion regarding the various consultation models and their advantages and challenges. These details notwithstanding, if consultation is deemed feasible and beneficial, the most prudent course of action is to clarify the goals for these services and discuss how they can be accomplished with the consultation style and services available.

Performance Feedback

Performance feedback has been used in educational settings to improve both teachers' adherence to classroom interventions and students' behavioral and academic performance (Mortenson & Witt, 1998; Noell et al., 2005). This strategy generally involves the use of a consultant, either a fellow teacher or a university or in-school consultant, who provides feedback on the extent to which strategies and lessons are implemented as they were designed. Measurements are taken on key elements of the program, and the consultant provides this information to the individual implementing the program. Studies have shown that receiving this information can be especially helpful in improving student outcomes. There is limited research on the use of performance feedback with SEL program implementation (Gueldner & Merrell, in press), but we believe that, similar to the research that has demonstrated the positive impact it has in the context of implementing a behavioral or academic intervention, it is likely that performance feedback can be an appropriate way to facilitate SEL.

Measuring Progress

Measuring and monitoring your students' progress during and after the implementation of an SEL program is critical to understanding the impact the program may be having, changes and accommodations that need to be made, and building a case for either continuing a successful program or discontinuing one that is not having the desired effect. We cannot emphasize this issue enough. Chapter 7 provides much more detail regarding the specifics on how to conceptualize this process and how to do it successfully. We wish to briefly mention it in this section as a way of orienting you toward the importance of including this planning phase, so this essential component is prioritized.

Managing Behavior

During the course of a school day, nothing detracts more from teaching academics than disruptions due to students' behavioral problems (also, fire drills!). We must emphasize the strength in classroom behavior management when the entire school ecology works seamlessly to foster positive relationships between and among school staff and students. Two primary and guiding factors promote successful behavior management in a school: fostering positive communication and relationships and structured and systematic approaches to schoolwide behavior managements. Walk into a classroom with this kind of rapport and you sense a distinct "tone." The teacher is conducting a lesson with a firm and engaging voice, he physically places himself in the room so that all students can easily see and hear him, students are listening attentively and actively responding to instruction. Research has demonstrated that teachers' verbal and nonverbal communication accounts for much of the positive "tone" by conveying a sense of interest in students, mutual respect and acceptance, and that unacceptable behaviors are not tolerated (Knoll & Patti, 2003). Positive behavioral interventions and supports (PBIS) is a structured and systematic approach that has vastly altered not only how behaviors in school are managed, but also the extent to which positive behaviors are proactively promoted (e.g., Sugai & Horner, 2002). Through PBIS, schoolwide and classroom-based strategies are universally adopted to teach and promote prosocial behavior. Behaviors requiring disciplinary action are managed through interventions (e.g., conducting a functional behavioral assessment that leads to a behavior management plan). Schools actively utilizing a systematic PBIS approach to school behavior are considerably ahead of the curve when it comes to managing behavior in the context of SEL programming. Students have an understanding of the basic behavioral expectations that occur across the course of their school day, whether it is in their classroom, in the hallways, during lunch, or waiting for the bus. An excellent starting point for learning more about PBIS is the U.S. Department of Education's National Technical Assistance Center on Positive Behavioral Interventions and Supports, located at *www.pbis.org.*

Why do we mention the importance of schoolwide behavior management in the context of SEL? Adoption and implementation of these general principles sets the stage for special behavioral expectations that are important when using SEL in the classroom. During an SEL lesson behavioral expectations should be no different than during a typical academic day. For example, students should be expected to be safe in the classroom (e.g., walking rather than running into the classroom), to be respectful to other students (e.g., use kind words, listen to another speaking), and to make responsible choices (e.g., come to class prepared). For continuity, these expectations and any associated management strategies (e.g., rewards given for observed and exemplary demonstration of an expectation) should be maintained throughout the course of SEL programming. Expectations that are special to SEL often include: (1) stating that although students are encouraged to share their thoughts and feelings, they should not feel pressure to share anything that makes them feel uncomfortable; (2) everything that is discussed in the classroom must be considered confidential; and (3) respecting fellow classmates is especially important when sharing thoughts and feelings that may be highly sensitive. These expectations should be clearly stated before any lessons are started, with opportunities for students to ask questions and receive clarification.

We have seen classroom teachers successfully increase the frequency that positive behavior is rewarded by using simple reinforcers that are highly interesting and relevant to their students. For many students, having the opportunity to share their experiences is reward enough. This situation often occurs with our middle school students whose developmental stage is conducive to learning about and expressing often confusing and painful emotions. For other students, sharing and participating may be anxiety provoking or may seem pointless and "boring." As you get a feeling for how your students are responding to the materials, you may wish to boost the frequency and type of special rewards you distribute for exhibiting safe, respectful, and responsible behaviors. You may also wish to consider having a "wrap-up" celebration to signal the completion of a program. We consider SEL to be a life-long learning process, but one that for students should continue throughout their academic tenure. Consequently, it is important to convey to students that the celebration does not signify the end of SEL, but rather a small reward they can look forward to for a job well done.

Conclusion

This section provided an overview of six primary areas that, if addressed successfully, will provide strategic assistance in planning and organizing SEL implementation efforts.

Attention to these areas will greatly improve the opportunities for school personnel to feel equipped to prepare not only the program materials, but also the surrounding support systems that are absolutely necessary to ensure student progress and all-around satisfaction. We encourage you to use Figure 3.1 as a checklist that condenses this information into a tool that can be used to prompt and monitor using these strategies. This next section discusses specifics for actual implementation of an SEL program in the classroom.

DELIVERY OF SEL

The previous section outlined several strategic areas for *planning* SEL implementation; now let's take a look at the "nuts and bolts" of *actual* implementation. Of course, as with anything new that is tried, there is always a mix of anticipation, excitement, and a hint of apprehension with getting started. You know that the students' first impression is vital to engagement and, obviously, the more positive that is, the better. You want instruction to flow naturally and you may find that getting some feedback would help you understand how the class is running and brainstorm modifications that can improve things. Engaging in many of the planning strategies in the previous section will set the stage; the following strategies will refine it.

Are We Teaching What We Intend to Teach?

One of the issues that surfaces time and time again in the literature and in practice is: *How do we know that a program is being implemented in the way that it was found to be effective when it was originally studied or researched?* In other words, programs are generally studied under carefully prescribed conditions, and in order to ensure the best chances for success, they need to be implemented as they were found to have a positive impact on students. Program designs are based on a tremendous foundation that includes scope and depth of theory and as well as previously tested evidence-based practices. In short, there are strategic reasons why specific SEL topics are included in materials and introduced in a particular order. In mathematics, students learn multiplication facts prior to diving into complex algebraic equations; the precision in which the scope and sequence of SEL concepts are similarly designed and delivered. How can we be assured that these steps are being followed?

> Monitoring the extent to which a program is being taught in the manner that is intended is a great way to maximize program implementation and improve results.

One way of measuring whether the programs are being taught in the way they were intended is to measure student outcomes. The logic here is that if students are gaining in knowledge and skill, then they must have been exposed to curriculum concepts that were deemed important to produce this result. This measurement is typically taken by testing students' knowledge via pencil and paper or oral examinations (e.g., quizzes, tests, in-class questioning). Clearly, there are limitations to this logic! Knowing student outcomes does not tell us whether all of the concepts were taught in the way they were found to produce positive results; it just tells us that students are performing at a specified level. Maybe they already knew the information. Maybe their knowledge was less than it could have been because half of the lesson content was omitted due to a fire drill one day.

Treatment integrity involves determining the extent to which the program/strategies were taught as intended, designed, and researched. Essentially, measurements are taken during program implementation sessions/teaching to determine the extent to which the interventionist (or teacher, counselor, psychologist, etc.) is using and delivering the program materials as designed and in the way in which they were found to be effective. Research has shown that student outcomes are directly related to the interventionist's use of programming materials (Witt et al., 1997). What this finding means is that measuring progress is not exclusive to testing students; it means that implementation efforts must be evaluated as well.

Of course, evaluating student outcomes is vital to tracking whether the program is having any effect (this issue is covered in more depth in Chapter 7). In terms of measuring implementation, there are two primary means by which this can be done. First, however, what is going to be measured? Typical practice is to define the essential areas of the program that, if implemented, should produce positive outcomes. Essential areas often include whether key concepts were taught, the extent to which they were taught (e.g., were they briefly mentioned or directly taught integrating relevant examples with opportunities for practice), the sequence in which the concepts were taught, the speed at which the lessons are to be covered over time, and the rate and volume of student participation. If you have chosen a commercially available program, we urge you to determine whether there are materials that can help you collect integrity data. If not, you may wish to consider designing a brief form that can measure the key components of the programs, that is, those that are considered absolutely necessary to ensure the success of the program. If this is the case, it will be helpful to meet with other instructors/interventionists to reach consensus regarding the essential areas. We have provided an example of a simple form that was created for effectiveness research with the Strong Kids curriculum (see Figure 3.1). The vignette at the conclusion of this section illustrates the process by which this form was created and should provide you with guidance on how to proceed with this valuable component of program implementation.

There are two primary methods by which treatment integrity can be measured. One method is to use a self-report checklist or rating scale (like the one just discussed) by which the interventionist rates him- or herself on the extent to which he or she implemented the program. This approach is relatively easy since a form can typically be completed within minutes and no additional technical support is needed. A major drawback to choosing this method is that it is a very subjective process, meaning that the accuracy of this rating is limited because the results rely solely on the perception of the rater. This issue is generally why a second method of measuring integrity is preferred. An impartial rater (generally another trained professional) conducts observations during program implementation. The rater uses the same form otherwise used by the interventionist. The difference is that the ratings can be less subjective, and during the observation session the rater may observe instructional, behavioral, or other issues occurring during the course of the session that may have gone unnoticed by the interventionist. This information can be very helpful not only to track

Implementation Checklist
Lesson 6: Clear Thinking Part 1

Observation start time: _____

I. Review

☐ Reviewed previous lessons'/assignments' main ideas (obtained 3–5 adequate ideas).

Circle one: Not implemented   Partially implemented   Fully implemented

Notes: _____

II. Introduction

☐ Introduced the concept of emotions and their varying levels of intensity.

Circle one: Not implemented   Partially implemented   Fully implemented

Notes: _____

III. Identify/Intensity of emotions, negative thoughts, and common thinking errors

☐ Used Supplement 6.1 as an overhead transparency.

☐ Teacher models example of feeling angry and where on thermometer.

☐ Students volunteer own examples.

☐ Teacher indicates that thoughts can co-occur with emotions.

☐ Students identify thoughts they had with emotions.

☐ Used Supplement 6.2 as overhead transparency and in-class handout.

☐ Teacher reviews each of the six thinking errors.

☐ Used Supplement 6.3 as an overhead transparency.

☐ Discussed the six scenarios and identified thinking errors.

Circle one: Not implemented   Partially implemented   Fully implemented

Notes: _____

IV. Closure

☐ Teacher reviews several main ideas from the lesson.

Circle one: Not implemented   Partially implemented   Fully implemented

Notes: _____

V. Homework handout

☐ Supplement 6.4 is distributed.

Circle one: Not implemented   Partially implemented   Fully implemented

Notes: _____

Observation finish time: _____

Percentage of components implemented:

FIGURE 3.1. A sample checklist for evaluating fidelity or intervention integrity of an SEL lesson.

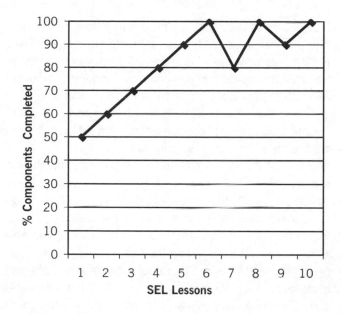

FIGURE 3.2. An example of graphing successful teacher implementation of the lessons in an SEL curriculum, using percentage of lesson components completed as the target.

the extent to which the program is implemented as intended, but also to troubleshoot and brainstorm solutions from another angle. Using this method requires that the rater have some training with the materials and rating form and for the interventionist to be open and prepared to receive feedback on his or her performance. Again, research has demonstrated the powerful impact measuring integrity and providing feedback can have on teacher and student outcomes, but there must also be a willingness to engage in this process. An additional component to this process worth considering is graphing the results from each observation session. Research has shown that a visual graphic of performance can help increase the extent to which programs are followed as intended (Balcazar, Hopkins, & Suarez, 1985). An example of what this might look like is shown in Figure 3.2.

VIGNETTE: Measuring Program Implementation

It's the start of a new school year, and Gabriella Jackson is looking forward to meeting her sixth-grade language arts students. There is always a sense of renewal and hope that comes with the beginning of a new class of students. Ms. Jackson looks forward to introducing and supporting them through the transition from elementary to middle school, which for some students can be challenging as they adjust to becoming more academically independent. This past summer, she attended a training session for a new SEL curriculum that promises to help sixth-grade students learn "resiliency" skills to cope with stress. Ms. Jackson is really looking forward to trying the new program, as are several other sixth-grade teachers in the building. They plan to use a couple of rating scales to measure student progress over the next 6 months and, because they are interested in teaching the program as close as possible to how it was designed, they've also decided to track their instruction and delivery for the next 6 months.

Unfortunately, the program does not include a "treatment integrity" worksheet or checklist. Having asked for 2 hours of release time, the teachers meet to develop their own system. Ms. Jackson prepared an outline that highlights the primary components that should be included in this measure. She presents them to the group as follows:

1. What are the primary components of each lesson that we want to make sure we teach well? These are the ones that we must focus on.
2. We need to measure the extent to which each component is taught. For example, not at all, a little bit, in its entirety?
3. We need to provide an opportunity to notice and record any observations we have during instruction where things didn't go so well or something could be changed.
4. We can either rate ourselves during instruction or observe one another for one-third of the lessons to make sure we are covering the content and provide feedback on our performance. Observing one another will be more accurate and useful; we should consider asking for occasional coverage for a couple of classes so that we can help one another or see whether the school counselor or psychologist would be interested and able to serve in this capacity.

Ms. Jackson provided this information to the team, and they were able to reach consensus with these items so they could begin tracking program implementation. The school psychologist was able to assist them with the observations and data collection, which gave the teachers insight into areas that needed adjustments as well as points of instruction that were going well. They also received feedback on how students were interacting with the materials—for the most part, really well and engaged. When it came time for the team to report to administration on the results of the program to date, the teachers were able to provide documentation of the extent to which they implemented the program as it was designed and consequently link the program to the positive student outcomes that were measured. These data helped to convince the administrative team that the program should be adopted across all middle school grade levels, beginning in the next school year.

PAYING ATTENTION TO INSTRUCTION

Effective instruction is an area where most school personnel have a solid foundation and should feel relatively comfortable. When implementing SEL initiatives, attention to instruction is also important when considering that this content is typically delivered through classroom-based instruction! In addition to using examples from students' daily lives and using role plays and discussions to make the material relevant and reinforcing (Gresham, 2002; Joseph & Strain, 2003), many SEL programs rely heavily on additional evidence-based instructional principles. For example, it is widely accepted that effective instruction uses "scaffolding" in order to introduce new concepts, build fluency, and continue to introduce new and complementary concepts that "build on" one another. Sometimes scripts are used to guide teachers through precise wording to be used in the lesson; limiting the amount of words used in the instruction as well as specifying the words to be used should ensure that students have a more accurate view and understanding of the content (Watkins & Slocum, 2004). Providing examples and nonexamples is a common evidence-based instructional strategy used to illustrate academic content and can be used to compare and contrast concepts that can range from maximally or minimally different (Kame'enui & Simmons, 1990; Watkins & Slocum, 2004). Take, for example, the emotions *happy* and *sad*. These emotions are a good starting point to highlight a maximally different emotional concept; most would agree that sad is usually the opposite of happy. However, when one compares the emotions happy and elated, these emotions share common features (e.g., smile, light heartedness, relaxed) and have some minimal differences (e.g., elated is typically "more" happy and often compared to feeling jubilant, excited, ecstatic, but it is certainly not sad).

Because we know that effective instruction is linked to students' academic success, it is quite generalizable to view SEL instruction in the same way and work hard to make sure instructional quality is good. This is where monitoring treatment integrity comes in. If you can measure and monitor the quality of instruction, you are well on your way to creating an effective model for SEL programming. I (B. A. G.) am currently working on a daily basis with mental health professionals

> **Delivering SEL content is enhanced by the use of effective instructional principles. Scaffolding concepts, using carefully selected wording, illustrating examples and nonexamples, and providing frequent opportunities to respond work together to produce social and emotional achievement.**

who work outside of education, discussing the value of attending to these issues. Those of you working in the educational field, who have had formal training in instructional principles or at least exposure and brief training, should easily understand the emphasis placed on this topic and be more prepared to assume responsibility for ensuring that effective instructional practices can lead to positive student outcomes.

PRACTICING SKILLS ACROSS SETTINGS AND OVER TIME

We can all remember experiences we've had learning a new instrument or sport—it takes practice to perform your skills under a variety of circumstances (e.g., feeling nervous, inclement weather, playing in front of a crowd of spectators) and to improve with time. I (B. A. G.) distinctly remember my years of musical "training" by way of weekly lessons, the daily practice for no less than 30 minutes, and the ultimate successes as I progressed from simple tunes to more advanced, memorized pieces. But because the practicing was a daily grind most times—the music was classical, and I preferred more contemporary music—it did not feel relevant or fun. Likewise, this is how learning a new skill can feel for your students. Learning about feelings, emotions, interpersonal relationships, and healthy ways of expression *can* be fun! And practicing in the classroom, home, and community can increase the likelihood that the skills will improve and become more fluent and polished.

Practicing SEL is like any other practice: finding frequent and regular opportunities to be exposed to and practice new SEL concepts, practicing under a variety of conditions (e.g., first in the classroom, then the hallways and cafeteria, on the playground, and at home or in the greater community). To encourage this process within the confines of a school day is challenging and, consequently, we offer the following suggestions:

- Focus on teaching the concepts and skills that are outlined in the materials as being the most important. These were found to be the essential elements that should bring students the most gains if they learn and practice them.
- Keep in mind your audience: Young students will have a shorter attention span and will only be able to sit through direct instruction for a brief time. If they are asked to listen longer than what is developmentally appropriate, they will become bored and some of the content will go unnoticed. Consequently, look for opportunities during the day to reinforce the content through examples and happenings in the classroom, in the hallways, and during lunch and recess. This is also true for older students who are able to sustain attention for longer periods of time.
- Highlighting examples of the content either just discussed or covered a few weeks ago will give life to the instructional materials in a way that should make sense to students, activate their memories, and develop more robust connections. For example, you may find that language arts lessons contain common social situations or ethical dilemmas that you can apply to SEL concepts, or a dispute between classmates can be used to practice the problem-solving skills that were just reviewed in last week's lesson. Look for ways to infuse the materials—examples abound and your students will learn and benefit!

INCLUDING FAMILIES IN SEL

One of the best ways to promote SEL and increase the likelihood that students will apply these skills to other situations is to include families. In order to do this, we must look for ways to include caregivers in the entire process. This means that these efforts should ideally go above and beyond sending home a flyer letting families know that their child will participate in an SEL program. It is vitally important to get to know the people who comprise your school community: parents, grandparents, caregivers such as foster parents, siblings, other extended family members. As we discuss in more detail in Chapter 5, we can mistakenly make sweeping generalizations about the community, the pervasive socioeconomic standings, and cultural considerations that may present unique considerations. However, understanding the family unit in which your students reside can really make a difference with sustaining SEL.

At this time, the school is the primary community institution in which children will be exposed to SEL programming. We look forward to more agencies, such as primary care facilities, having the capabilities to give caregivers and children SEL information and to provide complementary services. Until then, the school serves as primary clearinghouse for SEL programs. In order to do this, schools must make efforts to get to know our families and help them to feel welcome. Many families do not feel welcome in their neighborhood schools. This is not necessarily because schools are inhospitable, but they can be intimidating buildings to walk into, especially if caregivers had negative school experiences themselves. About a year ago, I (B. A. G.) walked into a middle school to support a graduate student in data collection for her dissertation. It had only been a year since I had stopped working as a school psychologist after practicing for more than a decade. Upon checking in, I actually felt a little nervous. I did not know the staff, it was clear everyone else knew their way around the building, and there is that undeniable pang of dread walking into the staff lounge and not knowing a soul! Although everyone was friendly and helpful, I was reminded that I had walked into a culture that I did not totally understand. I cannot imagine how our families feel coming into a school for the first time, under duress, or not speaking English. We encourage you to brainstorm with your colleagues ways

> **Caregivers need information on SEL to help their students practice the concepts at home and in the community. As educated role models in the community, caregivers are responsible to get this conversation going.**

in which schools can collaboratively and unilaterally take small steps to help families feel welcome; the goal is to have them engaged in their student's education, which now includes SEL.

In order to help families talk about feelings, cope with uncomfortable emotions, deal with stress in a healthy way, and manage interpersonal relationships, caregivers need information! Send newsletters, have an open house, create "link letters" that highlight the content of each SEL lesson and send them home with students, post them on the school's website, give them ideas on how to talk about SEL concepts at home, ask them how often they talk to their kids about feelings. Just help them get the conversation going! A positive relationship with the school is a step in the right direction for caregivers supporting education.

ADAPTING SEL PROGRAMMING FOR SPECIFIC POPULATIONS

We are regularly asked, often about three-quarters of the way through a presentation or workshop, "How do I modify and adapt the materials you are talking about to use with students who have autism/cognitive impairment/learning disabilities/traumatic brain injury/behavior problems/are non–English speaking/(fill in the blank)?" This is an undeniably important and challenging question as we strive to meet all children's needs in this pluralistic society. Chapter 5 reviews and discusses the social and emotional needs of children from varying cultural backgrounds and how SEL can be applied. This next section focuses primarily on using SEL programming with students who have developmental and learning delays as well as behavioral problems.

Students with Cognitive Impairments

Many teachers working with children who have cognitive impairments (e.g., mental retardation) and learning disabilities would like to use SEL programming, and in many cases are already doing so by weaving concepts into instruction throughout specially designed instruction. The question is, how can existing programs be adapted if they were not originally designed to be used with this population? In an age where evidence-based practices are expected, this issue poses quite a challenge, as there are limited programming options for this population. Despite this concern, we offer a few suggestions for consideration.

Like all typically developing children, students with cognitive impairments also require instructional materials to meet them at their current level of functioning and challenge them so they acquire new and useable information and skills. Several differences emerge between these groups, however, especially as children mature. Children with cognitive impairments typically process and acquire information at slower rate, necessitating the use of a repetitive and integrative instructional style to help encode the material into memory. The amount of information that can be covered in a typical 45-minute instructional block in a general education classroom cannot feasibly be covered for children with cognitive delays. There is too much information that requires introduction and mastery in this amount of time, and often it is difficult for these children to sustain attention when the concepts become increasingly complex. Consequently, it will take more sessions and, therefore, more time to cover all of the content. In addition, all of the same content may not be appropriate. Because new SEL concepts are introduced at strategic developmental milestones (i.e., introduced when children are able to understand them), concepts that require more abstract reasoning skills, such as metacognition or "thinking about your thinking," may be challenging for some students, depending on the level of their functioning. Finally, the materials that these children are exposed to are used with chronologically younger children and consequently use language and graphics that can seem quite "childish."

Given these considerations, what types of SEL concepts are feasible? We recommend that, at a minimum, a focus should be placed on the basics of SEL and build from there as students are capable. These basics generally start with emotional education, specifically emotional knowledge skills. Research has demonstrated that the ability to recognize emotions in oneself and others is predictive of social behavior, self-reported internalizing symptoms in later elementary years, attentional control, and academic competence (Fine, Izard, Mostow, Trentacosta, & Ackerman, 2003; Izard et al., 2001; Trentacosta, Izard, Mostow, & Fine, 2006). In other words, the ability to recognize emotions can improve these areas of functioning. It is also difficult for children to use strategies for *managing* their emotions when they struggle with identifying their emotions, and they are often rated as less well-liked by their peers and teachers (Denham & Weissberg, 2004). Most SEL programs start with emotion identification principles as a foundational skill, and we believe this is an excellent place to begin. Other areas worth focusing on include monitoring the pace of instruction and providing opportunities for practice throughout the school day. This is key to introducing concepts at a rate that students can grasp and yet are not overwhelmed or frustrated. Did we say opportunities for practice? Yes! Students need every opportunity to identify an emotion and consciously experience how their body feels when they are happy, sad, mad, frustrated, scared, and embarrassed so they can learn how to recognize the "early warning signs" to take it to the next level—management. This means finding times outside of formal instruction to practice these skills. We talk more about this in just a moment.

Students with Autism Spectrum Disorders

Children and adolescents with autism spectrum disorders (ASD) may have other challenges when learning SEL material. Part of the diagnosis of an ASD is having a measured deficit in social and communication development and skills, making SEL all the more important, but also uniquely challenging for these students. In addition, the diagnosis of an ASD can include a vast range of intellectual and communication functioning. You may work with students who are highly verbal, yet have a very difficult time noticing nonverbal cues or cannot seem to identify their feelings in conjunction with associated bodily sensations. Other students are severely impaired with intellectual delays and limited expressive language capacities. These vast differences in functioning can make systematic programming complex for students with ASD.

As the field learns to better understand the social and emotional characteristics of children with autism in order to more accurately recognize ASD, the level at which we are able to intervene in areas of deficits lags behind. Researchers and practitioners continue to learn more about how persons with ASD perceive emotions or more specifically, why this is so difficult (see Gross, 2004 for a discussion). We have worked with many teachers, speech and language therapists, and mental health professionals who have diligently pieced together and integrated social and emotional skills training into everyday programming for these students. When it comes to *systematic* SEL programming for students with ASD in the schools, there is room for growth. Social skills programming is an example where advances in the field are leading to very relevant and feasible interventions. Teaching social skills to children with autism requires intense and repetitive instruction (Baron-Cohen & Bolton, 1993) however, the literature documenting the effective use of group instruction in a school setting has been quite limited (as discussed in Kroeger, Schultz, & Newsom, 2007). A recently published study addressed this issue by using a group instruction format to teach young children with autism social skills using video modeling technology (Kroeger et al., 2007) and demonstrated how intensive, repetitive skills training in a group could improve children's social skills and have parent satisfaction with the results. We propose that future work promoting SEL with students with ASD should not only continue to study the effectiveness of particular programming, but also consider the SEL rubric for planning for implementation across grade and developmental levels, taking into consideration the need for schoolwide support, strategic planning, and goals for sustainable practice.

General Principles of Adaptation

Perhaps one of the most universally tried and true approaches to modifying any program to be used with specific populations is the use of behavioral reinforcement principles that can increase the likelihood that students will engage, attend to instruction, practice the concepts, and learn and apply them to everyday life. This is certainly true when considering modifications that may enhance SEL programming for students with learning and/or behavioral problems. The pace of instruction and the amount of material that is feasible to cover in one session must be taken into consideration, as these students often require fast-paced, repetitive instruction allowing for regular breaks and extended time spent on one concept. Adding reinforcers for desired behaviors such as attendance, participation, sustained attention, and performance can increase behaviors that facilitate learning (e.g., attendance, participation, attention), improve performance, and make learning fun! For all of these children, finding time during the day where they find success and enjoyment should be a top priority, and what better time than during SEL instruction? Simply modifying your current classroom management strategies to increase rates and types of reinforcement (e.g., choosing a special activity, getting out of an undesirable task, group winning) is a relatively easy adaptation to existing programming.

In summary, modifications with these populations of students can be straightforward if you keep your primary goals for prevention and intervention in mind: providing an opportunity for students to learn the foundational SEL skills using effective instructional principles, at a level and rate that is developmentally appropriate; and using behavioral strategies that increase the likelihood that students will engage, attend, and enjoy being a part of social and emotional learning. We must emphasize again that modifications may need to be made in a way that formal investigation (research) was not conducted. We urge you to work with your school team to develop a plan that is mindful of evidence-based practices and works well for your situation. Regularly scan the literature and materials catalogues for new and evidence-based SEL programs that might be a great fit for your students with special needs. They are sure to emerge as the technology improves and, certainly, after publication of this book.

WRAPPING THINGS UP

Chapter 3 outlined the basics for beginning SEL programming and highlighted several considerations that should help you and your school attain the best possible start. We cannot emphasize enough the importance of and value in considering these aspects when you make plans for a new or existing program. Just as we recommended focusing in on the main points of any SEL lesson, here are the highlights from this chapter that are worth revisiting:

• *Advance preparation is key.* Have the materials ready, get to know the materials by working with them ahead of time, read up on concepts that may be unfamiliar, and estimate how long you will need to plan and implement each facet of the program.

• Consider obtaining *extra support* through trainings or consultation from an in-house or otherwise knowledgeable professional, or find a trusted colleague who can give you feedback on your performance. This process will help polish your skills and show you areas that may need some adjustment. You also can use this process to determine a way to measure the extent to which you are implementing the program.

• Plan to *reinforce* your students for participation. You can use existing schoolwide behavior management strategies and/or create a complementary plan to increase the likelihood that students will engage with and enjoy the material.

• Work with your school colleagues to find ways of including families in SEL programming. Use existing ways that caregivers are informed of their student's progress (e.g., parent–teacher conferences) and brainstorm for new ones to involve those families who will likely benefit from this connection and are hesitant to engage with the school.

• Adapt SEL programming to the needs of special populations. Remember to keep up to date on instructional techniques that work for these students, which will help to guide the modifications. *All* students can benefit from SEL!

Easy-Reference Checklist for Advance Preparation of SEL Instruction

Obtain the necessary materials.

☐ Have the manual.

☐ Look ahead to what materials are needed.

☐ Photocopies, transparencies, etc.

Know the content.

☐ Read the manual.

☐ Familiarize yourself with the materials.

☐ Access additional information via trusted Internet sources or other written materials.

Plan for the time that is needed for preparation and implementation.

☐ List the tasks that are needed to prepare and implement each lesson or activity.

☐ Estimate the amount of time it may take for each task.

☐ Document the amount of time it actually took.

☐ Plan your schedule accordingly to accommodate these time requirements.

Technical support: Training, consultation, and feedback.

☐ Determine whether there is time allotted for SEL trainings.

☐ Investigate resources that may provide training.

☐ Determine whether "In-house" personnel might be willing/qualified to provide trainings and/or ongoing consultation support.

☐ Are staff interested in receiving performance feedback and, if so, who could assist in developing this option?

Measuring progress.

☐ Identify assessments that can monitor student progress (see Chapter 7 for details).

Managing behavior.

☐ Foster positive relationships and communication.

☐ Does your school use a schoolwide behavior management system?

☐ Identify other incentives you can provide to increase student participation.

CHAPTER 4

Using Social and Emotional Learning to Foster Academic Learning

INTRODUCTION AND OVERVIEW

In the previous chapters, we reviewed a variety of SEL programming options, described how to go about choosing a program that is a good fit with your school and its needs, and provided ideas for how to implement these programs with fidelity, while understanding that adaptive flexibility in program delivery may be necessary. We hope you are encouraged to pursue these options and move forward with SEL in your school or organization. After all, there is clear evidence that SEL can benefit not only students' social and emotional development, but also their *academic* development and performance.

We are fully aware of the challenges that exist in "selling" SEL. The countless hours we have spent in faculty meetings, eating lunches in the staff lounge, or consulting on cases offers convincing evidence that there continue to be significant barriers to implementing SEL in a school setting. Many of the reasons for these challenges seem to make sense: The demands placed on teachers in this era of accountability often seem insurmountable. Comments expressing doubts, like the following example, are commonplace and understandable when we consider how to fit SEL into current school culture: "When could there possibly be time during the course of a school day to focus on SEL?", "How is this the school's responsibility?", "I have to make academics the priority, I'm not sure I can focus on social and emotional development," and "Shouldn't families be doing this in the home?" Given these legitimate concerns, we offer the following assertion: *SEL will only be fully accepted into mainstream educational priorities when there is convincing evidence, widely known and acceptable to educators, that social and emotional skills are inextricably linked to academic performance and that SEL*

> **The connection among social, emotional, and academic functioning is logical and well documented. Focusing on social and emotional development can lead to positive academic outcomes.**

programming can efficiently be integrated during a typical school day and positively affect academic performance. Research is building to support this claim; providing a roadmap and technical support on how to efficiently integrate SEL into a typical school day will lead to meaningful directions and application of the research.

This chapter focuses on the ways in which social and emotional skills affect academic performance when students are struggling, how positive social and emotional development can influence and enhance academics, and ways in which SEL strategies can be logically and efficiently infused into a typical school day. Intuitively, the connection between social and emotional skills and academic performance certainly makes sense. Consider the following scenarios as you reflect on the students you have taught over the years and the social, emotional, and academic skills they demonstrated in your classroom.

Scenario 1

Maya is a student in your third-grade class. It is November, and parent–teacher conferences are next week. You have had some concerns about Maya and are interested in talking with her parents, although you can't quite grasp exactly what is the problem. She seems to be at least average in her physical and intellectual development (e.g., she walks and runs like the other students in her class, her handwriting is legible and neat, and she seems to understand everything going on during academic instruction). The problem is that Maya is very quiet, never raises her hand to ask or answer a question, and rarely makes eye contact when you talk to her. At the parent–teacher conference, you learn that Maya is active in a community youth symphony and talks a lot at home. When you ask Maya's parents how they think she feels about school, they replied that they are not sure . . . the family usually does not talk about their feelings.

Scenario 2

You are a fifth-grade teacher with a particularly challenging class this year. Budget cuts persist and the number of students you have in your class continues to increase. You've noticed that several of the students are angry, irritated, and mean to one another almost on a daily basis. Ignoring their behavior is not working anymore and seems to be making the problem worse, since some of the other students are getting annoyed. You feel like your classroom is becoming a "pit of despair" or, at the very least, more negative than you had hoped. You're worried that the students won't be ready to take a big standardized test coming up, because you're having to spend more time dealing with their bad attitudes . . . they really can't be learning very much at this point, can they?

Scenario 3

You are a second-grade teacher at a new charter school. You have some concerns about a new student, José, whom you think is a sweet kid with lots of potential, but has some developmental problems that are noticeable to the other students. At lunchtime and on the playground, you've noticed that José often is alone. His classmates are close enough to him that they could definitely talk to him or ask him to play, but you haven't seen this happen. In fact, you are beginning to worry that one of the leaders in the class is starting to laugh at José and encourage some of the other kids to do the same. You wish there were some way to teach your students about individual differences, respecting others, and friendships. José seems to be doing okay in the classroom, but having taught middle school in the past, you have witnessed how mean kids can be to others having some kind of disability. If only there was a way to teach your students these skills before it is too late! You are worried José may lose interest in school, struggle to finish, and never reach his full potential.

THE CONNECTION BETWEEN SEL AND ACADEMICS

The previous scenarios illustrate "real-life" situations and merely skim the surface of many you must have experienced or observed. There are many students whose social and emotional problems have noticeably affected their ability to pay attention in class, complete and turn in homework, and get along with other students well enough to have a friend to sit with at lunch. Consider the number of referrals you have made for disciplinary problems, academic delays, and concerns that something was not quite right with a student's social and emotional functioning. One of the essential features of having a diagnosis of a psychological problem or a disability according to special education law is that there is some sort of impairment in functioning, either with activities of daily living, interpersonal relationships at home and at school, and/or with academic performance. This impairment is typically obvious to adult observers—it is the very "tell" that there are underlying issues that may be impeding a student's ability to succeed in an educational setting.

The Evidence for SEL Influencing Academic Performance

A significant amount of research has documented the connection between social and emotional development and academic performance (e.g., Catalano, Berglund, Ryan, Lonczak, & Hawkins, 2002; Durlak & Weissberg, 2007; Greenberg et al., 2001) and how SEL programming can help students learn (Zins, Weissberg, et al., 2004). To illustrate the practical application of these research findings, consider children who cannot regulate their emotions very well. Poor emotion regulation interferes with the very cognitive processes that are needed to attend to instruction, remember key concepts, and plan to complete homework—the ability to sustain attention, memory, and planning (Blair, 2002). In younger children, an association between emotion regulation and academic performance has been well established (see Howse, Calkins, Anastopoulos, Keane, & Shelton, 2003; Martin, Drew, Gaddis, & Moseley, 1988). A recent study found that kindergarten-age children who have problems with emotion regulation (as reported by their parents) experience more problems learning, are less productive, and less accurate in completing their work (Graziano, Reavis, Keane, & Calkins, 2007). Certainly, this research speaks to the young age at which academic performance is affected by emotional and behavioral skill deficits. Middle and high school-age students who have difficulty managing uncomfortable emotions and are therefore aggressive have subsequent problems with academic learning (Kuhl & Kraska, 1989). For some adolescents, problems with emotion regulation may manifest as chronic feelings of sadness, hopelessness, and fatigue. These emotion regulation problems typically result in "tell" behaviors that communicate that something is wrong: the teen is having a very difficult time getting out of bed in the morning, not attending class consistently and falling asleep during instruction, and struggling with low energy to initiate, organize, and complete the work that is required to pass the class. Of course, we must consider whether these circumstances are a case of "the chicken or the egg"; certainly, many students with learning problems experience ongoing frustration, disappointment, and interpersonal problems. However, in the case of students whose primary skill deficit is regulating their emotions, this problem can lead to difficulties managing behaviors and subsequent troubles with paying attention and following through with academic demands.

Given that students who have social and emotional skills deficits can be at risk for poor academic performance, how do we know that efforts to strategically infuse SEL into a typical school day are having a positive impact on the social, emotional, and academic lives of *all* students? The answers are in the research literature. Chapter 2 included highlights from the research associated with various SEL programs. As you probably noticed, the breadth of social, emotional, and academic domains that have been studied is impressive and is measured by student's self-reports of functioning, their performance on academic tasks, and teachers' and parents' reports and observations of students' functioning. You may have even participated in a study that used these methods to collect some of the data that contributed to this body of literature. One of the primary goals of SEL initiatives is to make programs accessible to all students, not just those who require extra support. That means that students in general education will receive SEL programming, typically during the course of the school day.

Unfortunately, one program cannot possibly produce positive effects across each and every social, emotional, and academic domain. This issue speaks not only to the limitations regarding the scope of the program, but also what effectiveness studies can evaluate with limited resources and timelines. For example, the Second Step program is globally considered a violence prevention program; consequently, research studies will generally evaluate whether the program can increase prosocial behaviors and decrease antisocial behaviors. The program is not necessarily designed to improve student motivation for learning, although this could be an adjunct benefit. Table 4.1 provides a summary of the social, emotional, and academic domains that have been studied in selected SEL programs. The range of domains studied is impressive and speaks to the depth and breadth of areas that can be positively affected by SEL programming.

Evaluating the Effectiveness of SEL Programming

Opportunities abound for researching the extent to which SEL programming affects academic performance and the mechanisms for this change. One of the primary roadblocks to meaningful evaluation is a difficulty with measurement methods. The scope of this chapter

TABLE 4.1. A Summary of Demonstrated Academic, Cognitive, and Social–Emotional Effects of Selected SEL Programs

Domains affected	SEL program
• Impulsivity • Prosocial behavior (caring and sharing)	I Can Problem Solve
• Motivation to achieve • Enjoyment of school • Conflict-resolution skills • Empathy and altruism	Caring School Community
• Organizational and study skills • Attention • Goal setting • Understanding of social and emotional situations • Frustration tolerance • Sadness and disruptive behaviors	PATHS
• Attachment to school and family • Suspensions and expulsions • Social interaction and age-appropriate behaviors	Raising Healthy Children
• Perspective taking • Problem solving • Socially aggressive actions	Second Steps
• Knowledge of healthy social–emotional behavior • Student-reported social–emotional assets and resilience • Peer relations • Student and teacher social validity of using SEL programs	Strong Kids
• Prosocial behaviors • Antisocial behaviors	Social Decision Making/ Social Problem Solving

does not permit an exhaustive review of the intricacies of this issue. One challenging area for measurement is determining the accuracy of measuring what we want to measure. Consider the variability that exists in assigning letter grades to assignments, quizzes, and tests among teachers, grade levels, schools, and districts. A "B" grade may not mean the same across these areas since many different standards and expectations can be associated with a "B." How about standardized tests, like those that are given individually (e.g., to students undergoing an educational evaluation) or administered as a group for statewide testing? The time and costs involved in administering individual achievement tests generally are prohibitive, and the limitations of standardized testing in general abound. They are generally given once every couple of years, certainly not often enough to monitor students' progress. Finally, many of the SEL programs are intended as universally delivered programs, meaning that all students get the same instruction, not necessarily according to their risk level. Out of 30 students in a classroom, maybe a handful are exhibiting social and emotional symptoms that you may be concerned with (give or take a few students depending on your situation). Measuring change in behavior is difficult when the majority of your students would be considered typical and within the normal limits of functioning. What many of the programs aim for is something akin to *inoculation.* Similar to receiving vaccines to protect against serious disease, healthy students receive small doses of information and skills that can be used directly to protect them against future stressors that will inevitably arise in their lives. Consequently, research efforts are working toward longitudinal or long-term studies to follow the impact of a program on students' social, emotional, and academic health over time.

For example, the extent to which students stay emotionally healthy and stay in school several years after participating in SEL programming are critical areas to study to continue establishing the effectiveness of these programs. The Raising Healthy Children program is an excellent example of using this model to study the effectiveness of their program over time.

> **The spirit of SEL is to reach all students and provide small doses of information over time, which will be used when inevitable stressors arise.**

The Influence of the Student–Teacher Relationship as an SEL Component

In addition to the impact SEL programming can have on social, emotional, and academic development and performance, the student–teacher relationship has been found to be directly related and relevant in a school setting. Specifically, students' adaptation to a school environment and deficits in emotion regulation can negatively affect the student–teacher relationship (e.g., Pianta & Stuhlman, 2004). A relationship characterized by warmth, low conflict, and encouragement can increase the likelihood that kindergarteners for example, will demonstrate appropriate behavior in the classroom. In order to facilitate these relationship-building behaviors, both teachers and students need to possess some basic social competency skills (Graziano et al., 2007). For example, in a typical American classroom it is generally considered appropriate for students to show that they are listening in class by looking at the teacher and not talking during the lecture. A student who is constantly talking or checking e-mail or text messages during class may convey disrespect and annoy the teacher. Certainly, we know through the literature and personal experience that when school professionals interact with students whose behaviors feel generally unpleasant, the tendency to provide warmth and encouragement decreases (Coie & Koeppl, 1990). As adults, professionals, and human beings, it is very difficult to continue providing warmth and encouragement when these qualities are not necessarily reciprocated, even from our young pupils. Given the fact that many of you have students in your classrooms who exhibit troubling social and emotional behaviors, and knowing that their educational performance may be directly influenced by the teacher–student relationship, candid recognition of these issues and strategic intervention is the first step to positive development.

In summary, consider the powerful effects of combining evidence-based SEL programming in a school environment that values and strives to cultivate positive student–teacher relationships. Not only can students learn and practice SEL skills that can lead to competence, but students also can form positive attachments to school and perform academically in a way that would not have been possible without these factors (Greenberg et al., 2003).

APPLYING SEL TO IMPROVE ACADEMIC PERFORMANCE

If you take a closer look at Table 4.1, you will notice the wide variety of social, emotional, and academic domains that are addressed across a sampling of seven SEL programs. Consider how each of these domains can interface with general indicators of academic performance: attending school, attending to instruction, completing work in a timely fashion, working at a level commensurate with ability and skill level, and retaining the information to perform on quizzes and tests. As you can imagine, a deficit in one of these domains might mean a student experiences some challenges. These domains can also be organized into three primary categories and are all vitally important to students' overall success: students' attitudes toward school, their behaviors in school, and their academic performance (Zins, Payton, Weissberg, & Utne O'Brien, 2007). Of course, one program cannot target every area of need. Let's look at how a selected program applies SEL strategies directly to factors influencing academic performance.

Consider how the Social Decision Making/Social Problem Solving (SDM/SPS) program (as reviewed in Chapter 2) influences academics. Students are taught problem-solving and social–emotional skills that are applied to social, emotional, and academic issues throughout the school day. The model was especially designed for students to learn the skills so well that they could be applied even when under stress. This certainly makes sense given that many of the problems we are faced with include emotions and feelings about the situation: "What should I do?", "What if I don't do this right?", or "I can't decide." In overlearning the concepts by practicing and applying them across a variety of situations and times, students will be more likely to be able to apply the skills with increased fluency and confidence.

First, students learn how to work in a group and recognize and regulate their own emotions. Learning these skills represents a critical step before engaging in any problem-solving process. Imagine, for a moment, that you are stuck in traffic and late for an important meeting. Your heart starts beating faster and your thoughts turn from what you want to talk about in the meeting to being worried that the person you are meeting with will be angry and *never* forget the fact that you were late! It is far more difficult to creatively and effectively deal with the problem in a way that maximizes the chances for success (e.g., call the person you are meeting with and explain the situation) if you are unable to recognize that you are feeling frantic in the first place. What if you could recognize your physiological reaction to stress (heart pounding) and identify your feelings (worried) and thinking errors (the person will *never* forget that you were late)? Doing so allows us (and our students) to use some coping strategies to calm ourselves to then engage in an active problem-solving process. After establishing a foundation for using these skills, students are taught the acronym FIG TESPN as the decision-making process whereby they can **i**dentify their **f**eelings, **i**dentify the problem, set **g**oals, **t**hink of solutions, **e**nvision the consequences, **s**elect the best solution, **p**lan it/try it, and **n**otice what happens. Students learn these steps through direct instructional methods in conjunction with frequent opportunities for practice across a variety of academic content (e.g., language arts, social studies) *and* applied to real-life situations.

Applying these skills to social and emotional areas seems to reinforce the skills students learn when applied to academic materials (Elias & Clabby, 1992). When students used the FIG TESPN rubric over the course of social–emotional and academic content areas that were relevant to their lives, their language arts and social studies skills showed improvement compared with students who did not use the rubric. Of course, we acknowledge that more research is needed to continue to determine not only the effectiveness of SEL programming on academic performance, but also the mechanisms by which positive influence can be produced and sustained.

INTEGRATING SEL THROUGHOUT THE COURSE OF A TYPICAL SCHOOL DAY

One of the most frequent questions that is posed when schools are considering implementing SEL for the first time is, "How can we efficiently integrate SEL into the normal course of a school day?" We know through our years of practice in elementary, middle, and high schools that time during the course of a day and even school year comes at a high premium and that change, no matter how promising the potential outcomes, is difficult to initiate. Stated simply, we know what we know and how to teach/counsel/administer in a way that feels comfortable and workable with significant time and monetary constraints, let alone our personal limits for starting new projects that will involve some stress. Given this typical state of affairs, you may find a variety of reactions among your school staff when the conversation gets serious about really doing something and addressing the social and emotional needs of students. Tackling a new initiative, in the context of a movement that must prioritize academic accountability to the point of funding contingencies, can be viewed as both invigoratingly challenging and undeniably daunting. Some school personnel may be truly excited to finally systematically address the social and emotional needs of their students— the thought of directly affecting this critical aspect of youth development is welcome and matches a mission to positively influence lives. Other personnel may feel completely overwhelmed and doubt that they posses the skills to implement such initiatives (after all, their education and training didn't exactly cover this material) or that this is even possible given all the competing priorities (e.g., general education instruction, meeting the needs of students with special education needs or with 504 accommodation plans, managing classroom behavior, attending IEP meetings, state testing expectations, etc. . . . whew!).

Typical Integration of SEL Concepts into Academic Content

Fortunately, most designers of SEL programming recognize this dilemma and are consciously matching what is known about promoting social and emotional development with the needs of educational consumers. Most educators are finding ways of logically integrating the content of SEL programming using academic lesson time and/or content to demonstrate examples, as well as utilizing usual and customary intra- and interpersonal issues that inevitably come up during the day and in a school setting. Consider the Strong Kids curricula: Each lesson was designed to be brief enough to be delivered during one block of academic instruction time (e.g., a language arts lesson), and teachers are encouraged to solicit pertinent real-life examples from students. Similarly, the SDM/SPS program integrates its problem-solving framework (FIG TESPN) across a variety of aspects of an academic curriculum so students have an opportunity to practice using a problem-solving strategy for a variety of situations (Elias, 2004). For example, in language arts, a problem-solving framework

> **SEL concepts can be integrated into academic programming by capitalizing on the issues that develop during the course of a normal school day. Academic content, such as information presented through literature, can also be applied to social and emotional issues and used to illustrate SEL concepts.**

might be used to consider the feelings of characters in a book, as well as the choices these characters are facing, and brainstorm possible solutions. Students may then be asked in a social studies class to use a similar framework for discussing historical or current events, and again in a health class where they are asked to consider how lifestyle choices may affect a variety of health factors and generate possibilities for alternative actions that can lead to positive mental and physical health. The Caring School Community program also uses an activity-based instructional model to teach how to identify emotions and use problem-solving skills. For example, literature is specifically chosen to teach how to identify particular emotions and then use a problem-solving strategy to help the characters make decisions.

One of the most important aspects of ensuring that students grow socially and emotionally is to expose students to SEL instruction across a variety of situations and contexts and use explicit instruction. Many schools accomplish this objective by adopting a carefully selected program, identified through a needs assessment, targeting specific social and emotional needs of the student body, and implementing the program across all the classrooms in one grade level or if possible, across all grade levels in a school. The advantages to this approach are clear: School personnel are on the same page regarding the information they are imparting to students, and students are receiving the same concepts as their schoolmates. This circumstance creates a naturally reinforcing setting in which students can practice their new social and emotional skills with consistent performance feedback, thereby increasing the likelihood that they will integrate the skills into their daily lives.

Determining Where and How to Integrate SEL in Academics

In Chapter 2, we described how to determine your school's needs and choose from a variety of SEL programs. Chapter 3 discussed the "nuts and bolts" of preparing for lessons, implementing the materials in the way they were intended, and considering support as it is needed. Deciding which grade levels should receive an SEL program or choosing the best academic content area into which SEL ideas can be integrated takes careful consideration as well. We urge you to include these issues as part of a needs assessment, as well as any discussions you will have with a planning committee. Answering the question "How can we efficiently integrate SEL into the normal course of a school day?" requires an investigation into current instructional practices and demands, as well as school personnel's interest in SEL and their knowledge regarding its importance and potential impact on students' social, emotional, and educational functioning. In our experience, we have found a health promotion course, language arts, and social studies to be the most logical venue for SEL programming at the intermediate, middle school, or high school levels. Talking about issues related to building emotional resiliency is a major part of promoting health. Language arts content typically involves literature instruction whereby students can discuss and analyze literary characters' emotions and behaviors, and social studies includes complex national and international dilemmas that provide ample opportunity for refining problem-solving skills.

One of the most glaring challenges in integrating SEL programming into a typical school day, week, and year is organizing the plethora of programs already in place so that some semblance of logic and order is apparent. It is all too common for a school to implement one SEL program in one grade for the purpose of addressing, for example, social skills, and another program implemented in another grade level focusing on problem-solving skills. Meanwhile, another elementary school in the same district is implementing a program on "character education" in every grade level, but to varying degrees among the classrooms.

> **Organization and planning are essential to successfully fitting SEL into existing school culture. Remember to identify the extent to which the program will meet the needs of students and how its implementation will be supported and sustained over time.**

Why is paying attention to this issue valuable? We can imagine that many of you reading this book are working in school systems in the United States that include a great diversity of languages spoken by the families of your students. One of us (K. W. M.) was recently in a middle school in southern California where more than 20 languages were spoken by students and/or their families. We think it's clear that such circumstances are a harbinger of things to come nationally. Its great to view this type of situation as a wonderful opportunity for educational and personal enrichment. Non-English-speaking students are typically considered English language learners (or similar identifier) and are often provided language instruction and support. Why? Generally, because students are asked to perform academically in the English language across their academic career. If science instruction were in Russian, math in Spanish, social studies in German, art and music in Chinese, and language arts in English, there likely would be quite a bit of confusion for students—that's a lot of instruction in several languages! Much like the richness that exists in diverse and multicultural learning environments, there are complementary components to SEL programming that may focus on different areas of social and emotional development (e.g., violence prevention, friendship building, problem solving, stress management) that exist under one umbrella: Social and Emotional Learning!

Implementing SEL programming is similar to academic instruction in that systematic organization and strategic coordination among a variety of social and emotional concepts (programs) are delivered in a way that maximizes efficiency and effectiveness because students and teachers use the same social and emotional "language" from preschool through high school. Here are a few issues to address when considering how to coordinate SEL in your school and district:

1. Has your school or district conducted a needs assessment? The results should give you information on the type of programming that is currently in place, what is working, what is not, and whether your school/district should eliminate unnecessary or ineffective programming and focus on what is needed and what has the greatest potential for working.

2. You should take into consideration the needs of each classroom, school building, and district. Preferably the district will want all of its school buildings to be "on the same page." Much like reading initiatives whereby a common reading curriculum is adopted, SEL programming adoption is quite similar. It is much more efficient to provide universal support and measure outcomes when schools are using similar programming choices—the same "language" is being spoken.

3. There are likely many programs either being used in your school or sitting on a shelf gathering dust in a storage unit on campus. Some programs are well liked and used in the way they were intended; others are implemented using "a little of this, and a little of that"; and others are totally abandoned either because they weren't working or they had great potential to work based on the research supporting them, but there just wasn't enough support either through finances, other resources, or attitude. Three important factors for program consideration include:

- To what extent is the program evidence based?
- How does it fit with the needs and goals identified through the needs assessment?
- How will your school support not only its implementation, but also sustain it over time?

To summarize, one of the most important areas for consideration when implementing SEL is to seriously address how the programming will be organized and coordinated. Doing so will increase the likelihood that students have more opportunities for practice using concepts that are presented in a similar manner across multiple classrooms and grade levels and thus fluently apply these skills to other life situations. You may also find that these efforts will streamline the process and eliminate unnecessary time and resources spent on activities that do not lead you to your goals.

PROMOTING SEL
IN STUDENTS' HOMES AND IN THE COMMUNITY

In addition to providing opportunities for practicing SEL skills in the classroom, hallways, lunch room, bus line, and playground, students will likely learn these skills with greater depth and breadth if they have opportunities for practice in other settings, such as at home.

For students to do so, their caregivers must have some understanding of basic social and emotional concepts. For some caregivers, this is second nature: they talk with their children regularly about feelings and assist with problem solving as issues arise. We would argue that for the vast majority of caregivers, knowing, understanding, and effectively applying SEL concepts with comfort and fluency is a rarity. Consider your own experiences with learning and using social and emotional concepts. Maybe you had excellent modeling at home or possibly at school with an adult—what a wonderful foundation! However, most adults have not had exposure to social and emotional instruction and generally feel uncomfortable and inadequate. It is only when problems arise or through participation in an intervention activity (e.g., individual or couples therapy) will adult caregivers be able to then model these skills for children.

Schools already recognize the importance of parent involvement, and we discussed the importance of including families in the section "Including Families in SEL" in Chapter 3. The reasoning behind including families extends beyond getting to know the members of your school community. Providing caregivers with even brief information regarding the SEL content that is being addressed in the classroom or school as a whole enables them to be a part of SEL implementation. Getting the information to caregivers and ensuring that they use it is an ambitious undertaking and an undeniably enormous challenge. That said, it's also a great start.

How can the school system get the community involved? Engaging in general outreach activities is probably the most direct method—newsletters home to parents, articles in the local newspaper regarding the innovation happening in the schools, open houses, presentations to the board of education, "talking it up" when you are participating in usual community activities. Educational and mental health professionals are ambassadors to the community; we represent all facets of our professions, and there are more opportunities to share than we often realize. We also believe it is important to educate other members of the community who have direct contact with our students and are interested in collaborating and coordinating care. For example, some of our students see mental health professionals such as psychologists, psychiatrists, counselors, and licensed clinical social workers to receive direct individual services. Much of the treatment they engage in with youth is based on similar principles of SEL—identifying emotions, managing stress, problem solving, learning to get along with others, understanding how others feel, goal setting, and evaluating progress. It is often helpful for these professionals to be aware of any SEL programming that occurs in the schools; the language is very often the same or quite similar, which should sound familiar when we work to "get on the same page." A fantastic indicator of progress will be when community resources inquire about the SEL programming available in the schools and seek to coordinate our services (and vice versa). In summary, we should strive for more use of a com-

Reaching out to members of the community who are also a part of students' lives is tantamount to reinforcing SEL. Physicians, psychologists, social workers, preschool teachers, day care providers, and other community members can promote social and emotional development by simply knowing that school-based SEL programming is available and supporting its continued research and implementation.

mon language, more opportunities for practice, and increased likelihood for students integrating social and emotional concepts in all aspects of their lives.

WRAPPING THINGS UP

This chapter highlighted the undeniable connection between social and emotional functioning and academic performance. Although most school professionals would not deny this claim, the biggest challenge is how to address this issue in a productive and effective manner. Fortunately, the area of SEL is deepening its understanding of how to integrate instructional activities into the normal course of a school day. At this time, providing instruction within the school setting is the most viable option, as it provides a captive audience for a relatively brief occasion in the students' lifetimes. Combining sound instruction and psychoeducational principles in this type of instruction is the surest route to success. Future challenges include continuing to find funding and supportive resources to refine and sustain these efforts, as well as including caregivers and community agents so students have universal exposure to SEL concepts and practice. Reproducible Worksheet 4.1, "Worksheet for Integrating Social–Emotional and Academic Learning in the Classroom," is a practical tool to help you plan for better integration of SEL and academics in your school. This worksheet may be helpful in identifying natural linkages between SEL and academic instruction and in brainstorming less obvious linkages between SEL and academics.

VINGETTE: An Elementary Teacher's Experience

Ms. Brown, a third-grade teacher in an urban school district, has been teaching for more than 20 years. Her school is part of a new initiative from the state legislature requiring the school system to address SEL. Over the past year, she has worked on the committee that was formed to evaluate the needs of the school building and determine the best way to address this new requirement. One of the most challenging issues for the school is deciding on the program to use; however, the committee had decided on a program that will "build resiliency" in their young students. In her teaching career, she has seen programs come and go and has used bits and pieces of content that she enjoys and that she feels works for her students. Ms. Brown is looking forward to using a program that promises to use explicit materials and provide suggestions on how to coordinate the program over several grade levels.

The district is allocating resources for only one program with the stipulation that support for training and resources be included. The selected program can be used in kindergarten through grade 3, and the teachers have secured release time to begin training and preparation. Although it was challenging to build consensus, the teachers decided that the program would be implemented during the course of the social studies or civics academic instruction time, once per week for the school year. They came to this conclusion because the results from the needs assessment indicated that students needed assistance with problem-solving skills, and this time block was the most flexible for teachers in terms of the activities associated with the content. In addition to deciding the time during the school day when the program would be used, the teachers decided to prioritize the following three items:

1. The committee chair will talk to someone in the district about determining a method to measure whether the program is having an effect on students' problem-solving skills.
2. The teachers and support staff will meet as a group twice per month to discuss problems, concerns, and solutions so they feel supported and free to talk about this new program. The staff will negotiate with administrators scheduled release time, up to 1 hour per month, to meet as a group.
3. The group committed to using the program for 1 year, with a review at the end of the year to assess student progress, gauge school personnel's opinions regarding the program, and to discuss ways for families to become involved.

Ms. Brown felt comfortable with this plan and reassured that the program did not have be implemented perfectly the first time around and that her fellow school staff was committed to giving this a try. She felt hopeful that she could at last participate in an organized and coordinated SEL program.

VINGETTE: A Middle School Principal's Experience

Mr. Gallegos is the principal of a suburban middle school. He is part of a districtwide committee interested in infusing SEL throughout the district. Mr. Gallegos is feeling particularly overwhelmed because he cannot imagine where a new program is going to fit into a typical middle school day. Part of the problem is the school has used several other programs over the past 10 years, and the school just adopted PBIS to help with school climate and student behavior. Fortunately, the district has realized the enormity of starting a new program and has approved release time to staff to get this new system up and running.

A site committee was formed and reviewed the data from the district's needs assessment. The outcome was evident: Middle school teachers are feeling overwhelmed by academic instruction, grading, and preparing for statewide testing. Despite this challenge, the physical education program is growing and developing with a new, yet experienced teacher. She (Ms. O'Shea) voiced interest in participating in the SEL initiative, as her area of interest is mind–body–health connections. Ms. O'Shea volunteered to teach the program in her health class and strongly suggested that there be a way to infuse the concepts from this class into other academic instruction time, in the hallways, and on the sports field. The committee brainstormed for quite some time and decided to use some of the extra release time they had been granted to conduct brief, 45-minute inservices once per month for the duration of the school year. The school psychologist, principal, and physical education teacher would rotate presenting information on the topics to be covered for the month, along with a handout of helpful tips for reinforcing this information across school settings.

Worksheet for Integrating Social–Emotional and Academic Learning in the Classroom

Name of SEL program/lesson to be taught: _____

Key SEL skills to be taught in this lesson: _____

_____

Key concepts to be taught in this lesson: _____

_____

Materials needed: _____

Academic skill areas specifically included in this SEL lesson/activity:

    ☐ Reading   ☐ Written language   ☐ Mathematics   ☐ Social studies

    ☐ Science   ☐ Technology   ☐ Health/physical education

    ☐ Other _____

Academic skill areas not specifically included in this SEL lesson/activity, but could be integrated easily with minor instructional modifications:

    ☐ Reading   ☐ Written language   ☐ Mathematics   ☐ Social studies

    ☐ Science   ☐ Technology   ☐ Health/physical education

    ☐ Other _____

My plan for infusing and integrating academic skills into formal SEL instruction:

_____

_____

_____

_____

My plan for infusing academic skills into SEL instruction through supplemental activities (homework assignments, practice, feedback to students, modeling, examples, etc.):

_____

_____

_____

_____

One Size Does Not Fit All

Adapting Social and Emotional Learning for Use in Our Multicultural World

with SARA CASTRO-OLIVO

INTRODUCTION AND OVERVIEW

Perhaps it is just a coincidence, but the number of situations that lead to untreated social–emotional problems of our culturally and linguistically diverse (CLD) youth is so immense that I (S. C.-O.) seem to hear about new cases on a daily basis. While I was preparing to work on this chapter, I received a phone call from a community leader in Dallas, Texas. Her voice transmitted profound sorrow as she talked about the needs of many members of her community. She mentioned that she has been touched by the many children who are dramatically affected by their parents being detained, and often deported, due to the immigration tension in our country. Her main concern was clear: Children in her community are suffering from family separations, stressors related to poverty and perceived discrimination, and these children do not seem to have the necessary skills to cope with such devastating situations. She stated, "It seems no one is prepared to help them."

We are aware that the previous example may seem a bit extreme to some readers. However, it is lived (directly or indirectly) by many children in our public schools on a daily basis. Our students' ability to cope with such major stressors has a direct impact in

Sara Castro-Olivo, PhD, is Assistant Professor in the Graduate School of Education at the University of California, Riverside.

the schools where we work. Having to deal with multiple stressors affects how students learn and interact with peers, teachers, and other adults. The pressure for those educating these students—already immense—is magnified even further when we realize that teachers might be the only functioning adults many of these children come in contact with, the only ones who can provide them with some resiliency and coping skills, or at least with some advice or support that could allow them to see a light of hope for the future.

Regardless of your views on diversity, it is our opinion that we must not be oblivious to the fact that CLD students tend to be exposed to major life stressors at higher rates than students from the mainstream culture. A combination of contextual variables such as: poverty, minority status, higher rates of single-parent households, rough neighborhoods, perceived discrimination, limited English proficiency, and/or illegal immigration status tend to be the reality of many of our CLD students (U.S. Department of Health and Human Services, 2001). All of these contextual variables have been linked to negative social outcomes such as high dropout rates from school, teenage pregnancy/parenthood, and involvement in delinquent and/or antisocial behavior (e.g., underage drinking and gang-related activities). Make no mistake about it: The high percentages of ethnic minority youth who make up such negative statistics illustrate a significant social problem (Gonzales & Kim, 1997).

> **We must not be oblivious to the fact that culturally and linguistically diverse students, as a group, tend to be exposed to major life stressors at higher rates than students from the mainstream culture.**

How do we help these children? How can we make sure that they will be able to use the SEL skills taught in the classroom in their daily lives? How can we prepare ourselves to be more effective? How can we be a voice of hope for these students? What do we do, if the only thing they seem to be concerned about is basic survival? Yes, these questions are overwhelming, especially when we start thinking about the numerous "extreme" situations many of our CLD students face. I (S. C.-O.) am personally besieged by these questions when I realize that I'll be working with many at-risk youth and I might not be fully prepared to help them. What do I do if I can't relate to their experiences? What do I do if they might think I don't understand their issues? What if they just cannot trust me because of the color of my skin? After going through an almost endless list of questions, I comfort myself by remembering that asking these types of questions and showing that I care is the first step to establishing a culturally responsive environment. By asking these questions, I get motivated to increase my awareness about the specific needs of the students with whom I work. *Being aware of the sociocultural factors that affect our students' well-being is the key to implementing successful culturally competent interventions.*

In this chapter, we explain the rationale for making cultural adaptations to existing published SEL curricula, as well as necessary cautions in making these adaptations. As an example, we recommend some steps interventionists could follow in order to make the delivery and instruction of the packaged SEL programs more culturally responsive. As you read the following sections, we hope you identify the current urgency for engaging in these activities in order to maximize the effects of SEL on CLD populations.

RATIONALE FOR MAKING
CULTURAL ADAPTATIONS TO SEL PROGRAMS

The main purpose of this chapter is to provide readers—those of you who plan to implement SEL programs in multicultural settings—with a rationale and recommendations for making appropriate cultural adaptations to these types of programs. It is imperative to understand why we should consider making cultural adaptations to existing evidence-based programs. After all, if you are considering implementing an SEL program in your classroom, you are very likely to care about your students' outcomes and would only want to implement best practices. The main goal of the following sections is to describe the potential impact these adaptations could have on our students' outcomes and the overall success of these programs. Making cultural adaptations is not just about complying with the ethical guidelines of our professional organizations, which require us to respect members of other cultures and aim to become culturally competent (Association of American Educators, 2003; American Psychological Association, 2003; National Association of School Psychologists, 2000). Making cultural adaptations is about increasing our chances of helping at-risk and underserved students, as well as increasing the chances of yielding positive outcomes for *all* students.

When it comes to social–emotional and other person-centered interventions, we emphasize the title of this chapter: *One size does not fit all.* Culture matters! Our students live, perceive, interpret, and behave according to what their previous generations (cultural predecessors) have taught them (Nasir & Hand, 2006). Making cultural adaptations to existing SEL programs not only allows us to engage in culturally sensitive practices by showing that we care about and understand these populations, but it also allows us to make the material more accessible and relevant to students from diverse backgrounds. In a sense, when we make cultural adaptations to an existing program we are looking for ways to use our students' prior knowledge to maximize their opportunity to acquire new skills. Using their prior knowledge allows students to identify, grasp, maintain, and generalize the new information in a more efficient manner (Beier & Ackerman, 2005). Using this instructional philosophy is very important when delivering SEL programs. After all, the main goal of SEL is to provide students with the social–emotional skills they need to successfully navigate/cope with *their* daily life circumstances. Therefore, it is imperative that students have the opportunity to internalize and generalize these skills in a way that matches their cultural reality. If our students are not able to connect the skills we teach them with their own lives, it's very likely that the skills we teach them in the classrooms will stay in the classrooms and will not be generalized to other settings (e.g., their communities, homes, and interactions with peers).

> **Making careful, appropriate, cultural adaptations to SEL is not just about complying with ethical guidelines that require us to respect members of other cultures and become culturally competent; it is about increasing our chances of helping at-risk and underserved students.**

By now you might be wondering how relevant this chapter is to you. Those of you who work in highly diverse settings might find it easier to adapt the information summarized in this chapter to our own practice. Even those of you who work in more homogeneous settings might have already noticed a rapidly growing diversity within your schools that has required you to make some changes in the way you interact with students. At this point, if you live and work in most parts of our nation where more than one culture is represented, you will find the information in this chapter relevant. Given the stark realities of worldwide economic and political stresses, CLD families are finding the need to move to areas that promise better jobs, healthier neighborhoods in which to raise their children, and better housing markets. Such migration within the country and from other countries is making even those schools that have been historically homogeneous become more and more diverse.

Even if the number of ethnic and linguistic minority students in your school is small or nonexistent, we are convinced that the world is changing rapidly, and that you will soon notice these changes in your area and find yourself looking for new ways to connect with the newly arrived populations. In the following section we review the most recent statistics available regarding the growing number of students from diverse backgrounds. These statistics clearly show that at one point or another every educator will find him- or herself having to consider making cultural adaptations to SEL and other programs to better reach their diverse students.

MAKING CULTURAL ADAPTATIONS TO SEL PROGRAMS: THE CHANGING CULTURAL LANDSCAPE OF AMERICAN SCHOOLS

The cultural and linguistic diversity in our public schools is greater than it has ever been in the history of this nation. The United States—always a pluralistic and culturally diverse nation in comparison with most other parts of the world—is experiencing unprecedented and continuing multicultural change. The increasing number of students of color and English language learners (ELLs) has led to new challenges to a field that historically has been led by Caucasian middle-class individuals. Being part of an increasingly diverse society requires educators to become more aware of the role culture plays in our students' cognition, perceptions, and behaviors. We can use such awareness to develop and implement interventions that are more likely to yield successful outcomes for these populations. In the following section, we provide a quick overview of the diverse populations in our schools and the prevalence of mental health problems among these students and providing access to appropriate services.

For those of us who have been involved in the American school systems (as educators and/or students) for the past couple of decades, it has been obvious that there is a rapid increase in the diversity of our schools. In a single school we can find high percentages of students from different ethnic, language, religious, sexual orientation, and/or socioeconomic backgrounds, to mention just a few types of diversity. We are able to detect a particularly large difference in diversity in the area of ethnicity alone. By comparing the proportion of ethnic minority groups enrolled in public schools in the late 1980s and those currently enrolled, we are able to see how rapidly our schools have diversified.

For example, in the late 1980s more than 70% of the overall school population in the United States was identified as Caucasian, 16% as African American, 10% as Hispanic, 3% as Asian, and 1% as other. A little more than two decades later we can see that the proportion of white students has decreased while the percentage of other ethnic groups has significantly increased. In 2008 the U.S. Department of Education (through the National Center for Education Statistics) released a report showing that ethnic minorities comprise more than 40% of our overall school population. Caucasians continue to be the majority—for now—at 59% of the overall school population. Hispanics now comprise 19%, African Americans 17%, and Asians and/or other are now 4% of the nation's public schools student body (National Center for Educational Statistics, 2008a).

With the increase in ethnic diversity has also come the increase of linguistic diversity and the educational programming needed to better accommodate this growing population. The number of students who are ELLs has increased tremendously. More than 11% of students enrolled in public schools receive ELL services. *Please note that this statistic does not account for those students whose primary language, or language of proficiency, is other than English but do not receive ELL services.* ELLs often do not receive English language development services either because those services are not available in their schools (because limited services only allow for those with more intense needs to receive services, or because of political mandates in some states that limit time in which ELLs may be taught in their native language) or because their parents decide to refuse such services. In certain states such diversity is much higher. For example, in California, more than 26% of students enrolled in K–12 public schools receive ELL services (National Center for Education Statistics, 2008a). Educating students with such diverse languages/backgrounds surely presents many challenges.

The statistics regarding the overall presence of diverse populations in our schools has clearly increased over the years. Unfortunately, certain other statistics about these populations have not necessarily changed. Although the percentage of CLD students has increased in terms of enrollment, they are still underrepresented in honors programs and graduation rates. Latinos have the highest dropout rates when compared with members of other ethnic groups, followed by African Americans and Native Americans. Ethnic minority students tend to be overrepresented not only in dropout rates but also in special education programs, especially under the category of learning disabilities and emotional disturbances (National Center for Education Statistics, 2008b). Students from ethnic minority backgrounds are also overrepresented in our juvenile correction systems, where *more than 60%* of the overall population are members of ethnic minority groups (Bonavita & Fairchild, 2001).

Although the needs of these populations are profound, little preventive research has been conducted to change their negative trajectories. At this point, we cannot even report a rough estimate of the prevalence of mental health problems on ethnic minority youth. Historically, there has been a poor national representation of these populations in epidemiological studies. Most studies that have examined the prevalence of mental health disorders on ethnic minorities have focused on adults, almost completely ignoring children and/or adolescents (Blanco-Vega, Castro-Olivo, & Merrell, 2008; Rumbaut, 2004). The few studies that have looked at the prevalence of mental health problems among ethnic minority children often have employed questionable, or less than optimal, methods for collecting such data. Most of these studies tend to overgeneralize findings of their limited samples to *all* members of a specific ethnic group, which signifies a tremendous limitation (Lopez, Edwards, Pedrotti, Ito, & Rasmussen, 2002). Mainly because of convenience of their sample, most researchers are usually not able to incorporate in their studies minority youth from various backgrounds (i.e., socioeconomic status, different levels of acculturation, language proficiency, etc., all of which strongly predict within group differences) (Martinez, DeGarmo, & Eddy, 2004; Rumbaut, 2004). At this point, we can only assume that prevalence of mental health disorders in cultural minority youth is at the same level (if not higher) than in their white counterparts (U.S. Department of Health and Human Services, 2001; Gonzales & Kim, 1997). Some community-based studies (not national datasets) have shown that some ethnic minorities are at higher risk for mental health disorders than members of the mainstream culture due to the multiple life stressors they usually face (Gonzales & Kim, 1997; Martinez et al., 2004). An important piece of information that we can be certain of is that these populations have less (and poorer) access to mental health services than do members of the mainstream culture. For the few who seek and receive services, those services are usually of low quality (U.S. Department of Health and Human Services, 2001; Serpell, Clauss-Ehlers, & Lindsey, 2007; Vega & Rumbaut, 1991). We argue that if members of these populations are not accessing services at higher rates, it is not because they do not recognize that they need help or have a problem. Perhaps members of these populations refrain from seeking services because they have been conditioned to believe that such services will not be aligned with their cultural values and beliefs. In other words, they may fear their values and beliefs are not going to be respected or accounted for by their mental health providers. As it is, mental health services tend to be overly stigmatized among some of these populations because of the shame it is perceived to bring to the families (Serpell et al., 2007). Not providing them with a culturally sensitive service would only confirm that mental health services are stigmatizing and even useless. Providing CLD populations with programs that are aligned to their cultural values will yield better results and acceptance by allowing them to notice the link between the services they are receiving and their cultural background (Lieberman, 1989).

> Most researchers and program developers are usually unable to incorporate into their studies minority youths from various backgrounds whose socioeconomic status, different levels of acculturation, language proficiency, etc., all strongly predict group differences. Perhaps many members of these groups do not seek mental health services because they believe that such services will not be aligned with their cultural values and beliefs.

Besides not knowing exactly how many students are experiencing mental health problems, very little has been done to help these populations overcome and/or prevent social–behavioral problems. Very few studies have been conducted to validate the effectiveness of preventive programs for CLD students. Most of the available programs have been developed to work under a specific context (i.e., general education vs. special education) and with a specific group (e.g., general population, children identified as having attention-deficit/hyperactivity disorder, children with severe behavioral issues). The main goal of most research studies on school-based preventive programs is to see whether the given program achieves the desired outcomes (e.g., increases social skills, reduces incidences of aggression, prevents substance abuse). Most of the researchers who develop sociobehavioral programs meant to be implemented in the schools have not looked at the role culture could play in their program's outcomes. For the most part, students from minority groups are rarely part of the programs' effectiveness studies, owing to the lack of convenient access to these populations. Little is known on the impact of culture on school-based interventions. However, the few researchers who have made cultural adaptations to preventive or targeted mental health services have shown promising results (Castro-Olivo, 2006; Kataoka et al., 2003; Lopez et al., 2002).

The field of community-based mental health services for families has provided us with a little bit more evidence on the benefits of making cultural adaptations to existing programs. Studies developed to assess the effectiveness of parenting programs or family therapy on culturally diverse populations have shown that making such adaptations is not just the ethical thing to do, but also that engaging in such activities promotes better results among these populations. For example, some of these findings have shown that culturally adapted programs are better accepted by members of CLD populations, which in turn produces higher rates of participation, satisfaction with the program, and generalization of skills. On the other hand, community-based researchers have been able to note that when the same programs (parenting and/or family therapy) are provided in a nonculturally adapted format, members of ethnic minority groups tend to be less engaged in the services, attend fewer sessions, and in many cases tend to withdraw prematurely from studies/programs at higher rates than members of the mainstream culture (Kumpfer, Alvarado, Smith, & Bellamy, 2002; Martinez & Eddy, 2005).

It makes sense to think that in order to increase the acceptance of treatments among CLD populations we must provide them with culturally adapted programs. Providing programs in a culturally sensitive manner will allow these populations to be more engaged because it will be easier for them to identify with the material presented, which will lead to an overall better experience that could dramatically improve their outcomes (Bernal & Sáez-Santiago, 2006; Kumpfer et al., 2002; Lieberman, 1989; Whaley & Davis, 2007). Making such adaptations is not always an easy task. Researchers have often questioned the appropriateness of making adaptations to standardized treatment protocols (such as structured SEL programs). Scientists usually are concerned that such adaptations could jeopardize the fidelity and integrity of the existing program. Most prevention programs are usually validated to work in the contexts similar to those in which they were developed and with populations similar to those initially included in field trials. SEL researchers and developers may argue that making cultural adaptations could drastically deviate from the context they used to validate their program and therefore may not yield the same positive outcomes (Castro, Barerra, & Martinez, 2004).

> **Culturally adapted programs are better accepted by members of CLD populations, which, in turn, produces higher rates of participation, stronger satisfaction with the program, and generalization of skills.**

In their 2004 article titled "The Cultural Adaptation of Prevention Interventions: Resolving Tensions between Fidelity and Fit," Castro, Barrera, and Martinez provided prevention-focused scientists with a strong rationale for making adaptations without having to worry about jeopardizing the fidelity of the existing evidence-based programs. They stated that failing to make cultural adaptations could be more detrimental than not having 100% program fidelity. According to this view—a point with which we agree—we must understand that as long as all of the *big ideas* (main philosophy, theory, and skills to be taught) of the program are maintained, the program's integrity is not jeopardized. Researchers should consider adopting an evidence-based program that can be easily adapted to serve diverse populations to more adequately facilitate their understanding of the skills and concepts as a tremendous advantage.

Table 5.1 has been adapted from Castro et al. (2004) to illustrate the many mismatches that can surface when trying to implement an evidence-based program designed mainly

TABLE 5.1. Potential Sources of Conflict between CLD Clients and Validated Programs

Group characteristics	Population for whom program has been shown to be effective	Current population	Cultural mismatches that could affect program's outcomes
Language	English	Spanish; limited English proficiency; multiple languages in the classroom	Students are unable to understand the material if language is not adapted.
Ethnicity	White, or ethnicity not accounted for	Ethnic minorities	Due to a conflict of beliefs, values, and/or norms; some examples might be irrelevant to them.
Socioeconomic status	Mainly middle class, or socioeconomic status not accounted for	Mainly low socioeconomic status	Limited resources and access to environments that would reinforce generalization of skills.
Urban versus rural context	Varies, mainly urban; context not necessarily accounted for	Varies	Youth from urban and rural areas have different needs.
Risk factors	Not accounted for, or only focused on a few controlled ones	Multiple	The intensity of the examples might need to increase for those populations with multiple risk factors.
Cultural competence of staff	Might not be needed if not dealing with CLD populations	A must!	Students must feel accepted and understood in order to trust and internalize the instruction.

Note. Adapted from Castro, Barrera, and Martinez (2004). Copyright 2004 by the Society for Prevention Research. Adapted by permission.

for the mainstream culture, with CLD populations. Some of these mismatches are very obvious. For example, when working with linguistically diverse students, especially those who have limited English language proficiency, the superficial adaptation of language must take place in order for these students to clearly understand the instruction. Not translating/interpreting the lessons into a language that the students could easily comprehend would represent an *unbreakable barrier.* Understanding the concepts and practicing the skills will be nearly impossible, which implies a significant mismatch between this population and the population who participated in the validation of the program. Students who participated in the validation process of the program were more likely to speak English fluently, thus having a tremendous advantage over non–English speakers. We could easily see how a language mismatch could jeopardize the overall outcomes of the program. We could argue that by not translating the program we are *not* providing linguistically diverse students with equal access to valuable SEL skills and to an intervention that could improve not only their social and behavioral outcomes, but also their academic performance.

Our view is that to work effectively with students who do not speak English fluently, we must either do a complete translation of the SEL lesson into the students' language of proficiency or adapt the lesson in ways that incorporate best practices for the instruction of ELLs (provide more visuals, frequent repetition of key concepts, constant checks for understanding, etc.). Teachers might also find the use of local expressions beneficial when working with students who live in communities that rely heavily on colloquial language to use local expressions (e.g., rural vs. urban language expressions, or vice versa; regional dialectal differences in colloquial English). Using a language that is easier for the students to understand and identify with makes the learning process a lot easier.

Castro et al. (2004) also pointed out another potential mismatch between the students'/participants' *ethnicity or cultural background.* As previously mentioned, most evidence-based program developers conduct their pilot/clinical trial studies with populations they have relatively easy access to (convenient recruitment), and in many cases, ethnic diversity is not represented in these populations of convenience. Using programs that were designed for and with mainly homogeneous populations limits our ability to predict how well members of other ethnic groups will relate to the values, beliefs, and norms addressed in those programs. When working with ethnically diverse populations it is important to know their backgrounds well enough to know whether they will find the values, beliefs, and skills taught to be useful. If your students perceive the program as irrelevant to their *cultural reality,* we think that the likelihood of them engaging in the lessons and then actually using those skills outside the classroom is very slim.

Other significant mismatches could include the number of risk factors within the target population. Most researchers tend to control for these factors when they conduct efficacy or effectiveness trials of SEL programs or other social–emotional interventions. In the real world of classrooms, we don't get to control for the number of risk factors our students come in with. An important risk factor to mention in this regard is strained financial resources that might limit the availability of CLD populations to SEL interventions, especially if those interventions are conducted only by a few teachers in their classes, in after-school programs, or in community settings that might require the students to pay for their own transportation and other related expenses for their parents (e.g., find a babysitter for siblings who will not be attending the program). To increase the match between your students and the program, it is very important to get to know the risks and protective factors your students are exposed to in order to make the examples provided in your instruction match their reality.

One of the most important mismatches between evidence-based programs and implementing interventions in school settings is the training the interventionists might have received on cultural competency. For the few studies that have focused on working with CLD populations, researchers made sure their staff were well trained on working with diverse populations, which means teachers will require similar training in order to yield the same outcomes (Kataoka et al., 2003). On the other hand, evidence-based programs that did not incorporate a cultural component in their initial studies might have lacked culturally competent staff, and therefore their curricula lack the information teachers will need to ensure a culturally responsive practice.

Given the limited research on school-based preventive interventions for CLD populations, we suggest that there are times when we should refrain from implementing evidence-based programs exactly as they have been packaged. To do what is best for our students, we should follow theory-based guidelines to make these programs more culturally responsive and appropriate. Adhering to best-practice guidelines for making cultural adaptations will help minimize the negative effects that are produced by "mismatches" between your students and the validation process that was originally used to develop the program. By making such adaptations we will also be maximizing the benefits of participating in such interventions. As previously mentioned, we have known for many years that members of minority groups are less likely to access mental health services. For many of these underserved populations, the schools are their only hope, and the most appropriate setting for receiving the mental health services they need (Serpell et al., 2007). Given the limited research on culturally adapted programs, we can assume that, although we might not necessarily improve the overall impact a given intervention can have on CLD students, by making cultural adaptations we can be certain that it would increase our chances of getting through to a population that has felt forgotten for many years (Whaley & Davis, 2007). We will be earning their trust and promoting their sense of belonging to our schools, which has shown to be one of the strongest protective factors for at-risk youth (Gonzalez & Padilla, 1997; Napoli, Marsiglia, & Kulis, 2003). By engaging in this work you will be at the forefront of a movement that could tremendously benefit a highly at-risk and underserved population.

We are aware of a possible controversy regarding any recommendation to modify existing SEL curricula or any other evidence-based programs. Some researchers and program developers may take the point of view that any modification to an existing curriculum or intervention could render it ineffective, because it would no longer be conducted under the conditions in which it was evaluated. We understand and respect this viewpoint. We also emphasize what we stated previously—*we are not advocating that you make wholesale changes to any program*. On the contrary, *it is critical to maintain the big ideas or critical components* of an evidence-based program if we are to have confidence that the intervention will result in the desired outcome for our students. These aspects of a program should always be kept intact.

What we think may be absolutely necessary to modify are some of the ways in which the program is delivered: the language, the examples, the communication nuances, all of which do not change the underlying theory or critical components of a program, but may be essential for its successful delivery with students. Our view is that such changes may be absolutely necessary if we are to have any chance of success in delivering some programs to students whose cultural background and language are different enough from the script of the program as to make it unapproachable to them. In other words, our recommendations for making curriculum and intervention adaptations are for purposes of cultural and linguistic *social validity*. Please keep these important points in mind and move cautiously as you proceed with making program modifications on your own. Remember that the big ideas or critical components of a curriculum must always remain intact, even as we carefully modify some of the nuances in the way we deliver them.

GUIDING PRINCIPLES FOR ADAPTING AND MODIFYING SEL CURRICULA

Working with diverse and vulnerable populations of students comes with great responsibility. The American Psychological Association, American Educational Research Association, and the Association of American Educators, among many other professional organizations, have recognized the need to inform those in their disciplines about the need to do no harm to those they serve, respect people from diverse backgrounds, and to work toward becoming culturally competent in their practice.

Of the various professional associations we have examined, the American Psychological Association (2003) has developed the most comprehensive guidelines for working with culturally and linguistically diverse populations. The American Psychological Association recommends that (1) we recognize that culture matters; we increase our cultural awareness when working with culturally diverse clients/students, including understanding and appreciation of the worldviews and perspectives of CLD populations; and whenever possible, we engage in culturally sensitive/responsive practice to ensure that we focus "on the client within his or her cultural context, using culturally appropriate assessment tools and having a broad repertoire of interventions" (p. 390).

Experts on making cultural adaptations to social–emotional interventions have embraced the previously mentioned ethical guidelines. The main goal for these guidelines is to help interventionists understand how easy it can be to adhere to our ethical guidelines when working with CLD clients/students. For those of us who grew up in homogeneous (or close to homogeneous) cultures, thinking about becoming aware about other peoples' cultures seems like a lifelong journey. Many of us fear not being politically correct when trying to learn more about other cultures or when trying to work with culturally and linguistically diverse students. The truth is that learning about other cultures does not have to be a dreadful task. Learning about other cultures is fun, rewarding, and an overall positive (even life-changing) experience for you and members of the culture you are learning about.

In my experience (S. C.-O.), members of different cultures have told me that they feel honored by my curiosity about their culture, and I certainly feel extremely honored when they share their rich cultural background with me. Learning about other cultures is definitely a rewarding experience for both sides.

Table 5.2 includes some general principles and specific strategies for making cultural adaptations to SEL materials. These principles and strategies, which are based in part on the main points of emphasis from the 2003 American Psychological Association guidelines, are included as part of the group leader preparation section of each of the Strong Kids SEL program manuals. We made a specific point to include these materials in the Strong Kids program manuals because of our view that all teachers and school-based mental health practitioners should be aware of these issues, and because at some point almost all of these professionals will be in a situation where it is best practice for them to make such adaptations, for the benefit of *all* of their students.

RECOMMENDATIONS AND EXAMPLES FOR ADAPTING SEL PROGRAMS TO CLD STUDENTS

Having now established the need and set the foundation for being able to make adaptations to SEL curricula for CLD students, we will move on to some concrete recommendations in this area, as well as some examples of doing so from our own experience. Although these recommendations and examples are designed to be useful across virtually *any* SEL program, we obviously do not have personal experience in making adaptations to every such program. Rather, it is our view that the general principles and strategies we have identified can be generalized across programs, although our specific examples in this section come from the process of making significant adaptations to a particular program. One of us (S. C.-O.) took on the major task of making cultural adaptations for a specific student group with the Strong Teens version of the Strong Kids programs (Merrell et al., 2007c), and conducted an empirical study of these adaptations. This particular example will be used throughout this section to bring home the reality of how to enact the general procedures we are promoting.

Before providing a list of recommendations and activities that you can engage in to make cultural adaptation of SEL programs (like Strong Teens) in your classroom, it is first useful to review the "big ideas" behind our primary example—the Strong Teens curriculum. Maintaining the *big ideas and theory* of the evidence-based program is the first step to making cultural adaptations to any program. After all, we want to make sure the program we implement yields similar outcomes for our students as it did for those who participated in the clinical trials or pilot studies. We strongly believe that by clearly understanding the

> Cultural adaptations to existing SEL programs must be done very carefully to ensure intervention integrity and fidelity. Maintaining the "big ideas" and guiding principles of a program are critical features of doing this work appropriately.

main goals and theory of any SEL program you are trying to implement, you will feel more comfortable about making cultural adaptations. Making cultural adaptations will allow for a

TABLE 5.2. General Principles and Specific Suggestions for Delivering SEL Curricula in a Culturally Responsive Manner

Get to know your students.

- Ask students about their cultural identities, activities, and rituals.
- Reflect on the dominant cultural variables in your classroom and how these aspects of culture affect how your students behave and think.
- Identify common successes and failures, problem situations, and challenging life circumstances confronted by your students.

Get to know your students' community.

- Visit the homes and families of students in your class.
- Identify a cultural liaison (a parent or community member who identifies as a member of the target cultural group) to help you learn more about your students' culture.
- Ask the cultural liaison to assist with the cultural adaptation process.

Deliver the curriculum in a manner that your students can understand.

- Change the language of each lesson so your students can easily understand the key ideas.
- Use examples and situations that match the lives of your students (e.g., change characters' names, include extended family, include children with physical impairments, use examples of problems that your students have experienced).

Encourage tolerance.

- Teach students ways to show respect for different cultural groups.
- Encourage and reinforce students for respecting the examples and comments made by their peers.
- Establish and enforce a classroom rule that teasing and name-calling are not allowed.

Adapt assessment tools.

- Adapt the assessment materials so the students can understand (e.g., language and context).
- Pilot test some of the assessment materials with small groups of students prior to implementing the curriculum to ensure that students understand the questions.

Become aware of variations within cultures.

- Do not assume too much about a student's culture or ethnicity.
- Avoid making overgeneralizations about cultural groups. Not all members of a culture act the same way.
- Examine your own values, assumptions, and worldviews and how these are the same and different from those of your students.
- Continually examine the accuracy and fairness of your assumptions about the beliefs and behaviors of different cultural groups.

Seek feedback.

- View adaptation as an ongoing process.
- Consult with students and community members about the relevance and accuracy of the adaptation efforts.
- Ask the students how well the curriculum is matching their needs and life experiences.

better implementation of the program's big ideas, which tend to emphasize the need for *all* students to learn and practice the SEL skills they can use in their own surroundings.

Review the Big Ideas of SEL

The main goal of the Strong Kids/Strong Teens curricula, which are similar to the big ideas of other SEL programs, is to prevent and reduce mental health problems among children and adolescents by providing them with relevant and easy-to-use social–emotional resiliency skills. The Strong Kids/Strong Teens curricula attempt to meet such goal by teaching students to:

- Increase awareness about their emotions/moods and potential symptoms of depression, anxiety, and other social–emotional problems.
- Better understand other people's feelings in order to be able to appreciate others' perspectives and be more efficient at problem solving.
- Better understand the connection between thoughts, emotions, and behaviors and learn how to monitor and modulate them.
- Become better at identifying maladaptive thoughts and irrational beliefs to be more efficient at reframing and thinking positively.
- Learn new skills that could help them to physically relax when they are under pressure.
- Learn how to use effective communication skills to be more effective problem solvers.
- Learn the importance of setting realistic goals and monitoring their behavior to achieve such goals.

It is imperative to keep the big ideas of a program in mind while engaging in the cultural adaptation process, implementation of the program, and reviewing the outcomes. By referring to these big ideas from our example, you'll see the strong connection between the goals of the Strong Kids/Strong Teens curricula (or any other SEL program) and the cultural adaptations and the interventions overall outcomes.

When Should You Consider Making Adaptations?

By now, you are probably thinking, "When should I consider making a cultural adaption to the SEL curriculum I'm currently implementing?" In our experience, every school teacher or interventionist we have seen implementing some type of SEL curriculum has made some type of cultural adaptation to the program, sometimes without even realizing that they are doing so. Remember, most of these programs are semi-scripted, which provides teachers and interventionists with the flexibility to change examples based on what they know about their students. For example, in Lesson 6 of the Strong Teens program, students are introduced to six different thinking errors. One of the examples in this lesson, "Making It Personal," is illustrated with a situation about a student who is blaming himself for his parents' divorce (Merrell et al., 2007c, p. 92). Based on the information you know about your students you might decide to use an example about bullying instead of the example provided in the script. Most of the cultural adaptations you'll make to the program are minor and easy to implement on the spot. The ones that are going to require a little bit more time and creativity are the adaptations targeted for highly at-risk populations. Both types of adaptations have key elements in common. For those on-the-spot adaptations and for the adaptations focusing on bigger issues, one of the most important elements is *knowing your students*. By getting to know your students we mean getting to know the risk and protective factors they are exposed to, as well as their values and beliefs.

Those of you who work with a highly diverse student population, or with large numbers of at-risk students, and are able to tell that many of your students share similar problems might need to engage in a more elaborate cultural adaptation process that will lead to better results for your students. Such adaptations are still going to be easy to implement, but might require a little bit of time to plan. First of all, such adaptations will still require you to teach *all the main skills* of the SEL program (always keeping in mind the big ideas of the program). The factors that you'll have to consider are the types of examples you should use to ensure that the skills taught are going to apply to your students. The main goal of the adaptations is to help your students engage and identify more with the material in order for them to internalize and generalize these skills to their daily lives.

The following recommendations are based on the available literature of best practices for cultural adaptations of existing curricula, our professional and personal experiences, and a linkage of American Psychological Association ethical guidelines. In order to make the material of SEL programs more accessible for CLD youth, we particularly recommend that you engage in the following activities, which will be discussed in the following sections:

- Get to know your students and the socioculturally related issues they might be experiencing in their local communities.
- Identify the most appropriate delivery system for your students. The main elements to consider when trying to develop a culturally appropriate delivery system are language, interactions, culturally specific examples/metaphors, and content/concepts (see Bernal & Sáez-Santiago, 2006).

Getting to Know Your Students and Their Context

Having a broader understanding about the situations, protective factors, and risk factors your students are currently facing will allow you to come up with examples and discussions that your students will easily identify with, and that will allow them to be more engaged in the instruction (Dumas, Rollock, Prinz, Hops, & Blechman, 1999; Lopez et al., 2002). Being able to relate and identify with the presented material will make it easier for them to transfer the skills you teach them in the classroom to their communities and other personal situations and settings. How do you get to know and understand their problems? Based on the available literature and from our own experiences, we can suggest that you conduct a focus group with students, parents, and other relevant community members. Allowing members of the target population to help you identify some of the culture-specific issues the students in your community might be facing will provide you with a deeper understanding of the community's perspective on these issues and will allow you to make valuable connections for future work. Your credibility with this population will also increase dramatically. Another advantage of getting community members involved is the assistance they often volunteer to provide. While conducting focus groups or meetings with parents and community leaders, I (S. C.-O.) have had many of them offer to provide a great amount of help to my efforts. I have had community members help me co-teach the program, help with translations or editing the translation of the materials, and provide me with specific examples to use during a lesson. I have even had community leaders offer to write grants to better fund our efforts. Community members often feel very excited when they see someone wanting to help their peers, and they tend to go out of their way to help facilitate the process.

Identifying the Most Appropriate Delivery System

To be culturally appropriate, a program must be delivered in a language that the target population can better understand and relate to. You might need to adapt the language of the program to reflect the setting you live in (urban or rural). You should ensure that the interactions between the people delivering and those receiving the program are positive for both, and that everyone can relate to and trust each other. Students must be able to sense that the interventionist understands their struggles and is genuinely trying to help them.

You will also need to use metaphors, stories, and/or examples that are relevant to the students' culture. It will also be imperative that you supplement the SEL program you are using with new content or concepts you think will be relevant for this group of students. For example, when I (S. C.-O.) use the Strong Teens program in my work with recent immigrants, I introduce a few concepts the program does not cover in the standard version but are relevant for this target population. Some of the new content and concepts I introduce in the culturally adapted version of Strong Teens for recent immigrant students are acculturation, acculturative stress, acculturative gap, and discrimination. When I work with recent immigrants, my main focus is to help them use the skills in Strong Teens to reduce their *acculturative stress* (i.e., counterproductive pressure an individual experiences when finding him- or herself in between two conflicting cultures; Chavez, Moran, Reid, & Lopez, 1997). Providing them with these new concepts allows them to own the skills the program teaches because it makes these skills more relevant to the issues they are currently experiencing. Finding out about the most appropriate service delivery is something you can easily do during your focus group or through a quick informal survey of your class.

In summary, Figure 5.1 illustrates the main ideas behind making cultural adaptations to the existing curriculum. The overarching goal, or first step, is to make sure that the program's big ideas or theory is respected and well maintained throughout the planning, adaptation, and implementation of the program. The second step is getting to know your students' culture (values, beliefs, customs, hardships, and other risk and protective factors). This is another overarching principle that will ensure the accurate implementation of culturally sensitive practices. Once you have made sure that you understand the big ideas of

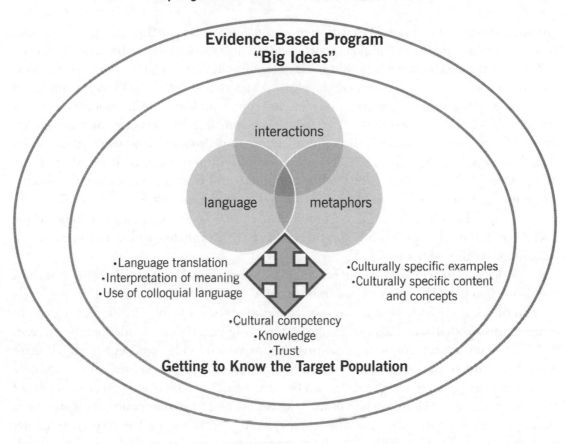

FIGURE 5.1. Key components of making adaptations for SEL programs to meet the specific needs of CLD learners.

the program, created a plan for maintaining them throughout the program, and gotten to know the target population, then you can start making the more dynamic adaptations, such as adapting the language of the existing program to one that would be better understood by your students, increasing your culturally responsive interactions (ongoing learning and respect of your students' cultures), and the use of metaphors or examples that would be relevant for the population you are working with.

LIMITATIONS OF ADAPTING CURRICULA

Many limitations could arise while adapting curricula. Some of these limitations include (1) overgeneralizing problems to members of the same ethnic group, (2) limited resources to run groups for students with diverse needs, and (3) ability to accurately evaluate the sociocultural problems your students might be facing and might need to be discussed during your intervention.

We are of the view that overgeneralizing can be the worst and most dangerous limitation of all. We must be aware that in addition to there being some notable differences between groups, there are also differences within any ethnic group (i.e., within-group differences). In fact, from a statistical standpoint, within-group differences tend to be larger than the differences we find between groups. Levels of acculturation, English language proficiency, and socioeconomic status are among the clearest factors that could make two members of the same ethnic group experience, interpret, and cope with situations in completely different ways. For example, two students who share a common Asian descent may have starkly different experiences related to their assimilation into mainsteam American culture, even though they may both be listed as "Asian American" with respect to their racial or ethnic group. One student could be a first-generation immigrant from a rural area of Cambodia, struggling to learn English and become adjusted to American culture, whereas the other student could be a fifth-generation Chinese American who is aware of his or her ethnic background, but who speaks only English and is fully assimilated within the mainstream culture in the United States.

Besides the danger of overgeneralizing, limited resources can also become a serious problem when trying to deliver a culturally adapted program. Students with differing levels of acculturation might have different needs and might need to be in different groups in order to ensure that the skills and issues they need to talk about are adequately covered. This situation would imply running multiple groups, which can become logistically difficult if you have limited time, resources, and conflicting ideas on how to do this. Also, accurately identifying the needs of your students can be a tremendous challenge if you are not part of their community and/or if you are not working closely with the community to identify your students' most pressing needs. Building home–school–community partnerships, conducting focus groups, and actively learning about cultural issues are key to addressing this challenge.

Finally, as we encourage you to make a serious commitment to reach all of your students in your efforts to deliver SEL programming—through making appropriate curriculum or program adaptations—we once more remind you to proceed with care. We are convinced that such adaptations can make all the difference in effectively delivering SEL to CLD students, so long as the modifications are focused on style, delivery, and subtle nuances that allow us to better connect with our students. These adaptations should not compromise the big ideas or critical features on which the program was built.

WRAPPING THINGS UP

We live in a dynamic and continuously changing society that is rich in diversity. In comparison with most other nations, America is defined by being diverse and welcoming of different cultures. As educators and clinicians, we are the first ones to introduce American culture to many children of CLD backgrounds. For many of these children we will also represent the only opportunity they have to receive some type of mental health services that would allow them to gain valuable skills to survive and better navigate their networks. SEL can provide students of any background with valuable knowledge and resiliency skills to succeed in our society.

Before assuming that any evidence-based SEL program would work equally for any student, regardless of their cultural background, we must do our homework. Dig in and learn more about your students and about the programs you are considering using with them! The goal of almost any SEL program is to help children acquire the skills they need to succeed at navigating their daily problems. Children's daily problems, and the way they cope with those problems, will be highly affected by their culture (their values, beliefs, and customs). Therefore, we must make sure that when instructing students from diverse backgrounds on SEL skills we engage in activities that would make our instruction more culturally responsive and relevant. Some of those activities include (1) getting to know your students, and (2) providing a delivery system that makes the instruction more accessible to them, like language, culturally relevant examples, metaphors, and concepts, all of which should be done by an individual who is committed to having sensitive and trusting interactions with these populations.

VIGNETTE: A Personal Reflection

We truly hope this chapter allowed you to understand the rationale for making cultural adaptations to programs that have already proven to work with mainstream populations. In my (S. C.-O.) experience, making cultural adaptations works from the moment you start recruiting participants. One of the first times I engaged in making cultural adaptations to an evidence-based SEL program, I was working in the role of the researcher trying to find out whether such adaptations were appropriate, help the participating students improve their socioemotional resiliency, and determine whether the program was perceived as valid. I must say that although some of the process (like translating the entire program) was very time consuming and daunting, the results of the adaptations were very positive and made my work very rewarding.

Many researchers will tell you that it can be very challenging to recruit people from underserved communities to participate in research studies, mainly because they tend to be skeptical of "research." When validating the cultural adaptations of the Strong Teens program for a Latino immigrant high school population, my experience was far from common. In my first visit to the classrooms where the intervention was to take place, I briefly described to the students my work and what the study was about. I spoke to them in their native language (Spanish). I clearly articulated my understanding of their needs and the reasons why I thought they could benefit from participating in the project. By doing this I showed them that I had done my homework in getting to know their needs, and some of the examples/metaphors I used during this introduction clearly resonated among them. During this initial introduction I had to make it very clear that although I strongly believed that they could benefit from participating, their participation was voluntary. I mentioned that those who were interested in participating needed to have parental consent forms signed and returned to the school a week away from my initial visit. I was happily surprised when, in less than 2 days, *all students* had signed their consent forms and had brought their parents' signed consent forms back to the school! Just talking about cultural adaptations helped us get 100% participation in less than 2 days. Other more experienced researchers were much more surprised than I was when they heard about the positive response. It was something unheard of in the research arena, especially because the students were not promised a monetary incentive for participating in the study. It was then when I realized that if these populations are not accessing mental health services, is not because they think they do not need them; it is because very few practitioners have tried to explain in a culturally sensitive manner what they can get from such services.

Once recruitment had been successfully completed, we had to start the preintervention assessment process. During this process, I made sure all the instruments I used were available in English and Spanish. All participating students had identified Spanish as their preferred language, as they had only been in the United States for 2 years or less. Students voiced that many of the questions listed in some of the instruments told stories similar to theirs. Students were very excited to start the program. Once the program started, we made sure to inform all participating students that all of the examples used to role-play or to illustrate new skills covered in each lesson had been suggested by members of their community who had participated in focus groups. We also informed them that some of the concepts in the lessons were included to help them understand the acculturation process and navigating two different cultures. We made it very clear that if they didn't agree with one of the examples, they could volunteer their own. Students reported that they felt empowered and comfortable during the lessons. The main interventionists were bilingual/bicultural teachers who had been trained to make their interactions with students as culturally sensitive as possible.

The results of this initial study were very promising. First of all, it showed that we had maintained the big ideas of the Strong Teens program because the overall results (effect sizes) were similar to those from studies conducted with students from mainstream populations. On top of getting similar positive outcomes from participating in this study, many of the participating students reported that they used the skills to solve some of the conflicts they were experiencing at home or with other peers (their cultural reality). They were very engaged during the lessons and more than 88% of them provided extremely satisfactory ratings to the program. They felt the program was very aligned with their needs as Latino immigrants and that they were likely to use the skills they learned in their daily lives (Castro-Olivo, 2006).

Making cultural adaptations to evidence-based programs might seem like a time-consuming task. Time is definitely a resource many educators lack, given the many demands and responsibilities we encounter in our public schools. I must say that the rewards you will receive from helping these populations will make the efforts and time you invest feel like time well spent, and unless you are making such adaptations for research purposes, all these activities can be done informally (which will take virtually no more time than what you would have taken to prepare for any given lesson). I must say that, for me, there is no bigger reward than walking to my office and seeing a musical card some of my students gave me to thank me for the "difference I make in their life." It brings a smile to my face every time I go to work!

CHAPTER 6

When Social and Emotional Learning in the Classroom Is Not Enough

Linking Students to Mental Health Services

INTRODUCTION AND OVERVIEW

This book reflects our effort to move mental health programming into the mainstream of school settings through the coordinated use of social–emotional and academic learning. Most of the chapters in this book are designed to help school personnel with the "A to Zs" of using SEL in school settings, with a particular emphasis on using SEL in a universal manner in classrooms and schools. Although such a universal approach has much to offer as a preventive mental health strategy, we are keenly aware that it will not fully meet the needs of the small percentage of students who have the most serious mental health problems and social–emotional deficits. Essentially, we need to recognize that sometimes SEL in the classroom is simply "not enough." Hence, the need for the current chapter, which is our effort to help you plan for and deliver coordinated SEL services to meet the needs of all students, including those who have the most severe problems. The chapter begins with another look at the three-tiered triangle of support model. Each of the three tiers within this model—including Tier 1/Universal, Tier 2/Targeted, and Tier 3/Indicated—is reexamined with the intent of helping you to plan SEL programming at each level in order to maximize the mental health benefits that will accrue to your most needy students. Following this review, the chapter moves into the specifics of planning mental health services, using a coordinated approach that takes into account various aspects of a student's environment, and that maximizes the use of available resources. Some brief case studies of some of the most typical severe men-

> Sometimes SEL in the classroom falls short of meeting the needs of students with the most intense mental health challenges. We also need to plan for delivering coordinated mental health services to meet the needs of all students, including those with the most severe problems.

tal health problems your students are likely to exhibit are included in order to provide some realistic context to your planning, including psychosis, substance abuse, and trauma. We then take an excursion into the territory of accessing mental health services in your community, including a look at ways of coordinating and planning care, and a brief overview of the types of mental health professionals who are likely to work in the community and may be good allies in your efforts. We conclude with a quick review and case study help to put the content of this chapter into a realistic perspective to help you feel confident about the strengths of using our recommended approaches to meet the mental health needs of your most troubled students.

ANOTHER LOOK AT THE THREE-TIERED PREVENTION MODEL

The three-tiered "triangle of support" model of preventive interventions was introduced at length in Chapter 1 and is referred to in other chapters. As we discussed previously, this model provides a terrific framework to plan for appropriate academic and mental health services for *all* students and at *all* levels of need. Making available a range or continuum of mental health services within school settings is one of the best illustrations of this three-tiered model. Given the focus of this chapter on enhancing SEL programming through offering mental health services in schools, this section is a very good place to reintroduce the three-tiered model and to briefly discuss each of its levels with this mental health emphasis in mind. The remainder of this section delineates some realistic ways that expanded school mental health services can build on the foundation of SEL programming in schools.

Tier 1 Strategies: Necessary but Not Sufficient

Many SEL efforts in schools—perhaps most SEL efforts—should be at Tier 1, or the universal level within the three-tiered prevention model. In graphic depictions of the triangle model that include color coding, Tier 1 is sometimes referred as the "green zone," which connects it to the idea that it includes all students, even if most of them—perhaps 80% of a typical school population—do not appear to be at heightened risk of developing significant social–emotional or mental health problems. In both theory and practice, general SEL programming helps all students, including those who are at elevated risk or who have intensive needs that may require more support than can be provided through a typical universal or "green-zone" SEL intervention.

In a previous discussion of using proactive strategies to promote student resiliency and social competence in school settings, we (Merrell, Levitt, & Gueldner, 2010) identified some of the ways that universal prevention programming can be best utilized to help keep lower-risk students from moving into higher levels of mental health or social–emotional concern. In our view, school-related risk and protective factors that most powerfully affect student success should guide universal SEL programming. Prevention researchers Hawkins, Catalano, and Miller (1992) noted that several school-related risk and protective factors tend to have a strong influence on student success and development. Current research indicates that key risk factors for future mental health and behavior problems include *early and persistent antisocial behavior, academic failure in elementary school*, and a *lack of attachment to school*. On the other hand, there are also several powerful protective factors that can be incorporated into school environments, including *a positive and caring school climate, development of positive relationships between students and their teachers*, and *effective academic instructional programming*. Schools that include universal programming aimed at the key risk factors and also focus on protective factors can help to prevent students from moving so quickly into a path of academic failure, antisocial behavior, and mental health problems. Combining both risk-reduction and skill-building efforts for your students' universal SEL programming may play a significant role in preventing your students from developing more intensive academic, social, or emotional problems.

> **The idea of *synergy* is that two separate entities end up working together to produce a more advantageous final outcome than if they worked separately. Sometimes, two preventive interventions delivered at the same time may result in better effects than if they were conducted separately and then added together.**

An additional way we can consider using Tier 1 SEL programming to help prevent students with latent risk factors from moving into the upper tiers of risk involves *using strategic combinations of more than one preventive intervention* at the same time. In the prevention science field, simultaneous use of multiple preventive interventions is known as an *integrated prevention approach*. The theory and rationale underlying this idea is that when multiple independent intervention strategies are merged into a single integrated prevention strategy, two types of benefits can occur: *additive effects* and *synergistic effects*. An additive effect occurs when you simply add the benefits or outcomes that come from separate programs. For example, a universal SEL program may enhance student's social–emotional competence and resilience, and a universal problem behavior reduction technique may result in increases in appropriate behavior and reductions in problem behavior in the school. Add them together, and you have the combination of the two benefits. A synergistic effect, on the other hand, is more complicated—and more intriguing. The idea of synergy is that *two separate entities end up working together to produce a more advantageous final outcome than if they worked separately*. In other words, the synergy of the two preventive interventions in this case might result in better effects than what would be expected if they were conducted separately and then added together. Consider the possibility of using an evidence-based universal SEL program such as one of those that are discussed earlier in this volume, while at the same time using a proven behavior management intervention. One possible synergistic effect of the two interventions in combination is that because of the complex positive benefits that may occur, academic outcomes might be enhanced at a greater rate, or bullying incidents on the playground or bus might diminish at a rate that exceeds what you would otherwise expect. This integrated prevention notion is still a relatively new idea in education and mental health, but it is definitely worth considering as a way to boost mental health outcomes for at-risk students within a Tier 1 prevention approach.

Tier 2 Strategies: A Little More

Students who are at the Tier 2 level of need with respect to social and emotional competency and resilience are those whose needs are best met with "a little more" effort than can be reasonably programmed into Tier 1 SEL interventions. Tier 2 students—roughly 15% of a typical school population by our estimation—may have heightened levels of social–emotional risk, or may be showing indications of early warning signs of mental health concerns or other social–emotional problems. Going back to some of the common color-coded uses of the triangle of support model, these students at the targeted or secondary prevention level of need are sometimes referred to as being in the "yellow zone" of preventive intervention. The yellow color—symbolic of a warning light in a three-color traffic signal—is a useful symbol in this case to remind us of the need to *slow down, prepare to stop,* or *be careful.*

Tier 2 prevention strategies can address the needs of students with similar risk factors, either individually or in small-group interventions that are aimed at preventing the onset of emotional or behavioral disorders (Kutash, Duchnowski, & Lynn, 2006). Such services go beyond the efforts found in Tier 1 SEL interventions, but are not as intensive as what are needed with Tier 3 students. Students who are at risk for mental health problems may commonly exhibit deficits in social and problem-solving skills, and they may also have a tendency to make *cognitive distortions,* or maladaptive perceptions and attributions regarding the way they think about things (Greenberg, Domitrovich, & Bumbarger, 2000). These types of social and cognitive factors may negatively affect students' abilities to develop and maintain positive relationships with peers and adults. They may also lead to academic underachievement. Given these risk factors, additional interventions designed to enhance social, cognitive, and academic skills are good targets for Tier 2 preventive interventions. Ideally, such interventions can be strategically added to the range of activities in these areas that are already being provided to students in the form of Tier 1 interventions that the entire class of students is receiving.

Although selection of specific Tier 2 interventions will depend on the specific manifestation and severity of the students' deficits or problems, our experience is that it is possible to provide effective Tier 2 programming by simply enriching existing SEL programming. Essentially, this enriched and targeted program enhancement creates a "high-octane" version of SEL for a few students who are already receiving general SEL strategies in the classroom. In our field trials with the Strong Kids programs, the following strategies were found to be especially useful in teaching SEL skills and concepts to students who had "yellow zone" levels of increased social–emotional need:

> **It is often possible to provide effective Tier 2 programming by simply enriching existing universal SEL programming.**

- Additional opportunities for practice of newly acquired skills.
- Additional opportunities to "show off" newly mastered skills in typical school settings.
- Immediate feedback on skill and concept acquisition.
- Higher levels of reinforcement for demonstrating appropriate SEL skills.

- Increased amounts of prompting or reminding of when to use skills.
- Break up SEL lessons or activities into shorter components if needed.
- Supplement and reinforce universal SEL programming throughout the week.
- Use smaller groups and more careful monitoring for role playing and practice groups when teaching SEL skills.
- Modify scripted SEL curriculum examples slightly to make sure that examples are realistic, relevant, and directly connected to the lives of students.
- Inclusion of basic positive behavior support strategies in conjunction with SEL programming.

These suggestions reflect relatively simple infusions of time and effort into existing SEL programming that all students should already be receiving, yet they have the potential to yield important dividends with your students whose risk levels put them in the Tier 2 "yellow zone."

In addition to basic enhancement of universal SEL strategies, there are times when Tier 2 interventions should take the form of specialized intervention strategies that are added to existing Tier 1 SEL interventions. Such additions are usually most effective when they are carefully planned out and delivered, not just haphazardly or unsystematically cobbled together. Such efforts may not need to be as intensive or as time consuming as what is typical in Tier 3, and they do not necessarily need to be delivered individually (i.e., 1:1), although that form of service delivery is always an option. Rather, specialized Tier 2 interventions are sometimes best delivered in small groups in settings outside of the general classroom. We have seen good examples of this type of service delivery in after school programs, and in "pull-out" programs offered by school counselors, school psychologists, or other interventionists at strategic times during the school day.

There are many evidence-based Tier 2 programs from which to choose (see Merrell et al., 2010, for more details). As examples, let's consider two programs that we are particularly familiar with and have directly observed as producing positive results for students who are socially and emotionally at risk.

The *First Steps to Success Program* (Walker, Stiller, Severson, Feil, & Golly, 1998) is a Tier 2 prevention program aimed at improving behavioral outcomes of preschool and primary grade students who show elevated levels of problem behaviors. The First Steps program includes two intervention modules—school based and home based—that may be implemented in unison to provide at-risk students with social–behavioral skills to help them successfully meet the academic and social demands of the school environment. The classroom-based component focuses on teaching target students adaptive behaviors that lead to academic and social success. Behavioral criteria are set each day, and the student is rewarded for reaching each behavioral criterion. The program typically requires 2 months or 30 program days for implementation. In conjunction with the classroom-based component, a 6-week home-based intervention provides students with additional behavioral monitoring and reinforcement for school success. A trained interventionist visits the student's home once a week for approximately 45 to 60 minutes and provides parents with activities to help build their child's social–behavioral competence. The lessons for the home-based component involve guides for parents, parent–child games, and other positive activities. First Step interventionists teach ways in which parents can help their child with skills such as communication, sharing, cooperation, limit setting, problem solving, friendship skills, and self-confidence. The evidence base in support of First Step is both extensive and impressive. This program appears to be particularly useful as a Tier 2 strategy for young students who are at risk for developing conduct problems and other externalizing disorders.

There are also some impressive Tier 2 preventive interventions that are focused on the internalizing domain. A good example in this realm is Clarke and Lewinsohn's (1995) *Coping with Stress Course*. Aimed at preadolescents and teens who are experiencing some symptoms of depression but who do not yet have a diagnosable "clinical depression," the Coping with Stress Course consists of 15 scripted group sessions, 45 to 50 minutes each, designed to teach students effective coping strategies and facilitate their emotional resilience in the face of troubles or setbacks. The course includes cognitive-behavioral techniques that teach students to recognize, challenge, and change irrational thought processes. A major focus of this program is to teach students effective and adaptive ways of coping with stress. Education regarding affect, cognition, and the link between these two spheres is the primary focus of the program. Each lesson includes role plays, cartoon drawings to illustrate major concepts, and group discussion activities that are tailored to the developmental level of the students. Although the lessons can be implemented in a school setting, it is recommended that trained mental health professionals (i.e., psychologists, counselors, social workers) serve as group leaders. Research by the Coping with Stress authors has demonstrated impressive reductions in depression symptoms among those students who participate in the course, with many treatment gains lasting at least 1 year following the intervention.

The First Steps and Coping with Stress programs are just two examples among potential offerings that are appropriate Tier 2 interventions for students with increased risk of mental health problems. Many other useful evidence-based programs are also available.

Tier 3 Strategies: A Lot More

If Tier 1 and Tier 2 symbolically constitute the "green zone" and "yellow zone," respectively, then an appropriate color for Tier 3 is the "red zone." As a metaphor for intensity of student mental health problems, the "red zone" as a symbol brings to mind terms like *stop, danger, powerful*, and, perhaps, *overheated*. Tier 3 includes a relatively small percentage of students—about 5% of a typical school setting—who need immediate and sometimes long-term attention because of the severity of their mental health and social–behavioral problems. Although these students may benefit from the types of primary and secondary prevention (Tier 1 and Tier 2) strategies previously described, their needs are so intensive that they typically require a much more concentrated and powerful intervention plan than is provided through Tier 1 or Tier 2 strategies. By definition, Tier 3 services are "indicated" services, and are considered to constitute a tertiary level of preventive intervention, which constitutes caring for individuals who have well-established problems or deficits. The intent of Tier 3 mental health services is to minimize the negative effects of the disorder or problem, to prevent worsening, and to help the person achieve the highest level of functioning that is realistically possible.

For children and adolescents who have developed severe mental health and social–behavioral problems, it is usually necessary to provide intense and coordinated interventions. In many cases, these types of intervention services require multiple professionals and coordination of services between schools and community agencies. Such coordinated and intense efforts are usually necessary if we are to effectively manage major problems and maintain adequate mental health. This type of intense effort may also be necessary simply to prevent future occurrences of severe symptoms.

Although there are many specific mental health interventions that are appropriate for Tier 3 types of problems and situations, it is not our intent in this chapter to cover individual programs or interventions in this realm. The reality is that most of the intended readers of this book—school psychologists, school counselors, school social workers, consultants, teachers, and administrators—will not really be in a position to be the ones who are individually planning and delivering indicated services

> **For children and adolescents with severe mental health problems, it is usually necessary to provide intense and coordinated interventions. Such interventions may require multiple professionals and coordination of services between schools and community agencies.**

at the Tier 3 level. Rather, most of you will have a role in providing mental health services to those students who have the most intense needs, but it is more likely to be an educational role or a coordinating and communication role, not the role of functioning as a primary care therapist. One of the key challenges of teachers and school-based mental health and support professionals is to develop an awareness of the mental health service systems available in their respective communities and to learn how to become an effective advocate for your most challenging students in linking them to comprehensive services within the school and broader community. Subsequent sections of this chapter offer solid advice on how to go about learning to navigate the available systems, but that is only one part of the picture. Another key focus is to help you to develop a perspective on effective school-based mental health practices. We also refer you to Figure 6.1, which provides a terrific array of recommended Web-based resources on school mental health services and models.

Our ideas about appropriate Tier 3 mental health services in school settings are informed by the notion of *wraparound services*, which are one of the more promising recent innovations in this area. This term does not denote a specific intervention or model of intervention. Rather, it is a "big idea" or concept that is based on the notion of providing individualized, community-based intervention services to children and youth, both in their homes and schools (Merrell et al., 2010; VanDenBerg & Grealish, 1996). Some states and local municipalities have adopted or even mandated wraparound services for children who have significant mental health concerns. This approach has been aided by expansions in the authorizing legislation for Medicaid at the federal level. The wraparound approach has also been stimulated by developments in social policy and social activism. Although there is not much empirical evidence either to support or refute the wraparound approach, it has a great deal of logical appeal because it helps to formalize the process and facilitate com-

- Centers for Disease Control and Prevention
  ww.cdc.gov
- Center for Mental Health in Schools
  smhp.psych.ucla.edu
- Collaborative for Academic, Social, and Emotional Learning
  www.casel.org
- Depression and Bipolar Support Alliance
  www.dbsalliance.org
- National Association of School Psychologists
  nasponline.org
- National Institute of Mental Health
  www.nimh.nih.gov
- Office of the Surgeon General
  www.surgeongeneral.gov

FIGURE 6.1. Suggested online resources for school mental health models and service delivery systems.

munication between professionals and families as plans are made and services are delivered to high-needs students.

Wraparound services, like other intervention strategies that require collaboration between schools and other community agencies, may involve referrals from school personnel to mental health, social service, and medical professionals. We think that referrals to professionals outside of the schools are appropriate—and may be essential—when students experience problems that are severe and/or chronic, their daily functioning becomes greatly limited, there is concern about the safety of the student or others, the interventions provided at school are not effective, or the student appears to be likely to benefit from some intervention that cannot realistically be provided in the school setting. Primary care clinics and emergency departments are often the first community resources that are accessed when students and families are in serious crisis situations. More commonly, families seek the advice of their primary care physician to obtain a referral to a mental health agency and, sometimes, an evaluation to determine whether medical interventions such as mental health medications could be helpful.

So what do we *really* mean by wraparound services? In practice, providing for a student who has serious mental health needs might look something like this:

A middle school student named Taylor has been a focus of concern among school staff for more than 2 years because of serious social skill deficits, depression, "odd" behaviors and thoughts, personal hygiene problems, and academic deficits. The school integrates an excellent SEL program seamlessly across the grade levels, and Taylor also receives individual counseling from the school social worker on a weekly basis, plus receives special education services for a learning disability and emotional disturbance (some additional academic support in a resource center, plus a weekly social skills training group run by the school psychologist). Despite all of these efforts, it is clear to the staff that Taylor's concerns are worsening, as evidenced by recent suicidal statements, increasing social disengagement, and exhibition of some characteristics such as rapid mood swings and incoherent statements. The student assistance team meets to discuss Taylor's case, with Taylor's mother present. It is decided that more services are needed than the school can provide through its regular support structure. A staff meeting is held at the school to discuss Taylor's case that includes the student assistance team members, two representatives from the local community mental health agency, plus Taylor's family physician. It is decided that Taylor should receive a psychiatric evaluation, which occurs within 3 weeks and produces recommendations for a change in medication. The staffing team meets again to discuss Taylor's intervention plan, and several new elements are put into place: a monthly check-in with the psychiatrist at the local hospital; participation in an intensive after-school care group four afternoons a week at the community mental health center (which includes a therapeutic group; intensive social skills training, and recreational therapy); elimination of the social skills training and individual counseling interventions at the school (so as not to replicate or confound the services to be provided in the community); the addition of a class-by-class check-in program and daily report card for Taylor, managed by the school counselor; the addition of an hour per day of intensive individual tutoring at school, provided by a special education consultant; and weekly home visits (with parent training and support elements) from the school social worker to Taylor's mother. It is agreed that the community wrap-around staffing team will meet at the school once per month for the immediate future to discuss Taylor's progress, and that each professional responsible for providing or monitoring services will bring to the meeting the appropriate progress data. In this way, Taylor is provided with a seamless home–school–community set of services to help mitigate his worsening problems, and to try and restore previous levels of social, behavioral, emotional, and academic functioning.

CULTIVATING AN ECOLOGICAL APPROACH TO MENTAL HEALTH ASSESSMENT AND TREATMENT

School-based mental health services have been strategically developed over the past two decades to integrate mental health services into an educational setting (Weist, Lindsey, Moore, & Slade, 2006). This structural approach allows information gleaned from a natural environment (classroom) to inform mental health treatment and for treatment to positively influence academic performance. The previous section described specific prevention and intervention efforts used across all levels of the continuum of care in the schools, and we clarified how students might progress through this model. To actually integrate mental health services into the context of a school system, research indicates that using an *ecological approach* to designing and implementing school-based mental health programming will produce sustainable and favorable outcomes. This section briefly reviews components of this approach, and you may wish to consider some of them as you contemplate how these ideas fit into your current system.

Bronfenbrenner's (1979) ecological model entails all of the natural environments in which children grow and develop, how these environments interact with and transform one another, and how they influence development. Designing the prevention and intervention methods described in the last section should include serious consideration of this model. For example, treatment proposals now consider goodness-of-fit between students' problems and current evidence-based treatments, the resources available to implement the treatment (financial, person-power, settings, materials needed and available), the impact treatment may have on family members and other students, and so on. Treatment that relies on resources that are not available may not be the best choice, and other options should be explored. The case for developing an integrated approach to education and mental health is similar. Mental health programs implemented in a school ecology will be most successful when pertinent ecological factors are considered, such as community needs and priorities, cultural issues that should guide program development, training for educational and mental health personnel that are strategic and complementary, available resources (financial and other), prioritizing parental involvement, and continuing to utilize known academic interventions (e.g., peer tutoring, evidence-based instructional principles) to improve social and emotional functioning.

In considering how to facilitate school-based mental health services, we encourage you to review each of the factors just mentioned. There are also emerging systemic trends and variables that can enhance program development. First, there is a growing movement to build partnerships between schools and community mental health services with the goal of building a "system of care" for children. Specifically, these domains of research and practice are increasingly working together to produce a public mental health care approach, delivered across ecologies (school, community) in an efficient and systematic manner (Weist, Axelrod Lowie, Flaherty, & Pruitt, 2001). It may be very beneficial to team with your local community mental health providers to determine where partnerships can be formed. Second, educational and mental health professionals work together with areas of overlap in respective practice as well as areas of distinctive expertise. Weist and colleagues discussed the unlimited potential for comprehensive mental health care for children when the "players" who are involved better understand one another's roles and expertise in promoting childhood development. We cannot agree more with this idea. Collaborative efforts (e.g., phone call communications, attending professional meetings and conferences) are continually challenged on a daily basis due to overscheduled work days, "turfing" to another provider or system of care to save time and resources, basic misunderstandings regarding training and experience, and day-to-day work challenges that are inherent in every professional's work environment. These challenges interfere with providing a continuity of excellent care, and we believe that reaching out across self-imposed boundaries is a first step in collaborating that can improve care for children. Finally, legislative and funding opportunities can fulfill students' mental health needs on a broad scale. The state of Illinois is an example of initiating and utilizing legislative action to promote universal awareness and implementation of SEL initiatives. Public monies and grant funding have provided much of the financial resources needed to carry out initiative related to mental health (e.g., Safe Schools Healthy Students). We strongly encourage you to investigate these options for advocacy and involvement.

EXAMPLES OF MENTAL HEALTH PROBLEMS
THAT REQUIRE COMPREHENSIVE CARE

At times there are circumstances when students need mental health services that exceed a school's limited resources. Despite ongoing work to expand mental health services in school settings, students may need community resources to access a specific type of care that is not otherwise available in the school. Examples of these issues may include, and are certainly not limited to, suicidal ideation and/or attempt, drug and alcohol abuse assessment and treatment, acute psychosis, severe and out-of-control behavior, threats of violence, trauma, homelessness, and other complex psychosocial stressors. On many occasions in our prior work as school-based practitioners, we have facilitated and coordinated such services. This process can be challenging. Not only can it be difficult to find the services that match a student's needs, but ensuring that students follow through with obtaining these services *and* coordinating them among multiple treatment providers can seriously obstruct the quality of care that is possible. The following brief case examples highlight mental health problems for which community agency assistance is indicated.

Psychosis

Javon was a 17-year-old male and a junior in high school when he was referred to the school psychologist for an urgent evaluation. His language arts teacher became very concerned when, during the course of reading a classic novel in class, he became very agitated, was mumbling to himself, and was talking like there was someone standing next to him. When the teacher asked Javon what was going on, he became angry, swore repeatedly at the teacher, and stormed out of the classroom. A brief evaluation by the school psychologist suggested Javon had actually been hearing voices for approximately a year, and recently the "voices" have sounded more threatening to Javon. The school psychologist knew that Javon needed a more thorough evaluation. Within 24 hours, Javon was evaluated in the emergency department of his local hospital and was found to be "gravely disabled" and needing inpatient hospitalization. After a 2-week stay, Javon went home after receiving an evaluation and psychotherapy by a mental health team that included a psychiatrist, psychologist, and licensed clinical social worker. The plan for his transition to home included ongoing medication management, weekly psychotherapy with his family, and meeting with the school to plan for his return. The school psychologist was asked to gather information from the outpatient providers to help with this transition.

Alcohol and Drug Abuse

Marci was a 15-year-old female attending school in a community generally considered to be affluent. In the past couple months, the school attendance officer had been calling her home to notify her parents of repeated absences—either select classes or failing to show up to school. When midterm report cards were delivered home, her parents discovered she was failing most of her classes. Earlier that week, Marci had been ticketed for underage alcohol consumption and she was grounded for a month. Her parents scheduled a meeting with the school counselor to obtain more information and develop a plan to get her back on track. The counselor inquired as to whether her parents suspected Marci was drinking and/or using illegal drugs on a regular basis because her drop in grades was so dramatic. Although Marci's parents didn't think this was the case, they agreed to take Marci to an alcohol and drug treatment center for an evaluation. During the course of this evaluation and through a routine toxicology screen, it was discovered that Marci had been using marijuana and cocaine on a regular basis. The treatment center recommended immediate and intensive treatment that would require a 30-day stay at the center and would include regular family psychotherapy. Marci was completely opposed; her parents agreed to the treatment. The school counselor asked Marci's parents to notify the school with Marci's anticipated date of return to school and obtained written permission to talk to the community treatment facility. As with all students returning to school after a lengthy absence, the school counselor would arrange for Marci and her parents to meet with him to determine how schoolwork would be made up so Marci could still earn credits toward graduation.

Trauma

Zelik was a 10-year-old immigrant bilingual female living in a rural community and in the fifth grade when she was referred to the school's student-support team. Her teachers were concerned about Zelik's increasingly apathetic behavior in the classroom. She had not turned in any work in about 4 weeks, seemed very distracted, and was increasingly irritable with her classmates. She also seemed tired and sometimes fell asleep in her morning classes. Her parents were asked to come to the school to talk more about the school's observations. Her parents spoke Spanish, and an interpreter was provided by the school district to provide translation services. Zelik's parents talked about their concerns with her sleep and eating habits: she was having nightmares almost every night and was barely eating the evening meal. They had also noticed that she was more irritable and was being disrespectful. When the school social worker asked whether anything "bad" had ever happened to Zelik, her parents said that their immigration experience had been very difficult for the family, as their initial housing arrangement did not work out and the family had been homeless for about 3 weeks. The student-support team decided that Zelik needed a school evaluation to determine whether there were any other supports they could provide and concluded that Zelik would probably benefit from a more thorough psychological evaluation. The challenge was in locating services in their rural community that would be accessible, considering that the family had limited resources to provide transportation. The school social worker contacted a community mental health center in a nearby town and helped the family schedule an appointment with a Spanish-speaking licensed clinical social worker. The school social worker was able to provide a voucher to the family to help with transportation costs, since the school had a grant from the federal government to assist rural communities with mental health care for school-age children.

These case examples provide a brief window into the severity and acuity of mental health problems that students face on a daily basis. Chances are that you are very aware of the psychological conditions that were just described and how they can potentially impede academic performance, let alone daily functioning with sleep, eating, social relationships, and overall well-being. The challenge is providing assistance to students that is feasible, effective, and within the scope of care that the school is required to provide. This next section outlines ways in which school personnel can actively assist students and their families in obtaining the mental health care they may need.

ACCESSING COMMUNITY MENTAL HEALTH SERVICES 101

A unique challenge for school districts is determining the extent to which they are required to provide psychological services to their students. This is a complex issue, and a direct way to address it is to talk to your administrative team to ascertain the district's policy on mental health referrals initiated by the school (e.g., how is this done, how is it worded to parents, and who will assume financial responsibility). Understanding these issues is especially pertinent when referring to community resources is emergent (e.g., a teen is threatening suicide) or as in most cases, the behaviors of concern are severe and chronic and comprehensive care is warranted.

Under what circumstances are referrals made, and to whom should students be referred? To reiterate, students in immediate crisis situations are often referred for emergent evaluations, either by an emergency department at a local hospital or to a treating provider, if the student has one. This includes students who you believe are in imminent danger of hurting themselves or someone else, or are impaired in a way that leads you to believe there is something wrong with them (e.g., incoherent, confused, grossly disorganized, unresponsive, responding to external stimuli). The vast majority of students who are referred are not so severely impaired, but require more treatment than is possible within a school setting. These situations may include needing clarification on psychiatric diagnosis that would directly influence school-based programming, suspecting a medical condition that is contributing to mental health and behavioral problems that are observed in the classroom, and helping a student and their family obtain mental health services that may be beneficial to them, but is otherwise not available in the school (e.g., drug treatment and treatment for abuse, neglect, and trauma). Some students experience emotional difficulties that are not necessary affecting school performance, but would benefit from treatment that caregivers choose to obtain in the community. Referrals are generally made via the designated mental health professional in the school building, often a school psychologist, counselor, or social worker. These professionals are an excellent source of consultation to assess a course

> **School personnel who refer students to community mental health professionals typically spend their career fostering relationships and continually network to find providers who can effectively serve school-age students and their families.**

of action. Figure 6.2 provides a brief checklist of areas that should be covered during the course of the referral process. We have also included a reproducible Worksheet 6.1, "Worksheet for Planning and Coordinating Community-Based Mental Health Care." This worksheet includes much of the same information found in Figure 6.2, but is organized in a practical format that may be used for guiding the process of initiating contact and making referrals to community-based mental health providers. Of course, you should make sure to follow all of your agency policies and procedures in this process, but our experience has been that many school systems do not have well-defined processes for this type of activity in place, so the worksheet may help organize your efforts.

Determining the "right" community provider to refer a student to can be confusing, but there actually is some logic to the process! School personnel who refer students to community mental health agencies typically spend their careers building relationships with these providers in order to continually update their lists of who can effectively treat school-age youth and their families experiencing a wide variety of problems. Treating children for mental health problems poses unique issues—they are not simply "little adults," and there are fewer mental health providers qualified to work specifically with children. Consequently, school personnel who coordinate community mental health services for students must continually network with community agencies to find psychiatrists, psychologists, licensed clinical social workers, licensed professional counselors, and other providers who offer specific treatments to match students' issues (e.g., psychotropic medications, drug and alcohol treatment, multisystemic therapy, group therapies). Networking is usually accomplished by contacting these agencies either to collect general information or it naturally occurs when a student receives services with the provider and the school is informed. We view this networking opportunity not only as a chance for schools to learn more about community services, but also as an opportunity for community providers to better understand the systematic services available in the schools as well as their limitations. In the spirit of efficiency, we

---

✓ Determine your school's referral policies and procedures.

✓ Identify and describe student's social, emotional, behavioral, and academic concerns.

✓ Consult with designated school mental health expert.

✓ List agencies or providers that can provide assistance and need to be informed (e.g., contacting the student's primary care provider).

✓ Contact student's caregiver and/or guardian.

✓ Obtain a release of information to exchange relevant information about the student with community agencies.

✓ Prepare and send a letter to relevant community agencies that describes behaviors observed and the impact on daily functioning.

✓ Follow up: Was the student connected with the referral agency? Has there been communication between the school and this agency? How can the parties involved in the student's care coordinate services?

FIGURE 6.2. Checklist for coordinating community-based mental health care for students.

[Date]

Dear Dr. [*insert name of primary care provider or other community provider*]:

I am writing on behalf of [*insert name of student*], a student at [*insert name of school*]. Over the past 6 months, we have become increasingly concerned about [*insert name of student*'s] behavior. We believe this student may benefit from collaboration between our school and the care you provide. The following is current, school-based information:

Grade level: [*insert grade level*]

Special education: [*yes, no; areas receiving services*]

Academic performance: [*grades, work completion*]

Attendance: [*absences, excused and not excused*]

Disciplinary record: [*referrals, suspensions, expulsions*]

Behavior: [*e.g., inattentive, problems staying on task, disruptive*]

Social: [*e.g., few friends, seems like a "loner," sits alone at lunch, fighting*]

Emotional: [*e.g., easily irritated, seems sad, expressed wishing never to have been born*]

Other: [*e.g., frequent trips to the nurse's office, neighborhood stressors*]

We look forward to collaborating with you to assist [*insert name of student*]. I can be reached at [*insert phone number*] between the hours of 8:00 A.M. and 3:30 P.M.

Sincerely,

[*insert name of letter writer*]

[*letter's writer's title*]

FIGURE 6.3. Template for sample referral letter to community mental health care providers.

have created a sample letter format in Figure 6.3 that can be used as a template for you to concisely convey relevant information to a community provider who is pressed for time.

What kinds of services are available through community mental health providers? Here is a general summary of specific mental health providers and their typical areas of practice. This description is not meant to be exhaustive, and certainly differences exist across agencies and communities.

Licensed Clinical Social Workers

Licensed clinical social workers (LCSWs) are typically trained at the master's and sometimes doctoral levels in social work and licensed to assess, diagnose, and provide individual and group psychotherapy to children and adults for a wide variety of mental health problems. They work in most community settings providing mental health services, including schools.

LCSWs have specific training in locating and understanding the vast array of community services available to children and families who have needs related to daily living, such as finding safe housing, accessing resources for domestic violence, and coordinating financial assistance to families in crisis via government-sponsored programs.

Licensed Professional Counselors

Sometimes known as a licensed mental health counselor, a licensed professional counselor (LPC) is required to have a master's degree in counseling or highly related field, has completed supervised clinical work, and is licensed by the state licensing board. LPCs' areas of specialization can vary and, therefore, it can be helpful to inquire into areas of expertise and experience. They are qualified to diagnose and treat a range of mental health problems and often work with a team of providers as part of a comprehensive approach to care. LPCs practice in a variety of settings, including community mental health agencies, private practice, and medical settings.

Licensed Psychologists

Licensed psychologists have obtained doctoral training in psychology, either clinical, counseling, or school psychology, and have completed a required amount of supervised clinical hours and passed an examination and peer review process to be eligible for licensure. They typically practice in community mental health settings, private practice, or medical settings, and are qualified to conduct thorough psychological evaluations, diagnose complex mental health problems, and offer individual and group psychotherapy. Some licensed psychologists conduct research and teach in academic settings, and in a small number of states, they may become licensed to prescribe psychotropic medications. Licensed psychologists also tend to specialize in either adult or childhood issues and may have particular areas of interest and specialization. Inquiring about these areas will help school personnel find a psychologist who best fits a student's particular needs.

Psychiatrists

Psychiatrists are physicians who have trained in medical school, a specialized residency program in adult psychiatry, and child psychiatry if they choose. Psychiatrists practice in similar settings as licensed psychologists. Their area of expertise is diagnosis and treatment of psychological problems, and they are specially trained to prescribe psychotropic medications. Some psychiatrists also include psychotherapy as part of the treatment they offer and may have particular areas of expertise and interest. It is important to inquire whether the psychiatrist is trained to treat children and whether psychotherapy is included in treatment. Many psychiatrists and psychologists collaborate to treat a child, where the psychiatrist prescribes and monitors medication and the psychologist facilitates psychotherapy. Having open and positive communication between psychiatry and psychology is a vital component to treating school-age children, as different providers often observe and detect varying issues during the course of assessment and treatment. Collaboration of care in this regard can provide a comprehensive approach to care that is not only in the best interest of the child, but also helps both domains of professional practice better understand the other's areas of expertise.

Pediatricians, Family Medicine Physicians, and Nurse Practitioners

These providers typically work in a medical setting, either in a primary care clinic or hospital, and provide general medical care to children and their families. They are increasingly being asked to manage psychotropic medications, such as those used to treat attention-deficit/hyperactivity disorder, and feel more comfortable doing so as they receive more training and have more on-the-job experience. Many hesitate to manage psychotropic medications used for more complex psychological problems such as depression and anxiety in children, bipolar disorder, Tourette syndrome (a specific type of tic disorder that often has psychosocial complications), and psychotic illness. A visit to a primary care provider is typically the first place that caregivers take their children when there is concern about social, emotional, and behavioral functioning. It is imperative to rule out organic or medical causes for these problems. School personnel can obtain releases of information to talk to these providers to explain the behaviors that are observed in school. Although it may be challenging to coordinate this communication due to hectic school and medical practice schedules, we have found most primary health care providers eager to collaborate.

To summarize, if we adopt an ecological approach to childhood development, we must recognize the roles that various community "players" have in facilitating social, emotional, and behavioral growth, particularly when serious mental health problems occur. In the last section, we briefly described the services available through a variety of mental health professionals in the community, all dedicated to children's health. The key here is not only becoming familiar with these professional resources, but also brainstorming ways to collaborate across school, home, and community. Many of the students who need intensive mental health services have very complex psychosocial issues that require multiple disciplines to coordinate case conceptualization and treatment. This can be a time-consuming process and we urge you to use your training, skills, and experience to initiate this collaboration in a way that works for you and advocates for students.

WRAPPING THINGS UP

There is no question that the complexity, variety, and severity of many of our students' mental health problems can be absolutely overwhelming. But that is a reality we must face up to if we are to be truly effective at meeting the academic and mental health needs of *all* students. The good news is that there have been many positive developments in recent years in school-based interventions—including SEL—that can help us be more effective. Figure 6.4 includes some suggested additional readings that we think will provide you with a more solid foundation in school mental health issues than can be created from this book alone. A

Berman, A. L., Jobes, D. A., & Silverman, M. M. (2005). *Adolescent suicide: Assessment and intervention* (2nd ed.). Washington, DC: American Psychological Association.

Brown, R. T., Carpenter, L. A., & Simerly, E. (2005). *Mental health medications for children: A primer.* New York: Guilford Press.

Merrell, K. W. (2008). *Helping students overcome depression and anxiety: A practical guide.* New York: Guilford Press.

Nastasi, B. K., Bernstein, R. M., Varjas, K. M., & Moore, R. B. (2004). *School-based mental health services: Creating comprehensive and culturally specific programs.* Washington, DC: American Psychological Association.

Sprague, J. R., & Walker, H. M. (2004). *Safe and healthy schools: Practical prevention strategies.* New York: Guilford Press.

Weist, M. D., Evans, S. W., & Lever, N. A. (2003). *Handbook of school mental health: Advancing practice and research.* New York: Springer.

FIGURE 6.4. Suggested additional readings on school mental health issues.

positive way to look at these sometimes daunting problems is to consider that you are not on your own in dealing with them, but are part of a larger school system and community that may include a great deal of expertise to meet your students' needs. To that end, some of the key aspects of using SEL and community-based resources to help your students with the most intense needs include:

• Within the three-tiered "triangle of support" model, we can maximize Tier 1 or universal services to all students in order to maximize the mental health impact on those students with the most severe needs. Some of the most promising strategies in this vein include strategic combinations of differing Tier 1 interventions, using an integrated prevention approach.

• Many Tier 2 interventions are available for students who are at risk for mental health problems. These interventions may be used in the general classroom setting, or in special programs that target smaller numbers of students. Enriching universal classroom-based SEL programming to provide a "high-octane" version of SEL for at-risk students is one example of a good Tier 2 strategy, as it uses manualized or scripted intervention programs designed specifically to provide early preventive interventions for students who are most at risk.

• Students whose intensive mental health needs place them in Tier 3—usually about 5% of a school's population—may benefit from SEL programs that are combined with specific additional supports and resources. One of the most promising efforts in this regard is the use of wrap-around services—a comprehensive plan of support and intervention across the school, community, and home settings—to help keep mental health problems from worsening and to restore students to their optimal level of functioning.

• As you plan for coordinated mental health services across the school and community settings, we urge you to consider the total ecology of a student's life in planning for such services and to consider issues such as community needs and priorities, cultural issues, available resources, parental involvement, and continued use of effective academic interventions as you move forward with coordinated care.

- Most communities include a variety of mental health practitioners who are available to help you support your students who have the most intensive mental health problems as you strive to provide a coordinated system of care. Some of the professionals in your community most likely to be of assistance in this regard include licensed psychologists, licensed clinical social workers, licensed professional counselors, psychiatrists, and primary health care providers, including pediatricians and family practice physicians, and nurses who have expertise in mental health care.

VIGNETTE: A School Counselor's Experience with Coordinating Mental Health Care

A school counselor working in an urban low-socioeconomic-status school district was recently granted a small amount of money from a community foundation to implement a new SEL program that helps children understand others' perspectives, develop empathy, and learn about emotions. So far, the students have really enjoyed the program, and the progress-monitoring data that's been collected indicates that students are able to identify their feelings and conflicts have been reduced in the classroom. Marcus is an 8-year-old biracial boy who attends an urban elementary school and has participated in this program for about 7 months. Marcus has always seemed shy and reluctant to interact with other children, and despite participating in the program, these difficulties have not improved. The school counselor talks with the school principal, and together they decide to have Marcus participate in weekly counseling for a month with the school counselor so that more information can be gathered to better understand how to help him. During the course of these sessions, the school counselor suspects Marcus may be experiencing a great deal of anxiety and has been for many years. She contacts Marcus's caregiver, his grandmother, who also expresses concern about this same issue. They decide that Marcus may benefit from a visit to his primary care provider (PCP) for an updated physical and that it is likely Marcus may need more support. Fortunately, his academic performance is within average limits and there have been no disciplinary problems. The school counselor agrees to write a brief letter to the PCP so the school's concerns are shared and Marcus's grandmother will make an appointment. They schedule a time in 2 weeks to talk again, after Marcus has had a chance to see his doctor. The school counselor wrote the letter and faxed it to the PCP. After several attempts at contacting the PCP and returning her messages, the two providers have a brief phone conversation about Marcus's behaviors. The PCP expresses appreciation for this contact, as the information was found to be helpful and instrumental in guiding Marcus and his grandmother to a community agency that can provide further support.

Worksheet for Planning and Coordinating Community-Based Mental Health Care

Name/age of student: _____

Names/contact information for student's parents/guardians: _____

_____

Date parent consent/written release of information obtained: _____

In the following space, summarize the student's major social, emotional, behavioral, and academic concerns that have led to this request for community-based care. Use additional space and attach additional reports or supporting evidence as needed.

```
┌─────────────────────────────────────────────────────────────┐
│                                                             │
│                                                             │
│                                                             │
│                                                             │
│                                                             │
│                                                             │
│                                                             │
│                                                             │
│                                                             │
│                                                             │
│                                                             │
│                                                             │
│                                                             │
└─────────────────────────────────────────────────────────────┘
```

List agencies or providers that should be informed regarding a referral and that are cleared for a release of information: _____

_____

_____

Notes on follow-up and outcomes:

CHAPTER 7

Assessment and Evaluation Strategies in Social and Emotional Learning

INTRODUCTION AND OVERVIEW

Anyone who is familiar with the day-to-day workings of K–12 schools anywhere in our nation understands the increasingly prominent role played by assessment and evaluation. From developmental screenings of preschoolers to state graduation competency tests for high school seniors, students are well aware that testing is something that is essentially woven into the fabric of their school experience. Teachers are often the ones who are assigned the task of administering these tests. Although they may have completed their preservice professional education training with very little formal training in educational assessment, teachers often end up learning assessment skills on the job, and by default often become seen as experts, whether or not they feel that way or actually possess technical assessment expertise. And administrators . . . well, let us put it succinctly, if not bluntly: In our age of educational accountability, the careers of school administrators can be made or derailed based on the performance of their schools on standardized testing that is required by state departments of education and the federal NCLB. You know—the assessment results and "report cards" that make the newspapers, that cause leadership and resource dominoes to fall, and that realtors use to convince potential home buyers that the home of their dreams is in a "good" school district.

But as we shall see, there is a still a bit of a disconnect between the general fervor for testing and assessment in our schools that we see in relation to standardized academic achievement assessments, and the efforts that are being promoted (and seldom if ever mandated) in the realm of children's social and emotional competence. Given this somewhat paradoxical state of affairs, we have endeavored to present you with all the basic tools you need to at least start moving forward with assessment and evaluation of SEL competences. To that end, this chapter begins with an overview of the general issues in assessing SEL competencies, including the most common assessment methods, a suggested strategy for assessment in this area, and brief reviews of some promising and mostly newer assessment tools that are now available in this area. We then detail a simple four-phase model for using assessment in a way that will help you solve problems. Following a discussion and examples of how the emerging three-tiered model of student supports in education can be used to guide our decision making in the realm of social and emotional skills, we then show how SEL competency assessment can be done using very brief experimental measures in a novel way to help you monitor SEL intervention progress with the individual students for whom you have the most concern.

ASSESSING SEL COMPETENCIES

Our combined experience in designing, implementing, and researching SEL programs has convinced us that with a few exceptions, assessment of students' SEL competencies—the actual behaviors, skills, and personal characteristics that we are trying to positively affect—is mostly an afterthought. There are some reasons why assessment is often put in this lowly position, regardless of the role that various professionals play in the SEL process. First, designers of SEL programs (us included), tend to put most of their energy, research and development efforts, and personnel resources into the content of the curriculum and into ways of ensuring that the content is acceptable to those who will be using it. For most program developers, assessment strategies become of interest only when they get to the point where they need to start thinking about producing evidence regarding the impact of their programs. Second, most teachers and practitioners are justifiably focused mostly on intervention. If they are interested at all in assessing the impact of their interventions, it is often because of external pressures to show evidence that what they are doing is resulting in improved student outcomes. Therefore, if there is any attention at all to assessing students' SEL competencies, it is generally later in the process, and assessment tools are often hastily selected based on what is easily available or what someone else is using. Third, even many research scientists who study the impact of SEL interventions (us included), tend to focus most of their attention on the design of the research study and the practical aspects of implementing the study, such as determining treatment fidelity, making sure that interventionists are on track, and dealing with the day-to-day concerns of running a study. To be fair, assessment of student outcomes is generally important to researchers who investigate SEL programs, but there is also a notable lack of good assessment instrumentation available that is designed exclusively with SEL competencies in mind, and validated specifically for that purpose.

In addition, not only are children's social–emotional assessment tools in shorter supply than tools to assess their cognitive or academic performance, but most of the available and validated assessment tools in the social–emotional realm are *pathology oriented*, meaning they focus on children's problems, disorders, or dysfunction, and tend to overlook social and emotional competencies or strengths (Merrell, 2008a, 2008b). Thus when developers, prac-

> **Accurate assessment forms the basis of effective intervention. Unfortunately, assessment of SEL competencies is mostly an afterthought.**

titioners, or researchers do try to select appropriate assessment tools to evaluate the impact of SEL, they are often faced with the choice of either measuring positive characteristics that don't quite capture the full measure of what is included in the SEL program (such as social skills rating scales or self-concept measures) or selecting problem behavior or psychopathology scales (such as child depression scales or conduct problems scales), and trying to evaluate the impact of a positive, strengths-based program based on whether it produces reductions in students' problem symptoms. Unfortunately, neither of these options is what is most needed if we are going to accurately assess or measure the range of student competencies and characteristics targeted by SEL programs.

Despite the challenges related to effective assessment of SEL competencies, it appears that we may be on the cusp of a new era in social–emotional assessment of children and adolescents. There are unmistakable signs that we are beginning to see a movement toward comprehensive strengths-based assessment that is on equal footing with the wide range of assessments available for disorders and problems. We are certainly not even close to that point yet, but a solid foundation in this area is being established (Beaver, 2008; Jimerson, Sharkey, Nyborg, & Furlong, 2004).

> We may be on the cusp of a new era in social–emotional assessment of children and adolescents; there are unmistakable signs that we are beginning to see a movement toward comprehensive strengths-based assessment.

Assessment Methods

In a widely used graduate textbook on social–emotional assessment of children and adolescents, we (Merrell, 2008b) have proposed that there are six basic methods of assessment that fall within this general domain:

- Direct behavioral observation
- Behavior rating scales
- Self-report instruments
- Sociometric techniques
- Projective–expressive techniques
- Interviewing techniques

There are a few examples of hybrid assessment methods that cross more than one category, or of assessments that don't neatly fit into any single existing category, but these six general methods represent the vast majority of available and validated social–emotional assessments for children and adolescents. Each method has its place, but projective–expressive techniques, although they remain popular in some quarters, are fraught with reliability and validity concerns that call their use into question, especially when assessment results are to be used for making high-stakes decisions (see Merrell, 2008b, for a comprehensive discussion of this issue).

If we take projective–expressive assessment out of the mix when considering assessing SEL competencies (a wise choice, given that none of these procedures to date have been designed specifically with SEL in mind), we are left with five assessment methods to consider. Realistically, these five types of assessments are not equally appropriate or relevant to assessing SEL competencies, although all have their place for other specific purposes.

Sociometric techniques (assessment procedures that require students to rate or otherwise evaluate the social or emotional status of their peers) have been shown to be very useful for research purposes and to have strong psychometric properties, but they are simply not practical for using in assessing SEL competencies, because they require active parent consent for every student in a classroom or group, even if only one of those students will be administered the assessment. In addition, sociometrics tend to focus on social reputation or status rather than specific social competencies.

Direct behavioral observation can be a highly valid method for assessing social behavior and is considered by many researchers to be the most naturalistic and scientifically defensible way of assessing children's social–emotional characteristics. That said, direct observation is most useful for problem behaviors rather than for social competence, and it has seldom been used or validated for purposes of assessing child characteristics that are not easily observed through external means, such as their mood, knowledge of healthy social–emotional behavior, or ability to engage in alternative thinking strategies. In addition, direct behavioral observation can be problematic for assessing social–emotional intervention outcomes when only limited number of observations can be conducted (say one or two, which is often the case), because researchers are increasingly finding that several direct observations of social behavior may be needed for a reliable estimate (see Merrell, 2008b).

Interviews with children and adolescents are among the most widely used of all social–emotional assessment methods. Although they vary widely in level of structure and reliability, interviews are a standard and trusted method of assessment with children and adolescents, because they allow one to get information directly from the child. That said, interviews are not recommended as a primary method for assessing SEL competencies, because very few if any have been developed and validated for this specific purpose, and because extensive time would be required to administer interviews to an entire class or group.

Recommended Methods and Assessment Tools

When we take out the four methods that appear to be of less use for assessing SEL competencies of students, we are left with two methods—behavior rating scales and self-report assessments—that have been widely used and validated for assessment in this domain. We now move into a discussion of both of these methods for use in assessing students' SEL competencies, with an emphasis on tools that are specifically relevant to SEL. In limiting our focus in this manner, we will necessarily be skipping over some of the most valid and widely used assessment tools in these areas—the Achenbach System of Empirically Based Assessment (ASEBA) and the Behavioral Assessment System for Children, Second Edition (BASC-2) come to mind as the most recognizable examples—because they are designed mostly for measuring problem behaviors, or don't quite capture the breadth or depth of SEL competencies that a developer, practitioner, or researcher would likely want to include in their selection of assessment tools.

Some examples of specific assessment tools in these two areas that appear to be especially germane for assessing SEL competencies are briefly described as examples, although we make no claims that our review is intended to cover everything that has been developed and is available. Our selection of tools in this

> **Behavior rating scales and self-report assessments are the most widely-used and researched methods in assessing SEL competencies.**

section includes measures that are either commercially published or easily available within the public domain in some other way, and searchable via the Internet. These examples have all been selected because of their solid research base and technical properties. Because some of the available assessment systems include both behavior rating scales and self-report assessment tools, we have not grouped our selection of assessments according to these categories. Rather, we present them alphabetically and note in our description what methods are used in the assessments.

Behavioral Emotional Rating Scale—Second Edition

Developed by Epstein (2004), the Behavioral Emotional Rating Scale, 2nd Edition (BERS-2) is a true cross-informant or multimodal assessment system for evaluating personal strengths and competencies of children and adolescents ages 5 through 18, given that it includes a parent rating form, a teacher rating form, and a student self-report form. There are 52 items on each version of the BERS-2. These items measure a variety of positive characteristics and strengths of students, specifically including interpersonal strength or social competence, involvement with family, intrapersonal strength (within-child assets), school functioning, affective strength, and for older youths, career strength (work habits and adjustment, occupational interests). This assessment system is designed to be used in planning for student services, evaluating the impact of services and programs, and making eligibility and placement decisions for special programs. These scales are standardized and norm-referenced, based on large and representative samples of children and youths. The Youth Rating Scale and Parent Rating Scale were normed only on students without disabilities, whereas the Teacher Rating Scale was normed on samples of students with and without disabilities. Supplemental norms are included in the manual for students with behavioral and emotional disorders. The test manual includes tables for converting raw scores to percentile scores and scaled scores for the subscales and total score. The total score is referred to as the Composite Strength Index. Technical properties of the BERS-2 are adequate to strong, and it has a growing research base that includes use in several outcome studies of innovative intervention programs. The BERS-2 is an exemplary strengths-based assessment system that is easy to recommend. We particularly like the range of items and subscales in this system. It is designed to assess a broad array of positive skills, attributes, and characteristics that are of utmost importance in SEL interventions.

Developmental Assets Profile

Developed by researchers at the Search Institute (2004) (a Minnesota-based nonprofit organization dedicated to promoting healthy youth development), the Developmental Assets Profile (DAP) is a self-report assessment tool for use with students in grades 6–12, or ages 11–18. The DAP is designed to measure positive assets in middle school– to high school–age children and youth, using 58 items that are based on 40 developmental assets within eight categories: support, empowerment, boundaries and expectations, constructive use of time, commitment to learning, positive values, social competencies, and positive identity. DAP scores can also be analyzed based on five different "context" score areas, including personal, social, within-family, school, and community contexts. The DAP can be administered by traditional paper-and-pencil method at any site, or in an online format on the institute's website (which also provides a scoring service). Both the online and paper-and-pencil assessment options may be used for either individual or group administration, and separate forms are used for each method of administration. Administration of this assessment requires 10–15 minutes on average. The DAP norming sample is reasonably large, and we consider its technical properties to be adequate to good, comparable to those of more widely known social–emotional assessment measures. Although the DAP was not developed with the specific intent of being used as an SEL assessment tool, we think it is a very solid match for this purpose. The items are strongly linked to important aspects of SEL competencies, as well as to outcomes that would be anticipated following successful implementation of a program. Although the DAP is strictly a student self-report assessment and does not have the advantages of being part of a multi-informant assessment system, it appears to be a potentially good choice in this area.

Devereux Student Strengths Assessment

A recent addition to the strengths-based assessment tools for children's social–emotional competencies is the Devereux Student Strengths Assessment (DESSA; LeBuffe, Shapiro, & Naglieri, 2009). The DESSA is a single 72-item behavior rating scale, to be completed by parents, teachers, or after-school care staff, targeting students in grades K–8. The 72 items on the full DESSA form are rated using a 5-point response format (never, rarely, occasionally, frequently, very frequently), with associated numerical values ranging from 0 to 4. The full rating form requires approximately 15 minutes for completion. A very brief eight-item screener version of the DESSA (called the mini-DESSA or 1-minute checkup) is also available for use in situations where a full screening is not required or not possible. The items of the DESSA are based on theories related to risk and protective factors of children, with a specific aim to focus on the protective factors that may play an important role in offsetting of mediating risk factors, or creating resilience. Thus the DESSA items are positively worded. The rater is asked to respond to the general item stem "during the past 4 weeks how often did the child . . . " as they rate specific items such as "offer to help somebody," "work hard on projects," and "ask somebody for feedback." The DESSA may be scored using hand-scoring paper profiles that are part of the standard assessment kit from the publisher, or using an optional online scoring and reporting program. DESSA items load into eight subscales that reflect commonalities among clusters of items: self-management, goal-directed behavior, self-awareness, social awareness, personal responsibility, decision making, and relationship skills. A total protective factors score—a summation of the individual item scores—is also obtained. The DESSA evidences careful development, with commendable attention to both theoretical issues and practical details of test construction. The nationwide norming sample is large and impressive, as are the psychometric properties and basic validity research. The DESSA appears to be advantageous for several reasons, including its specific focus on protective factors or resilience, its dual-rater (parent and teacher) target, its structural connection to the three-tiered prevention model that is increasingly popular in education, its strong technical properties, and the availability of the brief 1-minute checkup version of the scale. The DESSA's chief limitations appear to be the lack of a self-report version for use by students and the fact that it is intended to be used only through grade 8. These limitations may or may not be important issues, depending on the needs and aims of potential users. Overall, the DESSA appears to be a solid and welcome addition to the available assessments in this realm.

Emotional Quotient Inventory—Youth Version

Based on the notion of "emotional intelligence" that has been a part of psychological theory for many years and was popularized by journalist Daniel Goleman in the 1990s (Goleman, 1995), The BarOn Emotional Quotient Inventories are designed to assess social and emotional strengths and how effectively they are applied in practical day-to-day problems and situations. Although there are several Emotional Quotient Inventories developed by the same researchers and publisher, our focus is on the version used with children and adolescents ages 6–18: The BarOn Emotional Quotient Inventory—Youth Version (EQI-YV; BarOn & Parker, 2000). This student self-report instrument contains 60 items that are distributed across seven subscales: interpersonal, intrapersonal, adaptability, stress management, general mood, positive impression, and consistency index. A total emotional intelligence score is also obtained. A 30-item short form is also available, but is not reviewed here; it is conceptually similar to the regular version, but requires less time to administer and has slightly lower reliability. This assessment is available in an easy-to-use, self-scoring, paper-and-pencil format. The norming sample for the EQI-YV is large and impressive, and the psychometric properties are adequate. Because this assessment has the advantage of being part of a larger system of assessments that include primarily adult-focused measures, there are several published studies and retrievable professional presentations available on these companion measures. Although the notion of "emotional intelligence" is only one facet of what is incorporated within the broad spectrum of SEL competencies, we think that this measure does fit within the general domain, and there may be times when it could be a good choice as an outcome assessment tool, such as when the focus of SEL instruction will be specifically on enhancing students' practical applications of their social and emotional knowledge. We place this assessment on our recommended list, but not without noting its additional potential shortcomings with respect to its applications within SEL. Like the

DAP, it is limited to only self-report and thus does not have comparable parent or teacher rater versions available for cross-informant assessment. And second, despite the publisher's claim that the items are written at about a fourth-grade reading level, our experience in this area (and with this particular scale) is that the reading level may be too difficult for students who have poor reading ability—especially those students on the younger end of the intended age range, who may require assistance in decoding and understanding some of the more complex items.

Social–Emotional Assets and Resilience Scales

The most recent entry to the available strength-based assessment tools for assessing SEL competencies of children and youth is the Social–Emotional Assets and Resilience Scales (SEARS; Merrell, 2008c). The SEARS is a cross-informant rating system, consisting of self-report measures for children in grades 3–6 (SEARS-C) and adolescents in grades 7–12 (SEARS-A), a teacher report form for use with students in grades K–12 (SEARS-T), and a parent report form for use with children and adolescents ages 5–18 (SEARS-P). The four rating forms within the SEARS range from 52 to 54 items each, require approximately 12 to 15 minutes to complete, are available in a paper-and-pencil administration format, and use a common 4-point rating scale, where the rater is asked to evaluate how true each item has been for the target student during the previous 6 months (never, sometimes, often, almost always, or always). The items across the four rating forms are conceptually similar and were designed to tap the same constructs (e.g., coping skills, social–emotional competence, self-regulation, problem-solving ability, emotional knowledge, empathy, global self-esteem), but differ slightly in terms of setting and contextual wording of the items. In the case of the two student self-report forms, there are also some minor wording and content differences based on developmental differences between children and adolescents. The four primary forms of the SEARS system can be used for group or individual screening as part of a multi-element individual assessment battery, as outcome measures for SEL intervention programs, and for research purposes. In addition, short forms of the SEARS measures are available for use in individual progress monitoring of SEL interventions, including use within a response-to-intervention framework for determining how well students are responding to a planned intervention. The components of the SEARS system were normed and standardized on large and representative samples of children, adolescents, parents, and teachers. Raw scores are converted to percentile ranks and to score levels that are keyed to the three-tiered prevention model of student need (*core* instruction for 80% of students, *supplemental* instruction for 15% of students who are at-risk, and *intensive* instruction for 5% of students who are at highest risk). The SEARS assessment has been shown to have strong psychometric properties, including high reliability, validity, and clinically useful items, and to be sensitive to changes in students' social–emotional competencies and assets that result from participation in SEL programs. Given that one of the foremost purposes

> **The SEARS assessments have been shown to have strong psychometric properties and to be sensitive to changes in students' social–emotional competencies that result from participation in SEL programs.**

for which the SEARS was developed was for use in intervention tracking and outcome measurement and that its item content represents a broad range of student strengths, assets, and social–emotional competencies, it fills a unique niche among the available assessments in this area.

Social Skills Measures

The five assessment tools and systems overviewed thus far—the BERS-2, DAP, DESSA, EQI-YV, and SEARS—represent important advances in strengths-based assessment of child and adolescent social–emotional competencies that simply were not available only a decade or two ago. In addition to these five strengths-based measures—which cover a broad range of SEL competencies—another type of assessment to consider is more focused social skills or social competence measures. Two representative assessment systems of this type are very briefly overviewed in this section, which reflect two widely used social competence/ social skills measurement systems. Although this type of measure tends not to cover the broad range of social–emotional competencies that are included in the content of the five assessments previously discussed, they have a long history of effective use in education and children's mental health settings, and they may be particularly useful in situations where the assessment of peer relations and social skills are of primary importance.

The Social Skills Improvement System (SSIS; Gresham & Elliott, 2008) is a comprehensive system of social skills assessment and intervention tools for use with children and adolescents ages 3 to 18 years. The SSIS rating forms are an update of what was formerly known as the Social Skills Rating System (SSRS; Gresham & Elliott, 1990). The SSIS rating forms include cross-informant tools use by teachers, parents, children, and adolescents. The number of SSIS items range from 34 to 57, depending on the specific rating form and age level being assessed. Items are rated on a 3-point scale, ranging from 0 = never to 2 = very often. The SSIS consists of three measurement areas or domains: social competence (the main focus of the system, including five subscales), problem behavior (including three subscales), and academic competence. Raw scores are converted to standard scores, percentile ranks, and behavior levels, using either the standard paper-and-pencil hand-scoring system or with optional computer-assisted scoring software. The SSIS/SSRS has garnered more published research studies than any of the other assessments reviewed in this chapter, and it has strong technical properties. It is a very good choice as a screening, assessment, or outcome measure for users who want to focus primarily on the social skills and problem behavior area within a comprehensive cross-informant assessment system that is linked to intervention.

Another assessment system to consider for social skills or social competence is either the School Social Behavior Scales, 2nd Edition (SSBS-2; Merrell, 2002a) or the Home and Community Social Behavior Scales (HCSBS; Merrell, 2002b). The SSBS-2 is a social competence and antisocial behavior rating tool for use by teachers, normed and standardized for use in social behavior ratings of students in grades K–12. The HCSBS is a similar measure for use by parents of children and adolescents ages 5–18. Both scales contain 64 items—a 32-item social competence scale, and a 32-item antisocial behavior scale, each with three to four subscales and a total score. The social competence/antisocial behavior content focus of the system is unique in that its focus is exclusively on social and antisocial behavior, eschewing other types of competencies and problem behaviors to pinpoint nuances of peer social interactions (both positive and negative), social strengths, and social deficit patterns among children and adolescents. Raw scores are converted to subscale and total scores using a simple hand-scoring key that is embedded into the rating forms and converts raw scores to standard scores, percentile ranks, and social functioning levels. These scales have an extensive published research base, strong technical properties, large normative samples, and a very practical focus for users. They are both very good choices for use in screening, assessment, and outcome measurement in situations where the focus is on both positive and negative peer interactions and other forms of social behavior.

In summary, the seven assessments or assessment system that are briefly overviewed in this section provide a wide range of choices for professionals who are interested in assessing social–emotional competencies of children and youth. Each system or tool is somewhat unique, having distinct focus areas or purposes, but all have at least an adequate level of technical properties and practical advantages for which they are recommended. Table 7.1 includes a quick reference for the five social–emotional competency measures, including a brief description of the instruments, their intended target and focus, and a link to the websites for ordering or learning more about them. Table 7.2 includes similar information for the two social skills/social competence assessment systems that were described. This listing of recommended assessment tools will provide you with an excellent starting point for selecting tools and systems to meet your particular assessment needs.

USING ASSESSMENT DATA TO SOLVE PROBLEMS

Now that we have taken a brief foray into assessment methods and some specific tools that are especially useful for evaluating students' SEL competencies, let's look at how you might use such information in your day-to-day work. A comprehensive guide to the nuances and technicalities of assessment is

> **Considering assessment as part of a problem-solving process will help you both focus on the big picture of assessment and answer the most important questions.**

beyond the scope of this book, so we necessarily focus in this section on a few of the key aspects of using assessment data to guide your decisions in providing educational and mental health services. For a more in-depth guide to behavioral, social, and emotional assessment of young people, we recommend that you become acquainted with the contents of one of the standard graduate-level textbooks in this area, such as *Behavioral, Social, and Emotional Assessment of Children and Adolescents* (Merrell, 2008b).

One of the premises of the Merrell (2008b) assessment text is that behavioral, social, and emotional assessment—including assessing SEL competences—may be best used within the context of a four-phase problem-solving process. By following this model, it is less likely that you will ignore the "big picture" of the purposes of assessment, and that regardless of your specific purpose for wanting to assess SEL competencies, you will focus

TABLE 7.1. Quick Reference for Five Recommended Assessment Tools or Systems Focusing on Social–Emotional Competencies

Name of instrument or system	Focus	Age or grade range	Components and items	Publisher and related websites
Behavioral and Emotional Rating Scale, 2nd Edition (BERS-2)	Social–emotional strengths and career interests	Ages 5–18	Teacher, parent, and student self-report forms; 52 items	*www.proedinc.com*
Developmental Assets Profile (DAP)	Developmental assets within eight categories	Ages 6–18	Student self-report forms only; 58 items	*www.search-institute. org*
Devereux Student Strengths Assessment (DESSA)	Comprehensive assessment of social–emotional competences	Grades K–8	Teacher and parent forms; 72 items	*www.kaplanco.com www.studentstrengths. org*
Bar-On Emotional Quotient Inventory— Youth Version (EQI-YV)	Social–emotional strengths and "emotional intelligence"	Ages 6–18	Student self-report form only; 60 items	*www.mhs.com*
Social–Emotional Assets and Resilience Scales (SEARS)	Comprehensive social–emotional competencies, assets, and resilience	Ages 5–18 and grades K–12	Teacher, parent, and student self-report forms; 52 to 54 items	*strongkids.uoregon. edu/SEARS.html*

TABLE 7.2. Quick Reference for Two Recommended Assessment Systems Focusing on Social Skills or Social Competence

Name of instrument or system	Focus	Age or grade range	Components and items	Publisher and related websites
Social Skills Improvement System (SSIS; formerly known as Social Skills Rating System)	Social–skills, problem behavior, academic competence	Preschool through grade 12; ages 3–18	Teacher, parent, and student self-report forms; 34 to 57 items	*www. pearsonassessments. com*
Social Behavior Scales (SSBS-2); Home and Community Social Behavior Scales (HCSBS)	Social competence and antisocial behavior	Grades K–12; ages 5–18	Teacher and parent report forms; 64 items	*www. brookespublishing. com www.assessment-intervention.com*

on your assessment information in a way that helps you answer the most important questions. These phases, which are detailed for easy reference in Table 7.3, are briefly described in this section, with an emphasis on how these stages or phases might be considered within the context of SEL. For a full discussion of this model, we refer you to Merrell (2008b).

Phase I: Identification and Clarification of the Problem

In the first phase, the essential task is to answer some basic questions that will lead to articulating in a clear manner why you wish to pursue assessment in the first place. To do so, it is important to identify who is the focus of your assessment and why you want to gather assessment data. Usually, your students—or a particular student—are the focus of your assessment, but the purposes of obtaining assessment information can be complicated. Sometimes the perceived problem or question you wish to address is straightforward, and other times it is anything but that. For example, are you interested only in assessing your students' social–emotional competencies related to SEL, or are you also going to need to focus on problem behavior? Do you need to focus only on student-level skills and characteristics, or are you interested in learning more about such issues as classroom climate and

---

TABLE 7.3. Four Phases of Assessment as a Problem-Solving Process

Phase I: Identification and clarification
- Who is your main concern? (Individual student? Entire class or school?)
- What is the problem you wish to address?
- What is the intended purpose of the assessment?

Phase II: Data collection
- What information is needed?
- What assessment methods, procedures, and tests will best provide this information?
- Which of the potential means of gathering information are most appropriate for your students and this situation?

Phase III: Analysis
- Does the assessment information confirm the problem or answer your question?
- What other information do the assessment data provide regarding your students?
- How can the assessment information be used to answer specific referral questions?
- What factors appear to contribute to the problem or concern?
- Is any missing assessment information needed to better address this situation? If so, how can it be obtained?

Phase IV: Solution and evaluation
- Based on all the available information, what should be the targets for intervention?
- What appear to be the most appropriate types of intervention or programs?
- What resources are available to implement the intervention?
- Would it be useful to collect assessment data continuously during the intervention?
- Which means of assessment can be used to evaluate the effectiveness of the program or intervention?

---

peer relationship networks? It is possible that there will be more than one purpose for your assessment, such as diagnosing problems that may exist, evaluating the impact of an SEL program for purposes of accountability, or even to gather detailed data on individual students that may be used to develop an intervention plan or even to be used in determining eligibility for special services or programs.

Phase II: Data Collection

The second phase is where you gather assessment data. We recommend that you allow the purposes of the assessment and the characteristics of your students and the problems you are seeking to address guide the selection of assessment procedures and specific tools. Identify clearly what information is needed. Determine which assessment methods, procedures, and tools will best help you get the information you need. After you have made some decisions regarding what information is needed, consider carefully the specific nature of your students, the problems, and the particular situation to determine whether some means of information gathering may be more useful than others. For example, if you are more concerned about your students' peer relations skills and how well they accept each other socially, it would make more sense to select tools that will focus on these characteristics, rather than problem behavior rating scales or emotional intelligence measures. Ideally, you will be discussing these issues with your team, identifying the key problems you wish to target, determining the most feasible means of measuring the information (parent, teacher, or self-report), and aligning these goals with the rating tools that are available and fit within your budget.

Phase III: Analysis

In the third phase, you should analyze your assessment data in some detail. Some of the questions that may be most useful in guiding this process involve whether the data confirm the existence of a problem or skill deficit, identifying specific issues that may be contributing to the problems or deficits, and what, if any, further assessment data you may need. If additional information is needed, you need to consider whether it can be obtained without too much distraction from your main tasks, and if so, how you will go about doing that. Is additional information available from existing school records, or will it require new assessment? If new assessment is required, are there simple ways to obtain this information in a timely and cost-effective manner? Who will provide the information? These are the kinds of issues that need to be considered if you believe that additional information is needed but you have limited time and resources to generate that information.

Phase IV: Solution and Evaluation

Within this assessment as a problem-solving process model, the last step or phase is often the most difficult as you determine how to use the assessment information you have obtained to help you develop a solution to the problems you are concerned with or the questions you wish to answer. Ultimately, you may be interested in evaluating the effectiveness of the solution you develop, particularly if that solution involves selecting a specific SEL technique or program and delivering it to your students. Without formal assessment data that are closely linked to your needs, it will be very difficult to know or to show that what you did "worked." Ideally, the main targets for your interventions should be identified and selected first, based on all the information that you have gathered regarding your students' strengths, deficits, and problems. Second, identify the most appropriate types of interventions or programs for these targets, as well as any additional resources you may need for delivering the program. When an intervention is developed it is also advisable to consider how you might collect data on a continuous basis during the delivery of the intervention or SEL program, or whether this process is needed. For interventions targeted at individual students, continuous data collection may be essential for the success of the intervention, given that such information can help you determine whether you are on track. If you are focusing on an entire class or school for your SEL program, then continuous data collection may not be feasible, given the excessive time and effort it could require. In such instances, a simple pretest and posttest of your selected assessment tools may be sufficient to help you determine your success. Or if some classrooms are going to receive the SEL intervention and others are not, you might even consider trying a quasi-experimental design for your assessment, gathering data only at posttest (after the completion of the intervention) on *all* students, and then determining whether the assessment scores of the students who received the SEL intervention were meaningfully different from the scores of their peers who did not receive the intervention.

This simple model represents a practical, commonsense approach to assessment as a broad process for solving problems and answering questions. We encourage you to approach assessment of SEL competencies from a broad perspective, understanding that assessment is a means to a potentially valuable end, and not just another mandate for "testing" that may not have any direct impact on your day-to-day practice as a teacher or clinician.

USING THE THREE-TIERED MODEL FOR SCREENING AND ASSESSMENT

In Chapter 1, we extolled the virtues of the three-tiered prevention model that has become increasingly accepted in education and mental health settings. Also called the *triangle of support*, and sometimes referred to as by the generic label, "public health approach," this model of support has particular implications for how we might approach screening and assessment of skills and competencies that are integrally related to SEL. In this section we provide some practical guidance for making decisions with screening and assessment data in a manner that is consistent with the three-tiered model. First, let's clarify some terminology. *Screening* and *assessment* are terms that are sometimes used interchangeably. Although the actual mechanics of screening and assessment often look very similar—administering a self-report tool to your students, for example—there are some important differences in the purposes and aims for which screening and assessment are used (Merrell, 2008a, 2008b).

Screening involves the process of taking a larger group of students and narrowing it down to a smaller number of identified students based on some criteria or focus, whether it be mental health problems, social–emotional skills deficits, or disruptive behavior. Because screening is done with larger groups of students, and because it does not require precision, it is important to use screening tools and techniques that are brief, easy to administer, and directly connected to the construct of interest. Examples of screening procedures that have been used successfully in narrowing down a general population of students to a smaller group that may require additional attention because of their social–emotional problems or deficits include self-report tools, teacher rating scales, and teacher nomination procedures. Again, we emphasize that brevity of these tools is essential: It is not cost-effective or even feasible to ask a teacher to rate every student in the classroom using a 140-item behavior rating scale as a way to narrow down which students should be looked at more carefully regarding the potential for needing additional social–emotional supports. A very brief rating scale (10 to 15 items, for example), a standardized process for having teachers rank-order or prioritize the names from their class list on some criterion, or a very brief (10 to 15 items) student self-report scale for social and emotional skills may all serve this purpose more efficiently. With screening, it is acceptable to identify a few students who do not really have the concern in question (we call this a "false-positive" error), because those students will be easy enough to identify and move out of the screening group later. It is more important to make sure that your screening procedure does not miss students who really do meet your criteria of concern (we call this a "false-negative" error).

Assessment, on the other hand, may look like screening, but it tends to involve more of everything: more items, more instruments, more data points, and more complex processes for decision making. And whereas screening involves a broad process for narrowing down a larger group of students to a smaller group of interest, assessment focuses more on individuals or small groups. For example, a group of 4 students that has been screened from a classroom of 28 for the possibility of having significant social–emotional skill deficits might be good candidates for a few additional assessment procedures, to help determine whether they really meet the criteria in question. Another example involves referral of individual students who are already known to exhibit social–emotional skill deficits. There may be times when such a referral for further individualized assessment will be useful to help develop an appropriate (and customized) intervention plan for that student, or perhaps for helping to connect them to eligibility for needed individual services.

Take a look at Figure 7.1, which is a slight variation of Figure 1.2, with additional material to help clarify how the three-tiered model may guide screening and assessment decisions. Remember that the three tiers represent three levels of need: Tier 1 can be thought of as representing efforts that will help *all* students. More specifically, Tier 1 is often considered to represent the 80% of students in a typical school who *do not* demonstrate any significant concerns related to mental health problems or deficits in social–emotional competency. Thus a screening effort to identify students with potential deficits in social–emotional competence would initially involve all students in a classroom or group, but the screener would be used to quickly eliminate about 80% of the students. In our hypothetical classroom of 28 students, we would "screen in" about 6 students (or about 20% of the class) whose scores

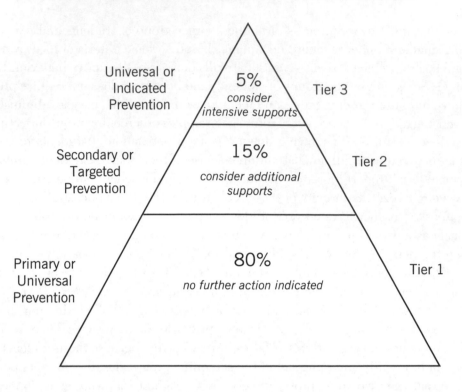

FIGURE 7.1. Another look at the three-tiered model of support for students with behavioral, social, and emotional problems.

indicate the highest levels of problems, or lowest levels of skills, and we would "screen out" the remaining 22 students (about 80% of the class).

As Figure 7.1 shows, Tier 2 represents about 15% of students in a typical school or class who have some concerns and for whom we should consider the possibility of additional supports. Given that our hypothetical screening process of 28 students resulted in the 20% cutoff giving us 6 students with the highest level of concern, we then need to look more carefully at these students to separate the Tier 2 and Tier 3 cases. Using the same logic as before, 15% of the 28 cases would give us about 4 students. In this case, our Tier 2 group would be the 4 students whose screening scores showed elevated concern compared with the 22 students who were "screened out." These students should be considered carefully, because their potential for risk may be elevated. Assuming the entire class is going to receive SEL instruction, it might make sense for these 4 students who are in Tier 2 to receive "a little more." Maybe some additional opportunities for practice and feedback of the skills they are learning would be useful. Perhaps some carefully engineered opportunities for them to play with or work with high-functioning students would be appropriate. In some cases, it might even be useful to supplement their general SEL instruction with some additional small-group instruction or skills training provided by the school counselor or school psychologist.

In our hypothetical class of 28, our Tier 3 or intensive needs students would be the 5% of the class that shows the greatest excesses in problem behaviors, or the greatest deficits in social–emotional competence. In this example, there are no more than two students who would fit our criteria. For a classroom teacher who knows his or her students well, there is often no surprise involved regarding which students fit into the intensive needs group—the teacher may have figured it out a long time ago. *But not always.* Students who have mental health concerns of the *internalizing* variety (depression, anxiety, social withdrawal, etc.) are not always on the radar of their teachers or other school personnel. A standardized screening process can help identify these students, assuming that the screening procedures or instruments reflect the right focus or content. Students who end up identified as Tier 3 cases generally require individualized intervention services of some kind. A comprehensive, individualized assessment (conducted by the school psychologist in most cases) may be useful to help better understand the needs of Tier 3 students and to help with intervention planning and possible service eligibility issues. In addition to the general SEL instruction that all students in the classroom receive and additional supports that Tier 2 students might receive, students who are accurately identified at the Tier 3 level often require intensive supports. Some examples of intensive additional supports that are consistent with our emphasis on SEL include "wrap-around" services that bridge the school and community, individualized social–emotional skills training, individual or small-group counseling, and the possibility of an individualized education plan.

In summary, the three-tiered model has a natural link to screening and assessment. The suggestions that we offered in this section will help you to make sense of screening and assessment information to make decisions that are consistent with the aims of this model and to plan for the needs of *all* of your students.

USING BRIEF ASSESSMENT DATA TO MONITOR INTERVENTION PROGRESS FOR INDIVIDUAL STUDENTS

Thus far in this chapter, we have provided a framework for assessing student competencies associated with SEL. Our discussion and examples have taken us through the basics of social–emotional assessment methods for children and adolescents, recommended assessment tools for assessing SEL competencies, a brief excursion into a sequenced model for using assessment data to solve problems and make decisions, and some examples of how to use screening and assessment data within the context of the increasingly popular three-tiered model of student support. Within these previous sections we focused primarily on using group-level data, such as screening students from entire classrooms or schools to identify possible Tier 2 and Tier 3 cases, and using a simple pretest and posttest design or a treatment group-control group design to see whether the use of SEL programming and interventions has resulted in meaningful gains for your students. Our discussion of using assessment data with individual students has focused primarily on hypothetical situations regarding how intensive needs students (Tier 3) may benefit from a carefully designed individual assessment. There is one more area of individually focused assessment that is essential to cover before we end this chapter: how to use brief and frequent assessment data to monitor intervention progress with individual students.

Because our focus in this volume has been primarily on using SEL as an instructional intervention with large numbers of students—groups, classrooms, schools, and entire school systems—we will not go into the details of how to plan, conduct, and evaluate individualized SEL interventions with single students. That area is worthy of coverage in its own right, and although the SEL movement has mainly focused on group applications within classrooms and systems, we think that there is no question that there will always be a need for individualized SEL interventions for Tier 3 intensive needs students. That topic, however, is not our focus in this volume, and we have space to include only limited content on use of assessment data with individual students in the remaining pages of this chapter. Our discussion and examples in this chapter will be very simple and straightforward. For those readers who are eager to learn more about methods of evaluating individualized educational interventions—especially using single-case designs—we recommend another book in The Guilford Practical Intervention in the Schools Series: *Evaluating Educational Interventions: Single-Case Design for Measuring Response to Intervention*, by Riley-Tilman and Burns (2009). Their book is a superb resource for using the tools of single-case design in evaluating the impact of educational interventions for individuals and small groups of students. Not only does it cover all the usual bases of single-case design in a very practical manner, but it does so by embedding the notion of response to intervention within its parameters. In addition, there are some excellent examples and tools, including clear instructions (and computer screen shots) for using the popular Excel software program to create and manage single-case graphs. We recommend this book highly!

Sticking with our focus on brief and frequent assessment data within busy classroom contexts to evaluate progress of individual students, we think it is possible to measure SEL competencies with the same general types of approaches that have been proven in the academic domain of skills (reading, writing, and arithmetic). According to Hosp, Hosp, and Howell (2007), some of the key elements that should be in place for this purpose include (1) continuous monitoring and frequent measurement, (2) an adequate sample of behavior of the key characteristics, (3) sampling those key characteristics as directly as possible, and (4) using data obtained through monitoring and measurement to ensure that the student is headed in the right direction. One of the challenges in following these guidelines in the social–emotional domain is that, as we have already indicated, the established measures we do have tend to focus more on problems than on competencies, and they tend to not be direct measures of behavior, but are more likely to measure how teachers and students *perceive* behavior. The former challenge we can do something about; the latter challenge is a work in progress, and we think that efforts

> **It is possible to measure SEL competencies using the same types of approaches that have been proven to be effective in the academic domain: 1. continuous monitoring and frequent measurement; 2. an adequate sample of behavior of the key characteristics; 3. sampling those characteristics as directly as possible; and 4. using data to ensure that students are headed in the right direction.**

to develop authentic and dynamic direct measures of social and emotional competence will be the focus of significant future research.

Earlier in this chapter—and in Tables 7.1 and 7.2—we detailed some recommended new assessment tools for measuring SEL competencies. Most of these tools require 10 to 15 (or more) minutes to complete and yet for frequent repeated measurement it is simply not feasible to use tools that require that much time. Rather, *very brief probes* are needed, tools that will make the process of monitoring progress of a student's SEL competencies similar to the use of brief oral reading fluency probes or math computation problems that have traditionally been used in curriculum-based measurement of academic skills. To solve this particular challenge, we suggest that you consider experimenting with small clusters of self-report or teacher rating scale items that are taken (or modified) from the tools are used for full-length initial screening or assessment of your students. Any of the tools presented in Tables 7.1 and 7.2 could serve this process, and, in fact, some of these tools actually include very brief short forms that are within our recommended upper limit (10 to 15 items) for frequent repeated measurement. Because SEL competencies are sometimes very individual in nature, we can't know in advance which specific items are going to be most sensitive for use with a target student in monitoring his or her response to an SEL intervention. This is an area where we clearly need more innovation.

An interesting and practical way to innovate with progress monitoring in this area is to carefully note the self-report and/or teacher rating items where the lowest level of competencies or highest level of deficits are shown, identify which of those characteristics are going to be most directly targeted in the SEL intervention that your group or classroom will receive, and then use that small number of items (again, we recommend no more than 10 to 15) as the basis for monitoring progress on a frequent basis (say, once a week) with the student(s) for whom you have the most concern. For example, let's assume that in your pretest of your classroom you used one of the self-report scales from Table 7.1, and it consisted of 50 or more items. Let's assume that you then identified for your student of concern the 12 items where the lowest levels of skill/greatest areas of deficit were noted. On a typical scale, the rating scale choices and subsequent scoring method for each item might be never = 0, sometimes = 1, often = 2, and very often = 3. Thus, you selected from the full assessment 12 items that you considered to be critical, and with each item having a maximum value of 3, you have an experimental scale that has a maximum value of 36. Assuming that your classwide SEL intervention targeted the skills reflected in those items, you now have the basis of a brief self-report for your target student to complete on a regular basis during the SEL programming (let's say once a week). You also have the basis for a 12-item teacher rating scale that you can use concurrently with the student-report progress monitoring tool, assuming you made appropriate adjustments in the item content (e.g., changing "Other kids invite me to play with them" from the student report to "Is invited by other students to play" on the teacher report). Thus you have constructed an experimental, individualized 12-item rating scale that is specific to the areas of greatest deficit of your student, based on those key items from the self-report where he or she rated "never" or "sometimes." Your measures can now be completed once per week by your student and by you. We think that completing such a probe would not require more than 2 or 3 minutes. The resulting scores can then be charted and plotted on a weekly basis. In this scenario, our progress monitoring of the effectiveness of your classwide SEL intervention for an intensive needs student is directly linked to the items you have created, and you now have a brief cross-informant (teacher and student) tool to gauge impact.

In Figure 7.2 we have provided an example—using a very simple A–B single-case intervention graph—of what the data from your experimental progress monitoring tools might look like, assuming these data were gathered in the context of an effective 12-week SEL program intervention designed to bolster the key skills related to your student's deficits in social–emotional assets, competencies, and resilience. Of course, our example shows an ideal positive outcome (we are optimists, and we also know that pedagogically speaking, it is important to start with a positive example!), and that you won't always have such positive outcomes. But our prior experience using such SEL curricula and simple measurement probes convinces us that outcomes such as are shown in Figure 7.2 are realistically attainable. We also think that the cross-informant aspect of our progress monitoring example (student report and teacher report) is a particularly salient aspect, because of issues relating to method variance and measurement error (see Merrell, 2008b), and because we realize that students who are at high risk may not always be the most accurate reporters of their own skills (see Merrell, 2008a).

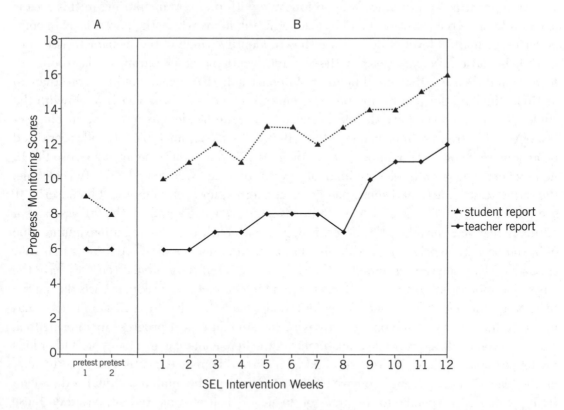

FIGURE 7.2. Sample progress-monitoring graph for brief student and teacher ratings of SEL competencies prior to and during intervention.

The type of experimental measurement we have advocated in this section is definitely worth a try. That said, we recognize that procedures like this are far from being perfected or considered a best practice at the present time. We offer this suggested procedure as a "big idea" and starting point for moving the field forward in an area where there has been almost no activity: applying the concepts of frequent and repeated measurement within a progress-monitoring and response-to-intervention approach to SEL competencies. In a related article (Levitt & Merrell, 2009) we have discussed in much more depth than in this chapter the possible technical and measurement problems that should be considered in such experimental approaches and recommended that practitioners and researchers who intrepidly follow our lead in this process be well grounded in their knowledge of measurement issues and the constructs (i.e., SEL competencies) they are monitoring. We encourage readers who want to learn more in this area to review the Levitt and Merrell article.

WRAPPING THINGS UP

By now we hope you have realized that assessment and evaluation activities can and should play an important role in your efforts to promote SEL in your school or agency. Although this area of assessment has not received the attention and resources that other aspects of behavioral or social–emotional assessment—and certainly not the attention that assessment of traditional academic skills has received—there is reason for optimism here. Not only are there some promising new strengths-based social and emotional assessment tools available for your use, tools that seem to have a very direct connection to SEL, but there also are some terrific emerging applications such as progress monitoring and response to intervention that appear to have great promise in the SEL realm. We have included reproducible Worksheet 7.1, "Social and Emotional Assessment Worksheet," as a practical tool you may wish to use in planning and summarizing your assessment data for individual students. This worksheet is built around the key premises of this chapter—that effective assessment should be linked to intervention, and that it is, in effect, a problem-solving process. Some of the key aspects of this chapter that we hope you remember include:

• Although schools are increasingly focused on assessment and evaluation activities, the bulk of the energy in this regard has been focused on the traditional academic domains, with relatively little (or next to nothing in most cases) focused on assessment of SEL competencies.

• The same essential reasons for assessing traditional academic competencies are also true for SEL competencies: Assessment forms the basis for identification of problems and solutions, and it is essential in determining effectiveness and accountability of programs we use.

• Within the realm of behavioral, social, and emotional assessment, several of the most widely used methods are simply not realistic, appropriate, or feasible when we focus them on the domain of SEL competencies.

• Our recommendation is that students' SEL competencies—at least at the present time and with the present available assessment tools—are best assessed using student self-report forms, teacher report forms, and parent report forms.

• Developments in strengths-based social–emotional assessment measures in recent years have great promise for use in SEL programming. We have overviewed several of what we think are the best of these measures.

• In many ways, assessment is best used when it is considered to be one part in an overall process for solving problems and making decisions. We have provided you with a straightforward four-phase model for using assessment to guide these processes.

• The increasingly popular three-tiered model of student supports in education—which was derived from earlier public health models—has particularly strong and useful implications for use in SEL programming in schools, including using screening and assessment data to make decisions regarding programming.

• Although most of our focus in this volume is on using SEL within schools, classrooms, and agencies—with groups of children and adolescents—there is also a need for understanding how to use SEL on an individual basis with your students who have the most intense needs. Our suggested experimental model of brief and frequently repeated SEL assessment probes offers an innovative way for you to determine whether your SEL intervention efforts are having the desired effect on individual students for whom you have particular concerns.

VIGNETTE: SEL Assessment in Action

Jaime, assistant principal and teacher at a small alternative high school of 200 students, needed no convincing regarding the potential benefits of SEL in his school. In fact, he had been an ardent advocate of SEL as not only a core part of the curriculum, but as the central curricular focus for a 30-day trial period that each potential new cohort of students went through to see whether they would meet the conditions (attendance, attitude, progress) required to be allowed to continue in the full alternative school program. Jaime knew that the SEL programming they were using was working very well and producing significant benefits for both the students and staff. There was no question that their students needed SEL. The student population at this alternative high school was mostly beyond being considered "at risk." These kids not only had the markers for potential negative outcomes, but most of them had already hit bottom. It was not unusual for students at this school to come to the 30-day trial or intake period directly from a substance abuse rehabilitation center, from juvenile detention centers, or after being expelled from regular high schools. Several of the students at the school were homeless, and many had serious family problems. In short, they needed every break and support they could get, and it was usually their experience—as well as the perception of all of the school staff, Jaime included—that the core SEL instruction they received for an hour each morning was providing a solid foundation for their success in school and in other aspects of their lives.

The problem Jaime faced was a skeptical school board and central administration. They demanded objective results and data to justify the relatively high cost of educating these students (the school purposely had a low ratio of students to faculty). Other than grades and graduation data, or anecdotal comments from successful program completers, *there were no data*. And the pressure mounted from the school board and central administration either to produce data that the extensive time spent in SEL was resulting in important gains or reduce SEL instruction to make room for more state-mandated courses. So Jaime spent part of his summer researching available tools for assessing SEL competencies. After selecting a tool that appeared to measure the constructs they were focusing on during their SEL intake process, and that had adequate technical properties, Jaime came up with a plan to assess the students as they went through the 30-day intake process, as well as students who were further along in the school program. Jaime's plan was a realistic and straightforward idea for assessment—not the kind of ivory-tower assessment plan that gets published in research journals—but it was just what the school needed, and it required a minimal outlay of time and resources. On the first day of the trial intake assessment period, each student completed a self-report measure. At the conclusion of the intake process, they completed the measure again, in a posttest fashion. Students at later points in the program were also assessed through both self-report and teacher ratings. There were six intake cohorts across the school year, each with about 25 students. With the help of a university researcher and graduate student who were interested in SEL, Jaime devised a schedule for scoring the measures, analyzing scores and running basic statistical tests, and then plotting the data.

After the first two cohorts of students, it was obvious that the subjective view of the teachers and students—that the SEL-focused intake process was making a meaningful difference—was supportable. In fact, the results exceeded initial expectations. By the end of the school year it was clear that not only were the students showing significant gains in SEL competencies—resilience, coping skills, problem-solving skills, emotion knowledge, peer relations—from pretest to posttest, but these gains were very large, even whopping in some instances. The same results were found with the students who were assessed at later stages in the program. Not only had they maintained the SEL competency gains assumed to be made in the intake process, they also were showing continual gains across their program, despite occasional setbacks. After analyzing the first year of data, Jaime presented it to the superintendent's team. These administrators, who were a data-savvy group, were most impressed. In fact, after they reviewed the data at some length and could find very little fault with it, they not only agreed to allow the alternative school to continue their intensive daily SEL programming for intake students, but they also made the presentation of these assessment results a priority and even a showcase at a school board meeting. More positives resulted from the dissemination of the data: favorable comments from a school board member, a general willingness to continue financial support of some programs that had previously been considered questionable, and some good public relations. Jaime was very pleased with the return on his investment in the assessments, and considered it one of the smartest moves he had made at the school.

Does this all sound too good a story to be true? Think again. Although we have changed the name of the vice principal/teacher and a few other details, this is a true story, and we were part of it. It was one of the most clear demonstrations we have ever seen of the positive benefits that can be attained from using even basic assessment procedures to evaluate the outcome of SEL programming. And if you do it right, using assessment to guide and evaluate your SEL programming can work for you, too.

Social and Emotional Assessment Worksheet

1. Student Information

Name: School:

Grade: Age:

Major concerns regarding student; reasons for assessment:

2. Summary of Assessment Information

Most important test scores, observations, and information from interviews or other assessment sources:

(cont.)

Social and Emotional Asessment Worksheet *(page 2 of 2)*

3. Problem Analysis

A. Major problems, concerns, diagnostic indicators, and so forth, that are indicated and supported by the assessment information.

B. Hypothesis regarding the possible origins and functions of any problems that are indicated. How might these hypotheses be tested?

4. Problem Solution and Evaluation

Potential interventions that appear to be appropriate for identified problems. Tools or methods that might be useful for monitoring intervention progress and evaluating the intervention outcome.

CHAPTER 8

Using Social and Emotional Learning within School Systems

Organizational Dynamics and Strategic Planning

INTRODUCTION AND OVERVIEW

This is just a guess, but we anticipate that many readers of this book, when they get to this final chapter, will take a look at the title and think "Why bother with organizational development and strategic planning? Can't I leave that stuff to someone else?" Or maybe, "What I'm really interested in are the interventions techniques and assessment tools from the other chapters. This systems and planning stuff is here if I need it, but I don't think I'll bother at this point." Are we right? Actually, we hope that we are wrong in our anticipation about how this chapter might initially be viewed by many readers, and that you are eager to dive into this important—no, essential—material. That said, our experience in promoting planning and system change strategies among a large number of educators and school-based mental health practitioners has taught us that we might need to convince many of you to soldier on and give this chapter a try. So for what it's worth, please consider the following plea: *This material is important*! Understanding organizational dynamics and strategic planning strategies will help you to maximize the effectiveness of SEL in your classrooms and schools. Still not convinced? We'll give it one more try: Our view is that if you master and utilize the information and strategies that we promote in this chapter you will be able to:

> **Understanding organizations and strategic planning processes is not just for administrators; it will help you to maximize the effectiveness of SEL in your classrooms and schools.**

- Get better SEL and academic results with your students in the long run.
- Maximize the gains that you make from using SEL.
- Convince administrators that investing in SEL is worthwhile.

- Encourage your colleagues to join you in promoting SEL among the students you serve.
- Put together a system of support that will help you and your colleagues in your efforts to promote mental health and academic success of your students.
- Make the case for allocating additional resources to promote SEL.

Are you convinced now? We hope so. Read on and you will find tools in this chapter to help you in the ways we have just described. We promise!

This chapter does not deal with the specifics of SEL intervention or assessment per se, as have the other chapters in this volume. Rather, it covers information that is critical to establishing a foundation for successful implementation and ongoing refinement of SEL in your school system. First, we overview the notion of schools or other agencies as dynamic and complex systems, borrowing key concepts from the organizational development literature, and considering the critical phases or steps that tend to be associated with enacting any organizational change, including SEL. Second, we focus considerable attention on some of the most important issues to consider in preparing for implementing or expanding SEL in your system. These are important strategic issues that are not necessarily connected directly to SEL, but will influence how well SEL is received and maintained in your school or agency. Five different aspects of strategic planning that are particularly important for efforts such as SEL are specifically overviewed, with practical suggestions for how to go about planning in each area. Finally, we present a case study vignette that describes the differences between two seemingly similar middle schools that attempted to undertake systemic efforts to include SEL in their curriculum, in which differing approaches were taken and strikingly disparate results were achieved.

SCHOOLS IN MOTION: UNDERSTANDING DYNAMIC SYSTEMS

In a related work, we (Merrell, Ervin, & Gimpel, 2006) included a chapter on facilitating systems and organizational change in schools, and noted that 21st-century American schools face challenges that were either unknown or were significantly less severe in previous eras. Among the key challenges we identified at this time include the following:

- *Technological advances*, including the need to incorporate these advances into schools and teach students to effectively navigate them, while simultaneously trying to combat some of the negative aspects of new technologies, such as increased access and exposure of students to media messages that promote negative and unhealthy behavior.
- *Changing dynamics of the American workforce*, including increasing economic and social pressures on families, increased competition from the globalization of the economy, immigration patterns, and increased cultural and linguistic diversity of individuals who comprise the workforce.
- *Increased heterogeneity of the student population*, including not only greater cultural and linguistic diversity of students, but also increased heterogeneity with respect to

their family constellations, socioeconomic stratification, neighborhood composition, and background experiences.

- *Expanding student needs*, as reflected by what seems like an ever-increasing percentage of students who are "at risk" in some way.
- *Increased demand for use of evidence-based practices and accountability* of schools (frequently from legislative mandates), often in the face of shrinking external supports and diminishing resources.

These are serious and complicated issues indeed. It's easy to look at the daunting reality of these challenges and feel overwhelmed by them, or think "It's just too hard; what's the use?" And yet, going back to our example at the beginning of Chapter 1, hope springs eternal, and when students arrive on that first day of school each year, there is always new hope. SEL can play an important role in helping schools and the students they serve to better navigate these types of challenges.

One of the primary reasons for highlighting some of these recent challenges is to illustrate the point that *schools are systems in motion*. Borrowing some language and concepts from the field of physics, schools can be considered *dynamic systems*, meaning they are in a constant state of adaptation to internal and external forces, power, and movement. When we think about schools in particular, the phrase *lasting change* is about as stark an oxymoron as there is. With respect to our school systems, change and adaptation is constant rather than lasting, and it will happen regardless of what we do or fail to do. Thus creating change in our systems through SEL or other innovative practices is not the foremost goal we should consider. Rather, it is better to think of what we can do to promote positive change and the healthy evolution of our school systems (see Grimes & Tilly, 1996, for a good discussion of this concept). Change, if anything, is a unifying feature of the challenges our schools face.

> **The term *lasting change* may be an oxymoron: Schools are dynamic systems, and change is a unifying feature of the challenges faced by our schools.**

When SEL efforts are introduced in schools that have not previously made it a major part of their system, there is not only the potential for positive change, but also some inevitable barriers and systems issues to consider if we are to go about implementing the program in an effective manner. We need to not only understand something about systems, but we also need to maximize the potential for SEL to produce the changes that we hope will occur.

The writings of organizational development experts such as Rummler and Brache (1995), give an interesting perspective on how to view the organizational change structure of schools. Traditional concepts of the structure of organizations tend to express a *vertical view*, meaning that the organization is considered to be hierarchical: top-down and neatly compartmentalized. This view of schools could be illustrated by the notion that the superintendent and school board run the school system, the principal runs the school, and each classroom teacher is compartmentalized neatly into a line of authority that runs directly to the principal, sometimes through a department chair or assistant principal. In reality, this view of schools as systems is simplistic and outdated; it does not help us to understand the complexity and richness of school environments as we attempt to implement SEL or related educational innovations. Thus the *horizontal view* of organizations is an interesting alternative. Although the principal is clearly the chief administrator and leader of a school, the horizontal view accepts that information, influence, and ideas run horizontally, meaning that individual classroom teachers can influence other teachers, and that specialists such as counselors, psychologists, and social workers can likewise influence teachers and be influenced by them. This perspective is particularly valuable when considering how we might go about introducing SEL in a school, or how we might expand its influence if it already exists on a limited scale. Although the principal will be critical to such efforts, his or her influence will not be sufficient by itself for this challenge. Thus relationships and communications among teachers and specialists—horizontal relationships, if you will—must be considered. In fact, there are individuals outside of the immediate school setting but who are important stakeholders in the system who must also be considered if we want to really make the best impact. More discussion of how to go about this process carefully is presented later in the chapter.

A final comment on schools as dynamic systems is that when an organization goes through a planned change that is intended to be beneficial (such as adopting or expanding SEL), there are some distinct phases of change that tend to occur. We need to be aware of these phases, and to plan specifically for them as we go about promoting SEL and other positive practices in schools. According to Adelman and Taylor (1997)—experts and leaders in the school mental health movement—the four critical stages of effective systems change (see Figure 8.1) are as follows:

1. *Creating readiness.* This first phase involves creating a culture or environment that is receptive to or ready for change. The development of *vision* is essential in this process, as is effective *leadership* (both formal and informal). Sufficient time needs to be set aside to create readiness for change, so that the individuals within the system (teachers, specialists, administrators, etc.) are invested in and prepared for it and don't see the change as being "foisted" upon them. Creating a formal or informal leadership team or planning group to help create buy-in and to help establish cultural readiness may be a helpful tool in this process.

2. *Initial implementation.* When SEL or any other new educational effort is finally started within a school, expect some bumps at first. During initial implementation it helps greatly to have individuals with some experience and expertise designated as *coaches or mentors* for those who may need additional support. During this phase it is often helpful to implement some ongoing or *formative assessment and evaluation* processes so that data can be collected to determine initial effectiveness and to guide modifications that may be necessary at this point.

3. *Institutionalization.* If including new SEL efforts in a school is going to be something that has a lasting impact, then the institution or system must have ownership of the innovation or program. If staff members from an external agency such as university or mental health center come into a school and deliver SEL without the school buying into and

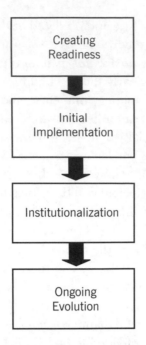

FIGURE 8.1. Four phases of systems and organizational change. Adapted from Adelman and Taylor (1997).

institutionalizing the new SEL process, you can be assured that the new program will wither away and eventually disappear after there are personnel changes or "the grant runs out." To make SEL part of the fabric of the school rather than a short-term experiment, we must facilitate a broad base of support and investment within the system.

4. *Ongoing evolution.* After an innovation or change has become part of a system—assuming the previous three phases were carefully considered and implemented—it is normal to expect that there will be continued evolution. Our experience has been that some teachers and administrators who are initially enthusiastic about implementing SEL in their school may grow weary of the ongoing demands, or may simply run out of steam. In addition, over time, even someone who continues to be enthusiastic about SEL may start to depart from the appropriate procedures for doing it, getting sloppy in the process. As a result, enthusiasm may diminish and the fidelity of implementation of the SEL program may decline. One way to avoid these negative outcomes after SEL has been planned, implemented, and institutionalized is to *conduct ongoing evaluation.* As we covered in detail in Chapter 7, assessment and evaluation data can not only steer you in the right direction if things are getting off course, but can also serve as a powerful motivator when they demonstrate positive results. In addition, consider the need for ongoing professional development and training and the possibility of ongoing refinements in the SEL implementation process as ways to keep SEL fresh, interesting, and rewarding for those who are charged with delivering it.

STRATEGIC PLANNING ISSUES

In Chapter 2, we discussed the process of selecting an SEL program. In doing so, we also tried to make the case for adopting SEL materials and using them with your students in a thoughtful manner. In this section we go a little further in this general direction of strategic planning and preparation for using SEL, building on what we have covered regarding systems and organizational change theory, and pointing out what we think are some of the most important issues to consider in your planning; with suggestions for how you might consider going about your advance preparations in a manner that will help lead to success. Of course, it is entirely possible to jump right into using SEL in your classroom or your clinic without putting too much advance thought into it. If you select good materials and use them as prescribed with your best teaching and clinical skills, you will probably make some positive gains with your students, even without the advance planning and preparation that we are promoting in this section. You might even make strong and relatively durable gains. That said, we think that putting time and effort into strategic planning and preparation will really pay off and will help you to make even stronger and longer lasting gains with your students. Attending to these types of issues up front is like putting money in the bank at a good and guaranteed interest rate: The dividends will accumulate in the long run, and you will maximize your impact.

In writing about successful implementation of SEL, Brandt (1999) noted that "when instruction is incidental rather than deliberate, it is difficult to determine the effects on students" (p. 178). In other words, when we engage in a planful process for teaching children and adolescents, we are better able to determine the impact of our instructional efforts. Furthermore, in discussing how to make SEL instruction more deliberate, Brandt noted several problem areas that tend to diminish the effectiveness and overall impact when SEL instruction is not carefully planned, and proposed that successful implementation is more likely to occur when the following elements are in place: *administrative support, time in the schedule, professional development,* and *teacher and parent approval.* We agree with Brandt's assertion. It has been our experience that well-intentioned efforts to incorporate SEL strategies and programs may be undermined if these four areas are not considered in the planning process. In this vein, we offer some suggestions across these four areas (with the addition of a related fifth area that we think is an important modification) that may help you avoid the pitfalls that are so often present when such planning efforts are not taken into consideration prior to SEL implementation. Figure 8.2 provides a visual reminder of what we think are the key strategic planning areas to consider prior to actually implementing SEL on any scale larger than a single group of students or classroom, and which are valuable for even individual classroom adoptions. These five planning elements are discussed as follows.

> **"When instruction is incidental rather than deliberate, it is difficult to determine the effects on students"** (Brandt, 1999).

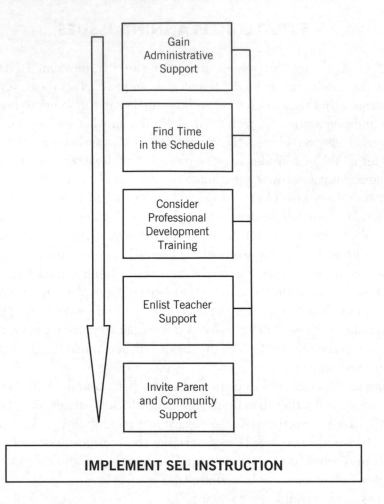

FIGURE 8.2. Recommended steps of strategic planning for implementing SEL in schools.

Gaining Administrative Support

Although teachers generally have a great deal of leeway in how they plan and deliver instruction—and the same is true for school-based mental health practitioners in determining how they deliver assessment intervention services—we suggest that obtaining "official" support from your administrator or supervisor as you undertake SEL efforts is a critically important step. At the school building level, the key person to get in your corner in this regard is the principal. Like the old saying goes, "the principal is your pal." At least he or she ideally *should be* your pal in these efforts. The principal is generally the most important person in setting the tone for the school. His or her support of your efforts may be absolutely essential if you are going to be successful and sustain your success. Principals are not only in a position to approve logistical and resource support of your efforts, but they also may be key in communicating the importance of SEL across the school, not just in individual classrooms. Principals who are engaged in and committed to SEL in their schools are in a position of great influence in this regard. Not only can they promote the aims of SEL in their day-to-day communications with school staff and students, but they also may be able to arrange professional development training, and help influence the school's leadership team or student assistance team to make SEL a high priority. Some of the ways you might try to positively enagage school principals in SEL include:

> Like old saying goes, *the principal is your pal.* At least he or she ideally *should be* your pal in promoting SEL in your school, if you want to do it well. The principal's efforts may be absolutely essential if you are going to be successful and sustain your success.

- Tell the principal why you are interested in SEL.
- Emphasize the benefits that your students may receive from SEL in the school.
- Especially, emphasize the link between SEL and academic success (see Chapter 4 for more details in this regard, as well as the excellent book edited by Zins, Weissberg, Wang, & Wahlberg, 2004).
- Show her some sample SEL materials.
- Invite him to visit your classroom when you are planning to infuse SEL into your teaching curriculum, or when you are intending to teach from a specific SEL program.
- Offer to discuss SEL at a faculty meeting.
- Suggest that you invite a local or regional expert on SEL to a faculty meeting— someone who is experienced in delivering SEL and who can speak with experience and authority on the benefits and practical challenges.

In summary, we think that the principal can be the strong link in your chain of success with SEL, and we encourage you to make your best efforts to enlist his or her support in your efforts.

If you are already in a leadership position within your school, we advise that you also consider enlisting the support of administrators at the district level, such as superintendents, assistant superintendents, and curriculum coordinators. In commenting on the importance of obtaining district-level support for SEL, Pasi (2001) stated, "A schoolwide program in social and emotional learning will require district resources in the same way it will require the active support and involvement of administrative staff within the school itself" (p. 37). This notion is especially true today as compared to earlier eras in education, because there is increased pressure these days on district- or system-level leaders for being accountable for student results. Because we are in an era when there is frequent turnover nationally among district-level school leaders (especially superintendents), it is especially critical that system-level leaders be consulted about SEL efforts, because new leaders may have different priorities than the old leadership team. Not only are system-level leaders in a position to promote the successful SEL efforts from one school on a larger scale, they are also often in critical positions for making resource allocation decisions. Our experience has been that, increasingly, system-level school leaders like superintendents and assistant superintendents are *attuned to data.* Thus when you consult with them regarding your SEL interest and efforts, it may be particularly important to provide them with evidence—the cold, hard facts (data)—regarding the effectiveness of SEL in producing important student outcomes. Chapter 7 provided a template for conducting SEL assessment and evaluation efforts to improve your efforts, and we encourage you to seriously consider those suggestions. Pointing out how SEL efforts help support district goals is also particularly important with system-level leaders, who need to consider SEL and any other area of emphasis within the larger context of many competing activities and limited resources.

Counselors, psychologists, social workers, and other school-based practitioners often have supervisors with responsibilities at the district or regional level, such as directors of student support services, special education coordinators, and pupil personnel services directors. These types of administrative leaders generally support the notion of SEL services and activities in schools. They may be important allies in the process of gaining administrative support for SEL. However, gaining their support seldom comes with an understanding that there will be a commensurate reduction in a practitioner's other responsibilities in order to make room for the new SEL responsibilities, particularly in the initial stages of adopting a program. It is generally very important to demonstrate to these types of supervisors how SEL supports existing efforts and may contribute to improved student outcomes. Again, consider the importance of data in making your case to a supervisor. Fortunately, there is a large body of general evidence in support of SEL, as we have seen in previous chapters. Using the information from this chapter to develop a plan for gathering program evaluation or student outcome data on SEL efforts may be a very important aspect of obtaining support from supervisors of mental health practitioners and other specialists.

Finally, consider that some leaders whose support may be crucial in your efforts to adopt and implement SEL are not administrators or formal leaders within the traditional vertical organizational flow chart. Some teachers or specialists are "opinion leaders" within their schools or within a system because of their influence and the respect they are accorded by their colleagues. It is usually easy to figure out who these people are. Whose views seem to be particularly influential with fellow teachers or with the principal? Who is the "go-to" person when there is a particular challenge that needs attention or a particular effort that needs to be launched? Who does the principal seem to especially listen to when there are difficult challenges to consider? The answers to these questions generally will lead you to the opinion leaders whom you may wish to informally consult in your efforts to adopt and implement SEL. Enlisting their interest and support may yield surprising positive results, particularly if they become personally engaged and invested in SEL efforts with their own students.

Finding Time in the Schedule

One of the most significant benefits of obtaining administrative support for SEL is that such support is probably critical if you are going to successfully navigate one of the underlying pragmatic challenges: finding time in the schedule for SEL instruction. Although, as we have already noted, teachers often have some leeway in how they approach their instructional tasks, they seldom have much flexibility in determining the overall curriculum and in deciding how to allocate time to various required components of the curriculum.

On the contrary, those decisions are often "top-down" matters, determined by school administrators, school boards, and state or even federal education policies. When we carried out the field testing trials for refining and validating the Strong Kids SEL programs, the reality of this situation was reinforced to us a great many times. It was not at all difficult to find teachers and practitioners who were enthusiastic about using SEL in schools. In fact, we often had more interest than we could adequately support. What proved to be a more significant barrier was figuring out *when* the programs would be implemented, and in many cases we had to make concessions in the research design and overall plan (shortening the length of lessons, combining lessons, skipping weeks, etc.) in order to work with teachers who were under great pressure to cover a large amount of required curriculum material within specified time parameters due to increasing state and federal accountability pressures on schools. Although we generally laud the aims of such efforts (and the emphasis on results and data), there are indeed costs to consider in terms of the difficulty in finding room and time for using prevention-oriented programming such as SEL.

As an example of this challenge, consider our efforts to conduct Strong Kids field trials at the high school level. We originally thought (and still do think) that ninth-grade health classes were an ideal venue—near perfect, really—for promoting SEL through the Strong Teens version of Strong Kids. The fact that SEL instruction would reach all students (these classes are required of all high school freshmen in most states), and that it would reach them at a relatively young and still somewhat malleable age—14 to 15 years—was compelling enough. Add to this rationale the fact that most states require some type of mental health component in their high school health curricula, and it seemed like a perfect marriage. However, making SEL happen in practice proved to be a great challenge. We sat through numerous meetings with health education department heads and assistant principals where they were immediately enthusiastic about SEL and our particular approach to it at the high school level. Then, after they told us how much they liked our program and our idea for a partnership, they tended to let us know what the parameters of their state and district-mandated curriculum goals included. By the time the mandated programs and particular content areas were accommodated (everything ranging from sexuality education to substance abuse information to nutritional counseling and obesity prevention), it was often very difficult (and sometimes impossible) to fit in a programmed and structured approach to SEL—Strong Teens or anything else.

Thus finding time in the schedule for SEL is often more than just a matter of teacher preference and planning. The active involvement and support of key administrators in finding ways to include SEL in the curriculum is indeed a critical consideration that you should not overlook. Although SEL instruction may eventually become part of the mandated educational curriculum (such as in the state of Illinois), this scenario is far from the norm. Planning for SEL that includes the active involvement of school administrators is much more likely to result in sustainable implementation than "go it alone" approaches.

Another way to consider how to embed SEL in the schedule is to infuse SEL instruction with other mandated topics to which it is naturally complementary. At the elementary level, we have often seen teachers successfully link SEL instruction to literacy instruction, particularly with the use of SEL materials that introduce new vocabulary words to students, and provide opportunities for reading and writing through carefully linked activities. At the middle school level, we have found that the language arts–social studies block classes are often an excellent place to include SEL instruction, and that the right SEL curriculum materials can enhance the aims of these classes. And don't forget our examples from Chapter 4 regarding how SEL can be infused across the entire curriculum to promote academic achievement. Even science and mathematics instruction can be linked to SEL activities in a potentially effective way (e.g., Elias, 2004; McCombs, 2004). But in using the *infusion* approach to SEL (where selected SEL activities and curriculum goals rather than an established formal curriculum are included with other academic subjects), it is important to understand that it will need to be done very carefully and methodically, or there is a risk that SEL will be eventually ignored and ultimately abandoned. As Brandt (1999) noted, "If SEL instruction it to be integrated with other classes, what will be done to make sure it is actually done rather than being squeezed out by competing demands?" (p. 179).

Considering Professional Development Training

Obtaining support for and finding time to implement SEL instruction are essential steps, but they don't necessarily ensure success. Even with those important issues covered, it is still possible for SEL programming to derail if other strategic planning issues are not anticipated, for example, the role of professional development for those teachers, administrators, and school-based mental health practitioners who will be actually delivering the curriculum.

Although most teacher contracts and school schedules stipulate that there will be a minimum number of hours or days per year devoted to staff professional development training, it is very difficult to gauge the impact of such efforts or the consistency with which they are carried out. There seems to be a general consensus that teachers tend to receive very little formal on-the-job training, and that the burden for mastering new materials or teaching techniques is generally placed directly on individual teachers. Given that the success of SEL efforts will be directly linked to how well a teacher or practitioner implements the curriculum or delivers the SEL activities in the classroom, the area of professional development prior to implementation should be carefully considered and built into the overall plan. It would be an ironic waste of time and resources if most of the pieces of SEL instruction were carefully planned and organized, only to have the outcomes with students be less than desired because those charged with the important responsibility of implementing the program did not receive adequate prior training or appropriate ongoing professional development support.

Packaged SEL programs vary greatly in their overall demands and requirements for training and professional development prior to effective use. On one end of the continuum, the Strong Kids programs are an example of an SEL curricula that was intentionally designed to require very little formal training and development prior to teacher-practitioner implementation. We designed the curriculum materials intentionally this way, because of our concern that teachers and practitioners may not have access to the resources required for extensive prior training, and because of our view that it should be relatively straightforward to achieve high levels of implementation integrity or fidelity in SEL. Our subsequent research validated our aim and goals, showing that even with as little professional develop-ment as a brief orientation meeting and prior reading of the lesson manual, teachers were able to achieve very high levels of treatment fidelity, and the curricula produced very strong social validity outcomes as well as positive student cognitive and behavioral outcomes (see Merrell & Gueldner, in press; Merrell, Gueldner, & Tran, 2008; Merrell, Levitt, & Gueld-ner, 2010; and Tran & Merrell, 2008, for reviews of the Strong Kids outcome research).

On the other hand, some packaged SEL programs are very complicated and expansive, and it is simply not feasible to expect teachers to be able to use them effectively and with high levels of adherence without extensive prior professional development training. Some packaged programs, such as Second Step and the PATHS curriculum, are of sufficient com-plexity and length to require specific training from qualified or certified experts, either on site at the school or at special training institutes prior to teacher or practitioner implemen-tation. If one of these types of more complex and thorough SEL programs are to be used, then it is especially important that the strategic planning process include time, materials, and financial resources for appropriate training and support of those professionals who will be delivering the programs.

Both approaches—the simple and straightforward SEL programs that require minimal prior training and the more extensive and complex SEL programs that require extensive prior training—have their place. It is not a matter of one approach being better than the other. The key issue to consider is what are the needs of the students and the demands and resources of the educational system, and which type of SEL instruction best fits within those parameters. In either case, prior and ongoing professional development training should be a carefully considered part of strategic planning, and not an afterthought.

Enlisting Teacher Support

We previously noted the importance of seeking out and soliciting support from "opinion leaders," that is, teachers or other school staff who are not in formal administrative leader-ship positions, but who have a great deal of influence among their peers in how new initia-tives will be accepted. Clearly, obtaining the input and support of such key staff members is important. We also wish to add that *rank-and-file educators*—the majority of teachers and professional staff members—should not be ignored in the strategic planning process. Although teachers may have little say in whether or how "top-down" mandates for curricu-lum programming are given to them, their acceptance of such initiatives is crucial to the overall success of such efforts. A case in point is the trajectory of the No Child Left Behind (NCLB) legislation, one of the most sweeping federal education reform efforts ever initi-ated. NCLB was the hallmark initial legislative victory for President George W. Bush, the first major effort that his administration was able to get through Congress—with bipartisan support—in the early days of his first term. Although key education leaders and agencies were consulted during the development of NCLB, there was very little, if any, input from frontline teachers in this process. After NCLB became law and schools began to learn how they needed to respond to the new legislation, it was apparent that many teachers were now expected to spend considerable time and effort preparing their students for the standard-ized educational achievement tests that would be used as benchmarks against which the school's success or failure would be judged. Although many teachers went along with the mandate for increased assessment and accountability, soon there was increased dissension from teachers who believed that the focus on standardized assessment and other accountability processes, hindered their ability to best serve their students. Grassroots opposition and backlash ensued, and reached the point where some states considered opting out of NCLB altogether (see Shelly, 2008). In subsequent revisions to this law, the focus on standardized assessment may likely be reconsidered and perhaps revised, in great measure because of the strong criticism from rank-and-file teachers that emerged over time.

Likewise, an enthusiastic teacher, principal, or superintendent who wishes to have SEL programming made part of the fabric of a school's general curriculum would be wise to involve teachers in the planning and preparation process. Taking into account and responding to the concerns and positive suggestions of teachers for creating an SEL plan that will actually be received with a measure of enthusiasm is an important endeavor. We suggest that at the individual school level, such efforts should include informal collegial discussions with teachers, invitations to observe SEL programming in action, offers to co-teach SEL modules or activities in their classrooms, informal discussions of SEL in the staff room, and formal discussions of SEL in staff meetings. At the systemwide level of influence, we suggest that including representative teachers on key committees to plan SEL is a critical step, as is consulting with representative individual teachers on the quality and feasibility of particular programs. This type of teacher involvement should be *genuine and reciprocal*, taking into account teachers' views on doing things differently as well as trying to enlist their support for SEL.

Inviting Parent and Community Support

A final issue to consider briefly in terms of strategic planning is whether and how to enlist the support of parents and other community members when new efforts to include SEL in classrooms and schools are being considered. This issue is complicated, because it is largely dependent on the composition and collective worldviews of individual communities and parent groups. For some teachers, clinicians, and schools, making specific efforts to invite parent and community support will not be a critical issue (although it is still advised), because their particular constituency is entirely or mostly supportive of the types of activities and goals that SEL involves. This situation has actually been our experience in many—and perhaps most—cases in which we have worked with school personnel to embed SEL assessment and intervention efforts into classroom or school routines. In such cases, it may not be necessary to exert the time and effort required to conduct a formal enlistment of support from parents and community members. That said, it is still advisable to communicate with parents and PTSO leaders regarding what will be happening when new SEL initiatives are undertaken, and in particular, how such efforts may benefit students. We have found that such simple home–school communications

> **Because SEL has much to offer in supporting the academic and mental health of students, we believe that simply getting the word out in a constructive and positive way will do a great deal to alleviate most concerns.**

have often resulted in a more interested and receptive climate for reinforcing and practicing newly learned SEL skills at home. These efforts are also a wonderful opportunity to reach out to caregivers who would otherwise be uncertain or timid about approaching the school and become actively involved, even though they are highly interested in and care deeply about their student's education.

On the other hand, there are communities in which inviting and obtaining parent support for SEL efforts—as well as the support of key constituencies in the community—may be important, even essential to the success of SEL. Our experience has been that parents and community leaders who might be described as "traditionalists" are in some cases suspicious of or even hostile to many efforts to include mental health programming or other types of educational programming that go beyond basic academics and citizenship training. They may see it is an unnecessary frill, something that detracts from more important matters, or even something that is subversive. Although such situations are probably not the norm, they exist in high enough numbers and with a strong enough outlook that they should definitely not be dismissed. As an example of this sort of SEL-resistant worldview, consider the experience that one us (K. W. M.) recently had in conducting a full-day training on SEL in schools for community mental health counselors and child development specialists who worked for a county mental health department in a very rural and conservative community. Although the participants in this training were very positive toward the idea of using SEL within their partner schools and eager to give it a try, it was clear that there was an underlying concern and tension regarding how such efforts might be received in some of their communities. During the discussion portion of the training, several participants noted their experiences with being on the receiving end of stiff resistance to mental health promotion and primary prevention activities from some parents who were members of conservative or fundamentalist churches that taught that such efforts were secular humanist attempts to undermine religion and exert inappropriate controls over the spiritual and mental functioning of their children. In some cases, ministers of these churches were actively teaching their congregants to resist such efforts. In other cases, the resistance did not come from religious fundamentalists, but from individuals or secular groups that were extremely conservative or libertarian, and viewed efforts to promote education outside of the basics as being unnecessarily intrusive efforts by the state, which would ultimately reduce the self-reliance of their children.

So what can be done in cases of organized resistance to SEL from parents or community leaders? Although we think that such instances will be relatively rare or nonexistent in the vast majority of schools, we do have some suggestions for overcoming resistance and building greater trust. First, consider the necessity of engaging your students' parents and other constituencies when you undertake new educational initiatives. Speaking of this type of resistance, Brandt (1999) noted that "public understanding and support will continue to erode unless schools establish a much higher level of public engagement than in the past" (p. 181). Some specific suggestions for overcoming the most challenging forms of resistance include holding parent meetings or other public meetings to explain the aims and strategies of SEL, and in some cases where it seems warranted, to consider creating a planning committee or task force that includes parents and other key community members, particularly individuals who are in the influential "opinion leader" position with other parents and community members. And in our view, simply communicating with your students' parents—frequently, clearly, and positively—will serve as a powerful means of preventing misinformation and mistrust, and promoting acceptance of SEL. Because SEL has so much to offer and can do so much to support the academic and mental health of students, we believe that simply getting the word out in a constructive and positive way will do a great deal to alleviate most concerns.

WRAPPING THINGS UP

This final chapter has dealt with some of the "big ideas" behind successful implementing of SEL in schools: understanding systems and how they change and evolve, and what types of issues you should consider as you strategically plan for implementing or expanding SEL in your particular system. These issues are often not considered essential by practitioners, but they are important. Taking the extra time to think about how to plan and prepare for SEL in your particular classroom, school, or system has the potential to maximize your effectiveness and pay valuable dividends in other words. Some of the critical issues to consider in this regard include:

• American schools of the 21st century are facing unprecedented pressures and demands, which in turn make SEL more important than ever but also can make it challenging to implement.

• Schools are dynamic and constantly evolving systems that sometimes have a great deal of complexity.

• Schools, like most organizations, go through certain predictable phases of change when innovations are implemented. The four stages of organizational or systems change discussed in this chapter as relevant to SEL include creating readiness, initial implementation, institutionalization, and ongoing evolution.

• Although it is possible to deliver SEL with success in your school or agency without giving too much thought to strategic planning, you are likely to get much better results if you attend to some critical planning issues, including gaining administrative support, finding time for SEL in the schedule, considering professional development training for those who will be involved in SEL, enlisting teacher support for SEL efforts, and inviting parent and community support.

VIGNETTE: A Tale of Two Schools

The experiences of two principals who established SEL programs in their respective schools illustrate the benefits of considering strategic planning and systems issues to enhance the impact of SEL. This vignette is based on an actual set of circumstances, but the names have been changed and certain other embellishments added for purposes of illustration.

The assistant superintendent and the director of student support services for the Mill Valley School District, with input from state department of education officials, agreed that their district should enhance their primary prevention and mental health promotion efforts at the district's eight middle schools. This was not to be a "top-down" approach where a particular program or plan was adopted for use districtwide. Rather, principals of the middle schools were given the directive to work with their staffs to devise a plan that made sense for their particular schools. They were given up to 18 months to develop and phase in a plan, and were to report back to the assistant superintendent annually on the impact of their efforts. A small grant from the state department of education and a local foundation made it possible for each school to have a moderate budget for the initiation and initial implementation of the effort, and the principals were given broad discretion in how they could spend the funds.

Two of the middle school principals were close colleagues who had taught in the same school together a decade earlier, and had completed master's degree programs together at the same university. They decided to go together to a national conference on mental health interventions for middle school students to survey ideas for possible programs and techniques to include as part of their school plans. Courtney, principal of Fox River Middle School, invited Pat, the school counselor at Fox River, to accompany them to the conference, whereas Taylor, principal of Central Middle School did not include another school staff member, thinking that other staff would be invited to provide their input after the meeting, to save funds that could be used to purchase of additional curriculum materials or training.

The conference had numerous breakout sessions on adolescent mental health, including several specifically on SEL strategies and programs. In addition, the conference had a large exhibit hall where many curriculum publishers and other vendors promoted their products. Courtney and Pat attended a few conference sessions together, and Taylor was at several of these sessions as well. The Fox River duo very quickly was impressed with a particular packaged SEL program that offered many advantages, was easy to implement, and fit within the budget. They immediately began to focus on this program, not only attending a session on its use, but spending a fair amount of time meeting with the publisher of the program in the exhibit hall. By the end of the conference they had determined this program was ideal for their school, and they made arrangements for an order for each of their teachers who had first-period block classes. They also made arrangements for a consultant from the publishing company to come to their school later that year to do a staff training. Taylor did not reach a decision so quickly, attending several sessions and meeting with some publishers, but mainly gathering information and making a list of several programs that might be good choices.

When the conference goers returned home and got back into their regular routines, they took differing approaches to moving forward with their schools' programs. Courtney called a meeting for the Fox River staff and let them know what had been decided, and when the training would occur. Taylor, on the other hand talked to the Central School staff about their mandate at the next faculty meeting, shared some basic information, and then established a workgroup of selected personnel—three teachers, the counselor, and the school psychologist—to work with leadership and staff to develop a plan.

By the end of that school year, Fox River staff had completed training and each of the first-period block teachers had implemented the SEL program for 11 weeks. The Central School staff, on the other hand, used the rest of that year differently. Staff training was provided with an expert on SEL from the state university, but mostly the efforts that year went into the workgroup reviewing programs, narrowing the possibilities, and talking to the other staff at the school. By the end of the school year, the workgroup recommended a particular program to the staff and to Taylor, the principal, as well as a time line for training and implementing the program the next year. After some discussion, a decision was made, and curriculum manuals and materials were ordered. They ended up choosing the same program that the Fox River principal and counselor had selected and already implemented at their school.

At the beginning of the second school year, the Fox River block teachers went ahead with implementing the program as planned, with no additional training or input, other than some questions and comments with the principal at the initial staff meeting of the year, and some occasional check-ins with him in the office or hallway. Pat, the school counselor, was available for consultation. By the middle of the school year, some of the teachers were departing signifi- cantly from the SEL program implementation manual, and one teacher had basically quit using it altogether, choosing to do her own version of SEL. No plan had been made for data collection or evaluation. By the end of the year, a hasty plan was put together to gather some evaluation data to respond to the assistant superintendent's request. The data were not particularly com- pelling or useful. Enthusiasm had waned from several of the teachers at this point, but it was assumed that the school would continue the course they were on for the next school year.

The Central School staff started the second year with a full-day inservice devoted to train- ing on the program that had been selected, and there were two breakout sessions for problem solving, goal setting, and feedback to the group. The final hour of the inservice was devoted to a plan for assessment and evaluation, led by the school psychologist, who had worked with the principal and counselor in developing the plan. The first lessons for the SEL program were not scheduled to be implemented until the second term of the first semester, allowing time for vetting the program with the PTSO and finalizing planning for consultation and data collection with the teachers. The first several weeks of implementation went relatively well, but consulta- tion and data collection procedures resulted in some retraining, because some teachers were implementing the program with low fidelity, and because the progress data indicated that some classes were gaining fewer skills than others. By the middle of first term of the second semester, the SEL program was running like a well-oiled machine, and the continuing data col- lection efforts showed consistent gains from the programs, as well as positive feedback from the teachers and students. By the last term of the year, plans were put into place for the prin- cipal and counselor to reinforce some of the main concepts from the SEL program in general school settings, such as morning announcements, an assembly, and in the hallways (posters were put in place). Assessment and evaluation data at the end of the school year showed sig- nificant student gains in knowledge and behavioral–emotional change, as well as strong social validity. The staff concluded the year looking forward to starting the next school year with SEL, and the assistant superintendent and school board used the Central School data as an example of the benefits that their schools could receive from SEL.

Thus we have two schools with the same curriculum and two very different outcomes. Why the difference, given that the same program was used and the two schools were relatively similar in terms of their student and staff composition? Clearly, the difference was due to atten- tion by Taylor, the Central School principal, to strategic planning, understanding the power of a community, and using knowledge of systems to get the best outcomes.

References

Adelman, H. S., & Taylor, L. (1997). Toward a scale-up model for replicating new approaches to schooling. *Journal of Educational and Psychological Consultation, 8*, 197–230.

Association of American Educators. (2003). *The AAE "code of ethics."* Retrieved October 1, 2008, from *www.aaeteachers.org/code-ethics.shtml.*

American Educational Research Association. (2000). *Ethical standards of the American educational research association.* Retrieved October 20, 2008, from *www.aera.net/uploadedFiles/About_AERA/Ethical_Standards/EthicalStandards.pdf.*

American Psychological Association. (2003). *Guidelines on multicultural education, training, research, practice, and organizational change for psychologists.* Retrieved October 1, 2008, from *www.apa.org/pi/multiculturalguidelines/scope.html.*

Balcazar, F., Hopkins, B. L., & Suarez, Y. (1985). A critical, objective review of performance feedback. *Journal of Organizational Behavior Management, 7,* 65–89.

Bar-On, R., & Parker, D. A. (2000). *BarOn Emotional Quotient Inventory—Youth Version.* North Tonowanda, NY: MHS.

Baron-Cohen, S., & Bolton, P. (1993). *Autism: The facts.* New York: Oxford University Press.

Beaver, B. R. (2008). A positive approach to children's internalizing problems. *Professional Psychology: Research and Practice, 39,* 129–136.

Beier, M. E., & Ackerman, P. L. (2005). Age, ability, and the role of prior knowledge on the acquisition of new domain knowledge: Promising results in a real-world learning environment. *Psychology and Aging, 20*(2), 341–345.

Bernal, G., & Sáez-Santiago, E. (2006). Culturally centered psychological interventions. *Journal of Community Psychology, 34*(2), 121–132.

Blair, C. (2002). School readiness: Integrating cognition and emotion in a neurobiolgical conceptualization of children's functioning at school entry. *American Psychologist, 57,* 111–127.

Blanco-Vega, C. O., Castro-Olivo, S. M., & Merrell, K. W. (2008). Social–emotional needs of Latino immigrant adolescents: A sociocultural model for developing and implementation of culturally sensitive intervention. *Journal of Latinos in Education, 7*(1), 43–61.

Bonavita, N., & Fairchild, M. (2001). Disproportionate minority representation in the juvenile justice system. *National Conference of State Legislature Legis-Brief, 9,* 30.

Brandt, R. S. (1999). Successful implementation of SEL programs: Lessons from the thinking skills movement. In J. Cohen (Ed.), *Educating hearts and minds: Social emotional learning and the passage into adolescence* (pp. 173–183). New York: Teachers College Press.

Bronfenbrenner, U. (1979). Contexts of child rearing: Problems and prospects. *The American Psychologist, 34,* 844–850.

Buchanan, G. M., & Seligman, M. E. P. (1995). Afterward: The future of the field. In G. M. Buchanan & M. E. P. Seligman (Eds.), *Explanatory style* (pp. 247–252). Hillsdale, NJ: Erlbaum.

CASEL. (2003). *Safe and sound: An educational leaders' guide to evidence-based social and emotional learning (SEL) programs.* Retrieved Februrary 5, 2009, from *www.casel.org/downloads/Safe%20and%20Sound/1A_Safe_&_Sound.pdf.*

Castro, F. G., Barrera, M., & Martinez, C. R. (2004). The cultural adaptation of prevention interventions: Resolving tensions between fidelity and fit. *Society for Prevention Research, 5,* 41–45.

Castro-Olivo, S. M. (2006). *The effects of a culturally adapted social–emotional learning curriculum on social–emotional and academic outcomes of Latino immigrant high school students.* Unpublished doctoral dissertation, University of Oregon, Eugene.

Catalano, R., Berglund, M. L., Ryan, J. A. M., Lonczak, H. S., & Hawkins, J. D. (2002). Positive youth development in the United States: Research findings on evaluations of positive youth development programs. *Prevention and Treatment, 5,* N.P.

Catalano, R. F., Mazza, J., Harachi, T. W., Abbott, R. D., & Haggerty, K. P. (2003). Raising healthy children through enhancing social development in elementary school: Results after 1.5 years. *Journal of School Psychology, 41,* 143–164.

Chavez, D., Moran, V. R., Reid, S., & Lopez, M. (1997). Acculturative stress in children: A modification of the SAFE scale. *Hispanic Journal of Behavioral Sciences, 19*(1), 34–44.

Child Development Project. (1988). *Caring School Community.* Retrieved December 1, 2008, from *www. devstu.org/pdfs/cdp/cdp_eval_summary.pdf*

Clarke, G. N., & Lewinsohn, P. M. (1995). *Instructor's manual for the Adolescent Coping with Stress Course.* Portland, OR: Kaiser Permanente Center for Health Research. Available for free download at *www.kpchr. org/public/acwd/acwd.html.*

Coie, J., & Koeppl, G. (1990). Adapting intervention to the problems of aggressive and disruptive rejected children. In S. Asher & J. Coie (Eds.), *Peer rejection in childhood* (pp. 309–337). New York: Cambridge University Press.

Coie, J. D., Miller-Johnson, S., & Bagwell, C. (2000). Prevention science. In A. J. Sameroff, M. Lewis, & S. M. Miller (Eds.), *Handbook of developmental psychopathology* (pp. 93–108). New York: Kluwer Academic/Plenum.

Collaborative for Academic, Social, and Emotional Learning. (2006). Casel practice rubric for school wide SEL implementation. Retrieved October 1, 2008, from *www.casel.org/downloads/Rubric.pdf.*

Committee for Children. (1988). *Second Step: A violence prevention curriculum* (1st ed.). Seattle, WA: Author.

Conduct Problems Prevention Research Group. (1999). Initial impact of the Fast Track prevention trial for conduct problems: II. Classroom effects. *Journal of Consulting and Clinical Psychology, 67,* 648–657.

Cowen, E. L. (1994). The enhancement of psychological wellness: Challenges and opportunities. *American Journal of Community Psychology, 22,* 149–179.

Crone, D. A., Hawken, L. S., & Horner, R. H. (2004). *Responding to problem behavior in schools. The behavior education program.* New York: Guilford Press.

Denham, S. A., & Weissberg, R. P. (2004). Social–emotional learning: What we know and where to go from here. In E. Chesebrough, P. King, T. P. Gullotta, & M. Bloom (Eds.), *A blueprint for the promotion of prosodal behavior in early childhood.* New York: Springer.

Doll, B., & Lyon, M. A. (1998). Risk and resilience: Implications for the delivery of educational and mental health services in schools. *School Psychology Review, 27,* 348–364.

Donegan, A. L., & Rust, J. O. (1998). Rational emotive education for improving self-concept in second-grade students. *Journal of Humanistic Education and Development, 36,* 248–256.

Dumas, J. E., Rollock, D., Prinz, R. J., Hops, H., & Blechman, E. A. (1999). Cultural sensitivity: Problems and solutions in applied and preventive intervention. *Applied and Preventive Psychology, 8,* 175–196.

Durlak, J. A., & Weissberg, R. P. (2007). *The impact of after-school programs that promote personal and social skills.* Chicago: Collaborative for Academic, Social, and Emotional Learning.

Durlak, J. A., & Wells, A. M. (1997). Primary prevention mental health programs for children and adolescents: A meta-analytic review. *American Journal of Community Psychology, 25,* 115–152.

Elias, M. J. (2004). Strategies to infuse social and emotional learning into academics. In J. E. Zins, R. P. Weissberg, M. C. Wang, & H. J. Walberg (Eds.), *Building academic success on social and emotional learning: What does the research say?* (pp. 113–134). New York: Teachers College Press.

Elias, M. J., & Bruene Butler, L. (2005). *Social Decision Making/Social Problem Solving curriculum for grades 2–5.* Champaign, IL: Research Press.

Elias, M. J., & Clabby, J. F. (1992). *Building social problem-solving skills: Guidelines from a school-based program.* San Francisco: Jossey-Bass.

Elias, M. J., Gara, M. A., Schuyler, T. F., Branden-Muller, L. R., & Sayette, M. A. (1991). The promotion of social competence: Longitudinal study of a preventative school-based program. *American Journal of Orthopsychiatry, 61,* 409–417.

Epstein, M. H. (2004). *Behavioral Emotional Rating Scale* (2nd ed.). Austin, TX: PAR.

Fine, S. E., Izard, C. E., Mostow, A. J., Trentacosta, C. J., & Ackerman, B. P. (2003). First-grade emotion knowledge as a predictor of fifth-grade internalizing behaviors in children from economically disadvantaged families. *Development and Psychopathology, 15,* 331–342.

Fixsen, D. L., Naoom, S. F., Blasé, K. A., Friedman, R. M., & Wallace, F. (2005). *Implementation research: A synthesis of the literature.* National Implementation Research Network. Retrieved July 20, 2005, from *nirn.fmhi.usf.edu.*

Goleman, D. (1995). *Emotional intelligence: Why it can matter more than IQ.* New York: Bantam Books.

Gonzales, N. A., & Kim, L. S. (1997). Stress and coping in an ethnic minority context. In S. A. Wolchik & I. N. Sandler (Eds.), *Handbook of children's coping: Linking theory and intervention* (pp. 481–511). New York: Plenum Press.

Gonzalez, R., & Padilla, A. M. (1997). The academic resilience of Mexican American high school students. *Hispanic Journal of Behavioral Sciences, 19*(3), 301–317.

Graziano, P. A., Reavis, R. D., Keane, S. P., & Calkins, S. D. (2007). The role of emotion regulation in children's early academic success. *Journal of School Psychology, 45,* 3–19.

Greenberg, M. T., Domitrovich, C., & Bumbarger, B. (2000). *The prevention of mental disorders in school-age children: A review of the effectiveness of pre-*

vention programs. Prevention Research Center for the Promotion of Human Development, College of Health and Human Development, Pennsylvania State University. Retrieved August 10, 2007, from *www. prevention.psu.edu/pubs/docs/CMHS.pdf*.

Greenberg, M. T., Domitrovich, C., & Bumbarger, B. (2001). The prevention of mental disorders in school-age children: Current state of the field. *Prevention and Treatment, 4*, N.P.

Greenberg, M. T., & Kusche, C. A. (1998a). *Promoting alternative thinking strategies: Blueprint for violence prevention*. Book 10. Boulder: University of Colorado, Institute of Behavioral Science.

Greenberg, M. T., & Kusche, C. A. (1998b). Preventive intervention for school-age deaf children: The PATHS Curriculum. *Journal of Deaf Studies and Deaf Education, 3*, 49–63.

Greenberg, M. T., Kusche, C. A., Cook, E. T., & Quamma, J. P. (1995). Promoting emotional competence in school-age children: The effects of the PATHS Curriculum. *Development and Psychopathology, 7*, 117–136.

Greenberg, M. T., Weissberg, R. P., O'Brien, M. T., Zins, J. E., Fredericks, L., Resnik, H., et al. (2003). Enhancing school-based prevention and youth development through coordinated social, emotional, and academic learning. *American Psychologist, 58*, 466–474.

Gresham, F. M. (2002). Teaching social skills to high-risk children and youth: Preventive and remedial strategies. In M. R. Shinn, H. M. Walker, & G. Stoner (Eds.), *Interventions for academic and behavior problems II: Preventive and remedial approaches* (pp. 403–432). Bethesda, MD: National Association of School Psychologists.

Gresham, F. M., & Elliott, S. N. (1990). *Social skills rating system*. Circle Pines, MN: AGS.

Gresham, F. M., & Elliott, S. N. (2008). *Social skills improvement system*. San Antonio, TX: Pearson.

Grimes, J., & Tilly, D. W. (1996). Policy and process: Means to lasting educational change. *School Psychology Review, 25*, 465–476.

Gross, T. F. (2004). The perception of four basic emotions in human and nonhuman faces by children with autism and other developmental disabilities. *Journal of Abnormal Child Psychology, 32*, 469–480.

Grossman, D. C., Neckerman, H. J., Koepsell, T. D., Liu, P. Y., Asher, K. N., Beland, K., et al. (1997). Effectiveness of a violence prevention curriculum among children in elementary school: A randomized controlled trial. *Journal of the American Medical Association, 277*(20), 1605–1611.

Gueldner, B. A. (2006). *An investigation of the effectiveness of a social–emotional learning program with middle school students in a general education setting and the impact of consultation support using performance feedback*. Unpublished doctoral dissertation, University of Oregon, Eugene.

Gueldner, B. A., & Merrell, K. W. (in press). Evaluation of a social emotional learning program using a consultation process integrating performance feedback

and motivational interviewing. *Journal of Educational and Psychological Consultation*.

Harlacher, J. E. (2008). *Social and emotional learning as a universal level of support: Evaluating the follow-up effect of Strong Kids on social and emotional outcomes*. Unpublished doctoral dissertation, University of Oregon, Eugene.

Hawkins, J. D., Catalano, R. E., & Miller, J. Y. (1992). Risk and protective factors for alcohol and other drug problems in adolescence and early adulthood: Implications for substance abuse prevention. *Psychological Bulletin, 112*(1), 64–105.

Hoagwood, K., & Erwin, H. D. (1997). Effectiveness of school-based mental health services for children: A 10–year research review. *Journal of Child and Family Studies, 6*, 435–451.

Hoagwood, K., & Johnson, J. (2003). School psychology: A public health framework I. From evidence-based policies. *Journal of School Psychology, 41*, 3–21.

Hosp, M. K., Hosp, J. L., & Howell, K. (2007). *The ABCs of CBM: A practical guide to curriculum-based measurement*. New York: Guilford Press.

Howse, R., Calkins, S., Anastopoulos, A., Keane, S., & Shelton, T. (2003). Regulatory contributors to children's academic achievement. *Early Education and Development, 14*, 101–119.

Izard, C., Fine, S., Schultz, D., Mostow, A., Ackerman, B., & Youngstrom, D. (2001). Emotion knowledge as a predictor of social behavior and academic competence in children at risk. *Psychological Science, 12*(1), 18–23.

Jimerson, S. R., Sharkey, J. D., Nyborg, V., & Furlong, M. J. (2004). Strengths-based assessment and school psychology: A summary and synthesis. *The California School Psychologist, 9*, 9–19.

Joseph, G. E., & Strain, P. S. (2003). Comprehensive evidence-based social–emotional curricula for young children: An analysis of efficacious adoption potential. *Topics in Early Childhood Special Education, 23*(2), 65–76.

Kame'enui, E. J., & Simmons, D. C. (1990). *Designing instructional strategies: The prevention of academic learning problems*. Hightstown, NJ: Macmillan.

Kataoka, S. H., Stein, B. D., Jaycox, L. H., Wong, M., Escudero, P., Tu, W., et al. (2003). A school-based mental health program for traumatized Latino immigrant children. *Journal of the American Academy of Child Adolescent Psychiatry, 42*(3), 311–318.

Knoll, M., & Patti, J. (2003). Social–emotional learning and academic achievement. In M. J. Elias, H. Arnold, & C. Steiger Hussey (Eds.), *EQ + IQ = Best leadership practices for caring and successful schools* (pp. 36–49). Thousand Oaks, CA: Corwin Press.

Kroeger, K. A., Schultz, J. R., & Newsom, C. (2007). A comparison of two group-delivered social skills programs for young children with autism. *Journal of Autism Developmental Disorders, 37*, 808–817.

Kuhl, J., & Kraska, K. (1989). Self-regulation and meta-motivation: Computational mechanisms, development, and assessment. In R. Kanfer, P. Ackerman,

& R. Cudeck (Eds.), *Abilities, motivation, and methodology: The Minnesota Symposium on learning and individual differences* (pp. 373–374). Hillsdale, NJ: Erlbaum.

Kumpfer, K. L., Alvarado, R., Smith, P., & Bellamy, N. (2002). Cultural sensitivity and adaptation in family-based prevention interventions. *Prevention Science, 3*, 241–246.

Kusche, C. A., & Greenberg, M. T. (1994). *The PATHS (Promoting Alternative Thinking Strategies) curriculum.* South Deerfield, MA: Channing-Bete.

Kutash, K., Duchnowski, A. J., & Lynn, N. (2006). *School-based mental health: An empirical guide for decision-makers.* Tampa: University of South Florida, The Louis de la Parte Florida Mental Health Institute, Department of Child and Family Studies, Research and Training Center for Children's Mental Health.

LeBuffe, P. A., Shapiro, V. B., & Naglieri, J. A. (2009). *Devereux Student Strengths Assessment.* Lewisville, NC: Kaplan Early Learning Company.

Levitt, V. H., & Merrell, K. W. (2009). Linking assessment to intervention for internalizing problems of children and adolescents. *School Psychology Forum, 3*(1), 13–26.

Lieberman, A. F. (1989). What is culturally sensitive intervention? *Early Child Development and Care, 50,* 197–204.

Lopez, S. J., Edwards, L. M., Pedrotti, J. T., Ito, A., & Rasmussen, H. N. (2002). Culture counts: Examinations of recent applications of the Penn resiliency program, or, toward a rubric for examining cultural appropriateness of prevention programming. *Prevention and Treatment, 5*(12).

Lorion, R. P. (2000). Theoretical and evaluation issues in the promotion of wellness and the protection of "well enough." In D. Cicchetti, J. Rappaport, I. Sandler, & R. P. Weissberg (Eds.), *The promotion of wellness in children and adolescents* (pp. 1–27). Washington, DC: CWLA Press.

Martin, R., Drew, K., Gaddis, L., & Moseley, M. (1988). Prediction of elementary school achievement from preschool temperament: Three studies. *School Psychology Review, 17,* 125–137.

Martinez, C. R., DeGarmo, D. S., & Eddy, J. M. (2004). Promoting academic success among Latino youth. *Hispanic Journal of Behavioral Sciences, 26*(2), 128–151.

Martinez, C. R., & Eddy, J. M. (2005). Effects of culturally adapted parent management training on Latino youth behavioral health outcomes. *Journal of Community and Child Psychology, 75*(4), 841–851.

McCombs, B. L. (2004). The learner-centered psychological principles: A framework for balancing academic achievement and social–emotional learning outcomes. In J. E. Zins, R. P. Weissberg, M. C. Wang, & H. J. Walberg (Eds.), *Building academic success on social and emotional learning: What does the research say?* (pp. 23–39). New York: Teachers College Press.

Merrell, K. W. (2002a). *School Social Behavior Scales* (2nd ed.). Baltimore: Brookes.

Merrell, K. W. (2002b). *Home and Community Social Behavior Scales.* Baltimore: Brookes.

Merrell, K. W. (2008a). *Helping students overcome depression and anxiety: A practical guide* (2nd ed.). New York: Guilford Press.

Merrell, K. W. (2008b). *Behavioral, social, and emotional assessment of children and adolescents* (3rd ed.). New York/London: Taylor & Francis/Routledge.

Merrell, K. W. (2008c). *Social–Emotional Assets and Resilience Scales.* Eugene: University of Oregon, School Psychology Program. Available at *strongkids.uoregon.edu/SEARS.html.*

Merrell, K. W., & Buchanan, R. (2006). Intervention selection in school-based practice: Using public health models to enhance systems capacity of schools. *School Psychology Review, 35,* 167–180.

Merrell, K. W., Carrizales, D., Feuerborn, L., Gueldner, B. A., & Tran, O. K. (2007a). *Strong Kids—grades 3–5: A social and emotional learning curriculum.* Baltimore: Brookes.

Merrell, K. W., Carrizales, D., Feuerborn, L., Gueldner, B. A., & Tran, O. K. (2007b). *Strong Kids—grades 6–8: A social and emotional learning curriculum.* Baltimore: Brookes.

Merrell, K. W., Carrizales, D., Feuerborn, L., Gueldner, B. A., & Tran, O. K. (2007c). *Strong Teens—grades 9–12: A social and emotional learning curriculum.* Baltimore: Brookes.

Merrell, K. W., Ervin, R. A., & Gimpel, G. A. (2006). *School psychology for the 21st century: Foundations and practices.* New York: Guilford Press.

Merrell, K. W., & Gimpel, G. A. (1998). *Social skills of children and adolescents: Conceptualization, assessment, and treatment.* Mahwah, NJ: Erlbaum.

Merrell, K. W., & Gueldner, B. A. (in press). Preventative interventions for students with internalizing disorders: Effective strategies for promoting mental health in schools. In M. R. Shinn, H. M. Walker, & G. Stoner (Eds.), *Interventions for achievement and behavior in a three-tiered model including RTI* (3rd ed.). Bethesda, MD: National Association of School Psychologists.

Merrell, K. W., Gueldner, B. A., & Tran, O. K. (2008). Social and emotional learning: A school-wide approach to socialization, friendship problems, and more. In B. J. Doll & J. A. Cummings (Eds.), *Transforming school mental health services: Population-based approaches to promoting the competency and wellness of children* (pp. 165–185). Thousand Oaks, CA: Corwin Press/National Association of School Psychologists.

Merrell, K. W., Juskelis, M. P., Tran, O. K., & Buchanan, R. (2008). Social and emotional learning in the classroom: Evaluation of Strong Kids and Strong Teens on students' social–emotional knowledge and symptoms. *Journal of Applied School Psychology, 24,* 208–224.

Merrell, K. W., Levitt, V. H., & Gueldner, B. A. (2010). Proactive strategies for promoting social competence and resilience. In C. Gimpel Peacock, R. A. Ervin, E. J. Daly III, & K. W. Merrell (Eds.), *Practical handbook of school psychology: Effective practices for the 21st century* (pp. 254–273). New York: Guilford Press.

Merrell, K. W., Parisi, D., & Whitcomb, S. (2007). *Strong Start—Grades K–2: A social and emotional learning curriculum.* Baltimore: Brookes.

Merrell, K. W., Whitcomb, S., & Parisi, D. (2009). *Strong Start—Pre-K: A social and emotional learning curriculum.* Baltimore: Brookes.

Michael, K. D., & Crowley, S. L. (2002). How effective are treatments for child and adolescent depression?: A meta-analytic review. *Clinical Psychology Review, 22,* 247–269.

Morgenstern, J. (2004). *Time management from the inside out, second edition: The foolproof system to organizing your home, your office, you life.* New York: Holt.

Mortenson, B. P., & Witt, J. C. (1998). The use of weekly performance feedback to increase teacher implementation of a prereferral academic intervention. *School Psychology Review, 27,* 613–627.

Nakayama, N. J. (2008). *An investigation of the impact of the Strong Kids curriculum on social–emotional knowledge and symptoms of elementary aged students in a self-contained special education setting.* Unpublished doctoral dissertation, University of Oregon, Eugene.

Napoli, M., Marsiglia, F. F., & Kulis, S. (2003). Sense of belonging in school as a protective factor against drug abuse among Native American urban adolescents. *Journal of Social Work Practice in the Addictions, 3*(2), 25–41.

Nasir, N. S., & Hand, V. M. (2006). Exploring sociocultural perspectives on race, culture, and learning. *Review of Educational Research, 76*(4), 449–475.

National Association of School Psychologists. (2000). *Professional code manual: Principles for professional ethics guidelines for the provision of school psychological services.* Retrieved October 1, 2008, from *nasponline.org/standards/ProfessionalCond.pdf.*

National Center for Educational Statistics. (2008a). *Number and percentage of children ages 3 to 5 and 6 to 21 served under the individuals with disabilities education act (IDEA), by race and type of disability: 2004.* Retrieved on October 10, 2008, from *nces.ed.gov/pubs2007/minoritytrends/tables/table_8_1b.asp?referrer=report.*

National Center for Educational Statistics. (2008b). *Table 2.1a. Percentage distribution of public elementary and secondary school enrollment, by race/ethnicity: Selected years, 1986 to 2002.* Retrieved on October 10, 2008, from *nces.ed.gov/pubs2005/nativetrends/ShowTable.asp?table=tables/table_2_1a.asp&indicator=2.1&excel=xls/table_2_1a.xls&excelsize=17.*

Noell, G. H., Witt, J. C., Slider, N. J., Connell, J. E., Gatti, S. L., Williams, K. L., et al. (2005). Treatment implementation following behavioral consultation in schools: A comparison of three follow-up strategies. *School Psychology Review, 34,* 87–106.

OSEP Technical Assistance Center on Positive Behavioral Interventions and Supports. (2008). What is schoolwide PBS. Retrieved September 9, 2008, from *www.pbis.org/schoolwide.htm.*

Pasi, R. (2001). *Higher expectations: Promoting social and emotional/earning and academic learning in your school.* New York: Teachers College Press.

Petersen, K. S. (2005). *Safe and caring schools: Skills for school, skills for life.* Champaign, IL: Research Press.

Pianta, R., & Stuhlman, M. (1995). Teacher–child relationships and children's success in the first years of school. *School Psychology Review, 33,* 444–458.

Prevention Research Group. (1993). *Promoting alternative thinking strategies.* Deerfield, MA: Channing Bete.

Riley-Tilman, T. C., & Burns, M. K. (2009). *Evaluating educational interventions: Single-case design for measuring response to intervention.* New York: Guilford Press.

Rumbaut, R. G. (2004). *Immigration, generation, and "Americanization": Empirical patterns and epidemiological paradoxes.* Paper presented at the National Hispanic Science Network on Drug Abuse, Fourth Annual National Scientific Conference, San Antonio, TX.

Rummler, G. A., & Brache, A. P. (1995). *Improving performance: How to manage the white space on the organization chart* (2nd ed.). San Francisco: Josey-Bass.

Search Institute. (2004). *Developmental Assets Profile.* Minneapolis, MN: Author.

Serpell, Z. N., Clauss-Ehlers, C. S., & Lindsey, M. A. (2007). Schools' provision of information regarding mental health and associated services to culturally diverse families. In S. W. Evans, M. D. Wesit, & A. N. Serpell (Eds.), *Advances in school-based mental health interventions: Best practices and program models* (pp. 18-2–18-17). Kingston, NJ: Civic Research Institute.

Shelly, B. (2008). Rebels and their causes: State resistance to No Child Left Behind. *Publius: The Journal of Federalism, 38,* 444–468.

Shure, M. B. (1990). *The What Happens Next Game (WHNG): Manual* (2nd ed.). Philadelphia: Drexel University.

Shure, M. B. (1992a). *I Can Problem Solve (ICPS): An interpersonal cognitive problem-solving program (kindergarten/primary grades).* Champaign, IL: Research Press.

Shure, M. B. (1992b). *Preschool Interpersonal Problem Solving (PIPS) test: Manual* (2nd ed.). Philadelphia: Drexel University.

Shure, M. B., & Glaser, A. (2001). I Can Problem Solve (ICPS): A cognitive approach to the prevention of early high-risk behaviors. In J. Cohen (Ed.), *Caring classrooms/intelligent schools: The social emotional education of young children* (pp. 122–129). New York: Teachers College Press.

Smith, B. H., McQuillin, S. D., & Shapiro, C. J. (2008). An installation–adaptation–diffusion model of university–community–school partnerships. *Community Psychologist, 41,* 43–45.

Solomon, D., Battistich, V., Watson, M., Schaps, E., & Lewis, C. (2000). A six-district study of educational change: Direct and mediated effects of the Child Development Project. *School Psychologist of Education, 4,* 3–51.

Sugai, G., & Horner, R. H. (2002). Introduction to the special series on positive behavior support in schools. *Journal of Emotional and Behavioral Disorders, 10,* 130–135.

Tran, O. K. (2007). *Promoting social and emotional learning in schools: An investigation of massed versus distributed practice schedules and social validity of the Strong Kids curriculum in late elementary-age students.* Unpublished doctoral dissertation, University of Oregon, Eugene.

Tran, O. K., & Merrell, K. W. (2008). Promoting student resiliency: Social and emotional learning as a universal prevention approach. In B. Doll (Ed.), *Handbook of youth prevention science.* New York: Routledge/Erlbaum.

Trentacosta, C. J., Izard, C. E., Mostow, A. J., & Fine, S. E. (2006). Children's emotional competence and attentional competence in elementary school. *School Psychology Quarterly, 21,* 148–170.

U.S. Department of Health and Human Services, Substance Abuse and Mental Health Administration, Center for Mental Health Services. (2001). *Mental health: Culture, race, and ethnicity—A supplement to mental health: A report of the Surgeons General.* Rockville, MD: Author.

VanDenBerg, J.E., & Grealish, M. E. (1996). Individualized services and supports through the wrap-around process. *Journal of Child and Family Studies, 5,* 7–21.

Vega, W. W., & Rumbaut, R. G. (1991). Ethnic minorities and mental health. *Annual Review of Sociology, 17*(3), 51–83.

Vernon, A. (2006). *Thinking, feeling, behaving: An emotional education curriculum for children/grades 1–6.* Champaign, IL: Research Press.

Walker, H. M., Horner, R. H., Sugai, G., Bullis, M., Sprague, J. R., Bricker, D., et al. (1996). Integrated approaches to preventing antisocial behavior patterns among school-age children and youth. *Journal of Emotional and Behavioral Disorders, 4,* 193–256.

Walker, H., Stiller, B., Severson, H. H., Feil, E. G., &

Golly, A. (1998). First step to success: Intervening at the point of school entry to prevent antisocial behavior patterns. *Psychology in the Schools, 35,* 259–269. Commercially packaged program materials are available from Sopris West Publishing, *www.sopriswest.com.*

Watkins, C., & Slocum, T. (2004). The components of direct instruction. In N. E.Marchand-Martella, T. Slocum, & R. C. Martella (Eds.), *Introduction to direct instruction* (pp. 28–65). Boston: Allyn & Bacon.

Weist, M. D., Axelrod Lowie, J., Flaherty, L. T., & Pruitt, D. (2001). Collaboration among the education, mental health, and public health systems to promote youth mental health. *Psychiatric Services, 51,* 1348–1351.

Weist, M. D., Lindsey, M., Moore, E., & Slade, E. (2006). Building capacity in school mental health. *International Journal of Mental Health Promotion, 8,* 30–36.

Whaley, A. L., & Davis, K. E. (2007). Cultural competence and evidence-based practice in mental health: A complementary perspective. *American Psychologists, 62*(6), 563–574.

Wilson, D. B., Gottfredson, D. C., & Najaka, S. S. (2001). School-based prevention of problem behaviors: A meta-analysis. *Journal of Quantitative Criminology, 17,* 247–272.

Witt, J. C., Noell, G., LaFleur, L., & Mortenson, B. P. (1997). Teacher use of intervention in general education setting: Measurement and analysis of the independent variable. *Journal of Applied Behavior Analysis, 30,* 693–696.

Zins, J. E., Bloodworth, M. R., Weissberg, R. P., & Walberg, H. J. (2004). The scientific base linking social and emotional learning to school success. In J. E. Zins, R. P. Weissberg, M. C. Wang, & H. J. Walberg (Eds.), *Building academic success on social and emotional learning: What does the research say?* (pp. 3–22). New York: Teachers College Press.

Zins, J. E., Payton, J. W., Weissberg, R. P., & Utne O'Brien, M. (2007). Social and emotional learning for successful school performance. In G. Mathews, M. Zeidner, & R. D. Roberts (Eds.), *The science of emotional intelligence: Known and unknowns.* New York: Oxford University Press.

Zins, J. E., Weissberg, R. P., Wang, M. C., & Walberg, H. J. (Eds.). (2004). *Building academic success on social and emotional learning: What does the research say?* New York: Teachers College Press.

Index

Page numbers followed by an f or t indicate figures or tables.

12/11